Achieving

Learning and Teaching

in Secondary Schools

Fifth edition

Edited by Viv Ellis

SAGE | LearningMatters

Los Angeles | London | New Delhi
Singapore | Washington DC

Learning Matters

An imprint of SAGE Publications Ltd

1 Oliver's Yard
55 City Road
London EC1Y 1SP

SAGE Publications Inc.
2455 Teller Road
Thousand Oaks, California 91320

SAGE Publications India Pvt Ltd
B 1/I 1 Mohan Cooperative Industrial Area
Mathura Road
New Delhi 110 044

SAGE Publications Asia-Pacific Pte Ltd
3 Church Street
#10-04 Samsung Hub
Singapore 049483

Editor: Amy Thornton
Production controller: Chris Marke
Project management: Deer Park
Productions, Tavistock, Devon
Marketing manager: Catherine Slinn
Cover design: Toucan Design
Typeset by: PDQ Typesetting Ltd,
Newcastle-under-Lyme
Printed and bound by MPG Printgroup, UK

MIX
Paper from
responsible sources
FSC
www.fsc.org   FSC® C018575

Library of Congress Control Number:
2013932594

British Library Cataloguing in Publication
Data

A catalogue record for this book is available
from the British Library

ISBN 978-1-44626-751-6 (pbk)
ISBN 978-1-44626-750-9

Contents

Part 4: Professional knowledge: inclusion

Preface to the Fifth Edition

The fifth edition of this successful textbook has been prepared just over half the way through the life of the Conservative–Liberal Democrat coalition government in England, first elected in 2010. That this book begins with such a sentence indicates the significant influence governments in England have on the frameworks and curriculum for initial teacher education (ITE). But the interest of governments in reforming teacher education is a global phenomenon and the directions in many parts of the world are the same: national professional standards based on 'core competencies'; a reduced role (at least rhetorically) for universities and much greater responsibilities on schools to lead ITE programmes; a closer focus on practice and a lesser role for 'theory', however defined; and, at the same time, perhaps contradictorily, the aspiration for teaching to be a Master's level profession. As I noted in my preface to the fourth edition, some fairly fundamental relationships and processes remain unaffected by these changes. Teachers are still prepared to teach in classrooms, to teach relatively large groups of children, in phases and groups organized according to the child's age and the children are expected to learn some fairly stable 'subjects'. Teachers need to be able to form appropriate relationships with these groups of children, to plan for their learning at the medium-term and in the short-term, and they need to be able to assess children's learning and the effectiveness of their teaching for a variety of purposes.

For the fourth edition of this book, all contributors updated their chapters and the edition included a new chapter on teaching as a Master's level profession and also a new chapter on pastoral care and citizenship. For this fifth edition, the chapters have been updated further, particularly to reflect the new Teaching Standards and SEN policies. In addition, appendices are provided that cross-reference the standards and competences in the other UK jurisdictions (Wales, Scotland, Northern Ireland). As we have for the last eleven years, the authors of this book offer it as support and guidance to student teachers and trainees during their ITE programme. Its purpose is not to replace face-to-face interactions with mentor teachers and tutors but to supplement them. Whatever the political complexion of the government of the day, the preparation of new teachers is an important task for any society as a whole and it is in this spirit that the new edition has been produced.

Viv Ellis
London
March 2013

Contributors

Rob Batho, formerly Senior Adviser, Secondary National Strategy

Jane Briggs, Senior Lecturer in Education, University of Brighton

Alan J. Child, Regional Director (North West), The Personal Finance Education Group

John Clay, formerly Senior Inspector for Ethnic Minority Achievement, London Borough of Greenwich and Adviser, General Teaching Council for England

Alaster Douglas, Reader in Education, Roehampton University

Viv Ellis, Professor and Head of Education, Brunel University

Patrick Fullick, formerly Lecturer in Education, University of Southampton

Rosalyn George, Professor of Education, Goldsmiths, University of London

Gary D. Kinchin, Senior Lecturer in Physical Education, University of Southampton

Kate Mackrell, Freelance Mathematics Consultant

Trevor Mutton, PGCE Secondary Course Leader, University of Oxford

Lynne Parsons, formerly Regional Adviser (Behaviour and Attendance), Secondary National Strategy

Miranda Peverett, Teacher of English, British International School, Valencia

Geraldine A. Price, formerly Lecturer in Specific Learning Difficulties, University of Southampton

Richard Pring, Lead Director of the Nuffield Review of 14–19 Education, England and Wales; University of Oxford

Sue Walters, Lecturer in Education, University of London, Institute of Education

Cathy Wickens, formerly Senior Lecturer in ICT Education, University of Brighton

Charlotte Wright, Teacher of English, Hanson School, Bradford

Acknowledgements

The editor and contributors would like to thank the following people for their support and assistance in the development of this book.

Ros George and John Clay for their contribution to the Introduction; the PGCE secondary English group at the University of Brighton (2000–2001); Tony Burgess; Maggie Miller; Deb Davies; Nicole Dingwall; Kate Spencer Ellis; Chris Childs; Graham Corney; Nathalie Manners; Julia Morris; Amy Thornton; Jennifer Clark; Alaster Douglas for his minor amendments to several chapters in this edition; Boda Sedlacek for outstanding administrative support.

For Jenny Irvine, Cathie Salisbury, Sally Carter Tabasso, Helen Smy, Aisling Walters, Lucy Fortnam-Paynter, Sarah Roberts, Nathan Munn and the other school-based mentors who have worked with this book in its various editions over the last eleven years.

PART 1
PROFESSIONAL ATTRIBUTES AND LEARNING

1
Introduction
Viv Ellis

This book was written for anyone undertaking a course of training leading to qualification as a school teacher in the secondary (11–18) phase. If this applies to you, then you may be registered at a university or college on an undergraduate degree programme with QTS, you may be taking a Post Graduate Certificate of Education (PGCE) course, or you may be following the new 'School Direct' programme led by one of the outstanding new Teaching Schools in England. Whatever the particular route, you will be based in schools for most of your time and working with tutors and mentors towards the same goal: becoming an effective new teacher and achieving the Teachers' Standards. This book offers you useful guidance and support during your initial teacher education and shows how the information and guidance it provides relate to the Teachers' Standards and the relevant educational research and inspection evidence.

The title of this book is *Learning and Teaching in Secondary Schools*. Our intention here is to emphasise the learning for two reasons: first, to acknowledge that this is what you – the trainee teacher – will be engaged in for a significant period and with some intensity. For this reason, the book addresses you directly, provides some classroom-based illustrations, and offers practical and reflective tasks and further reading to consolidate your understanding. The second reason is that fostering, developing, assessing, planning for and managing student learning is your primary role as a teacher. This may sound obvious but very often trainee teachers will initially focus on the performance aspects of teaching – how teachers look, behave and sound – rather than how and what their students are learning. We hope you will find it reassuring when we say that very good teachers do not need to be extrovert or overtly 'charismatic' performers; very good teachers listen to students carefully, think about what they see, hear and read analytically and treat students and colleagues with respect and sensitivity.

Learning to teach

Becoming a teacher is a rewarding, stimulating and challenging process. Do not underestimate the changes in your life and circumstances that may occur during this process.

This is not to say that undertaking a teacher training course will inevitably lead to divorce, stress-related illness or the decision to keep a small-holding on Skye. It is fair to say, however, that the process of becoming a teacher involves personal, intellectual and professional transformation and that, for many trainees, it requires them to consider what is important and meaningful to them for the first time. As a consequence, most trainees feel that – at the end of their initial training – not only have they learned a lot about teaching and learning but they have also learned a lot about themselves. For most, this acts as confirmation of their initial desire to teach and confirms that they have entered a profession that they will find rewarding. For some, however, whether early on or at the end of the course, it will confirm that teaching is not for them. This is an important decision that carries with it no sense of failure.

One of the most interesting writers about the process of becoming a teacher is the American psychologist Seymour Sarason, and his book *You Are Thinking of Teaching?* is recommended as further reading at the end of this introduction. Sarason's point is that any decision to enter the teaching profession must be an informed one: you must understand why you want to become a teacher and what it means to be a teacher (the responsibilities and the constraints):

> *If you conclude that teaching is for you, it should be on the basis that you know who and what you are, the ways in which you will be challenged, and that you are prepared to be other than a silent, passive participant in the socially fateful and crucial effort to improve our schools; that is, the particular school or schools in which you work.*
>
> (Sarason 1993, p. 4)

In addition to knowing why you want to become a teacher and that you understand its active and socially important role, Sarason also draws attention to the 'political' dimension of teaching, with which you might feel uncomfortable. Couched in the following terms, however, it is difficult to disagree with the view that teachers effect this kind of change:

> *It is unfair and unrealistic to expect teachers to change society. It is not unfair or unrealistic to expect teachers to change, in part if not wholly, the conditions in which they and their students experience personal and intellectual growth.*
>
> (ibid., p. 5)

The Teachers' Standards recognise that this kind of change is at the heart of the teacher's role.

The current context for teacher education and training

Teachers' Standards

In England, the Teachers' Standards (DfE 2012) replaced the standards for Qualified Teacher Status (QTS), the Core professional standards previously published by the Training and Development Agency for Schools (TDA), and the General Teaching Council for England's *Code of Conduct and Practice for Registered Teachers*. The standards apply to the vast majority of teachers regardless of their career stage and they define the minimum level of practice expected of trainees and teachers from the point of entry to the profession. Your initial teacher training provider will assess you against the standards in a way that is consistent with what could reasonably be expected of a trainee teacher.

The standards are presented in three parts. The preamble summarises the values and behaviour that all teachers must demonstrate throughout their careers. Part 1 comprises the Standards for Teaching. Part 2 comprises the standards for professional and personal conduct.

The preamble states:

> *Teachers make the education of their pupils their first concern, and are accountable for achieving the highest possible standards in work and conduct. Teachers act with honesty and integrity; have strong subject knowledge, keep their knowledge and skills as teachers up-to-date and are self-critical; forge positive professional relationships; and work with parents in the best interests of their pupils.*
>
> (DfE 2012, p. 7)

All the standards were underpinned by a document called *Every Child Matters* (discussed later) and the six areas of the common core of skills and knowledge for the children's workforce. It is intended that the work of practising teachers be informed by an awareness, appropriate to their level of experience and responsibility, of legislation concerning the development and well-being of children and young people expressed in the Children Act 2004, the Disability Discrimination Acts 1995 and 2005 and associated guidance, the special educational needs provisions of the Education Act 1996 and the associated Special Educational Needs Code of Practice (DfES 2001d), the Race Relations Act 1976 as amended by the Race Relations (Amendment) Act 2000, and the guidance on safeguarding children in education (DfES 2004a). This body of legislation is referred to as appropriate in the chapters that follow; all of it emphasises the importance placed on achieving educational inclusion in practice. It is worth noting that the coalition government is reviewing the qualifications framework for teachers.

In the other countries of the UK, there are also frameworks of Standards or competencies and these are reproduced in the appendices to this book.

Every Child Matters

In 2003, the Labour government in England took a new approach to the care, education and well-being of children and young people, following the tragic death of a young girl called Victoria Climbié. *Every Child Matters* was published (along with the Children Act) in 2004 and represented the national strategy for professionals working together on the well-being of children and young people from birth to age 19. The intention was that organisations such as hospitals, schools, social services departments, the police and voluntary groups team up in new ways, share information and work together so that young people have the support they need to:

1. be healthy;
2. stay safe;
3. enjoy and achieve;
4. make a positive contribution;
5. achieve economic well-being.

Together, these statements have become known as the five outcomes of the Every Child Matters agenda.

Secondary National Strategy

The Secondary National Strategy was also a key lever for the reform of teaching by the Labour government in England. There were six strands in the Strategy. These were:

1. English (including literacy across the curriculum);
2. Mathematics (including numeracy across the curriculum);
3. Science;
4. ICT (Information and Communications Technology);
5. Foundation subjects;
6. Behaviour and attendance.

The English and mathematics strands of the Secondary National Strategy were introduced to all schools in England in 2001 with science, foundation subjects and ICT following in 2002 and behaviour and attendance in 2003. The aim of the Strategy was to raise standards by strengthening teaching and learning across the curriculum. Literacy was one of the cross-curricular elements of the Strategy. Its main principles – derived from the Key Stage 3 strategy that came before it – were concerned with improving learning and teaching in the classroom and can be summarised as follows.

Set high expectations and give every learner confidence they can succeed
- Demonstrate a commitment to every learner's success, making them feel included, valued and secure.
- Raise learners' aspirations and the effort they put into learning and engage, where appropriate, the active support of parents or carers.

Establish what learners already know and build on it
- Set clear and appropriate learning goals, explain them, and make every learning experience count.
- Create secure foundations for subsequent learning.

Structure and pace the learning experience to make it challenging and enjoyable
- Use teaching methods that reflect the material to be learned, match the maturity of the learners and their learning preferences, and involve high levels of time on task.
- Make creative use of the range of learning opportunities available, within and beyond the classroom, including e-learning.

Inspire learning through passion for the subject
- Bring the subject alive.
- Make it relevant to learners' wider goals and concerns.

Make individuals active partners in their learning
- Build respectful teacher/learner relationships that take learners' views and experience fully into account as well as data on their performance.
- Use assessment for learning to help learners assess their work, reflect on how they learn, and inform subsequent planning and practice.

Develop learning skills and personal qualities
- **Develop the ability of learners to think systematically, manage information, learn from others and help others learn.**
- **Promote learners' confidence, self-discipline and an understanding of the learning process.**

The Secondary Strategy also emphasised the personalisation of learning, specifically by encouraging:

- exciting whole-class teaching, which gets the best from every child;
- extra small group or one-to-one tuition for those who need it, not as a substitute for excellent whole-class teaching but as an integral part of the child's learning;
- innovative use of ICT, both in the classroom and linking the classroom and the home.

Although the contract for the Secondary National Strategy was not renewed in 2010, it is expected that these principles will be embedded into secondary school practice.

The 14–19 curriculum

At the time of preparing the fifth edition of this book, proposals were once again under review regarding the 14–19 curriculum. The balance of subjects and modes of assessment for students in this age range have been a bone of contention for some time (see Chapter 11). There is potential here for radical change that may have a profound impact upon the way we organise our schools and colleges. But then again...

How to use this book

The chapters in this book are presented in what we hope is a logical sequence. The reality, of course, is that not all of you and not all of your courses will necessarily progress through the same sequence.

The chapters in the book are arranged into four parts:

1. Professional attributes and learning
2. Professional skills: planning and assessing learning
3. Professional knowledge: across the curriculum
4. Professional knowledge: inclusion

Each chapter is prefaced by a short statement that references the content of the chapter to the Teachers' Standards. Because of the nature of the Standards, you will see them repeated in a number of chapters. This is the nature of teaching and of learning to teach: the Standards are not activities that can be atomised or isolated within the whole of what teachers really do in classrooms.

In the classroom

Some chapters also contain vignettes that illustrate aspects of the content of the chapter in a classroom context. These are introduced by the heading 'In the classroom'. In Chapter 6, for example, some of the principles of formative assessment are illustrated in a dialogue between teacher and student. The classroom stories are not meant to be exemplary templates or models to be imitated, however. They are examples of individual cases and fully enmeshed in a particular context. You will find them useful as cases when formulating your own ways into teaching.

Practical and reflective tasks

Each chapter includes a number of practical and/or reflective tasks. You can use these tasks in a number of ways:

- to explore the relationship between the general principles outlined in the chapter and the policy of the schools in which you are training;
- to develop and consolidate your understanding of important skills or issues;
- to connect the principles informing your initial training and the practice of particular schools.

You may find that the tasks would be a useful focus for some of the ongoing work with your mentor.

Moving on

Some chapters in this book have sections entitled 'Moving on'. These are intended to offer suggestions to those of you particularly interested in the topic or theme of the chapter as to what you might like to read or do. These sections are in addition to suggestions for further reading.

Reading this book and engaging with the tasks alone will not enable you to become an effective teacher and to demonstrate achievement against the Teachers' Standards. This book can only support the intensive and interactive training you undertake as part of your course in schools and in higher education. The Teachers' Standards and the Award of QTS offer training providers – universities, colleges, local authorities and schools – the opportunity to design courses that regard teacher development holistically rather than as the 'ticking off' of separate technical competences that need to be 'evidenced' in wheel-barrows full of paper. Such courses acknowledge that values and dispositions (towards young people, to learning, to society, to teaching as a profession, etc.) accompanied by an understanding of how we learn and how we promote and assess learning, together with delight in a particular subject, and combined with skills of planning, organisation and communication are what effective teaching is all about. The contributors offer this book in support of such training programmes.

FURTHER READING FURTHER READING **FURTHER READING** FURTHER READING

Ellsmore, S. (2005) *Carry On, Teacher! Representation of the Teaching Profession in Screen Culture*. Stoke. Trentham Books. An entertaining and thought-provoking study of the charismatic, inner-city school teacher in film and what practising teachers have to say about this character.

Sarason, S.B. (1993) *You Are Thinking of Teaching? Opportunities, Problems, Realities*. San Francisco. Jossey-Bass. This is one of the best books available on the reasons why (or why not) to become a teacher. Sarason discusses the challenges that new teachers face in many aspects of their lives. He also explores issues of change in the lives of more experienced teachers. Although difficult to find in some libraries, this book is worth locating.

2
Teaching as a Masters' level profession: implications for beginning teachers
Viv Ellis

Introduction

In the shaded sections that precede the main chapters in this book, you will notice text that relates the chapter content to the Teachers' Standards. The section that precedes this chapter draws attention to the requirements to reflect on your own learning and development and to examine your teaching critically. Paragraph 14 of the Teachers' Standards outlines how *appropriate self-evaluation, reflection and professional development activity is critical to improving teachers' practice at all career stages. The standards set out clearly the key areas in which a teacher should be able to assess his or her own practice, and receive feedback from colleagues. As their careers progress, teachers will be expected to extend the depth and breadth of knowledge, skill and understanding that they demonstrate in meeting the standards, as is judged to be appropriate to the role they are fulfilling and the context in which they are working.* Academic qualifications such as Masters' degrees are awarded by higher education institutions and require the demonstration of a certain level of abstract or theoretical knowledge in order for the postgraduate, Masters' (or M-level) title to be justified. So conceptualising M-level work in initial teacher education requires some careful thought.

The move towards making teaching a Masters' level profession in England came as a result of the last Labour government's Education Secretary, Ed Balls', speech to the Association of School and College Leaders in 2008. Balls had noted that the country that so often performs at the very highest levels in international tests of reading, mathematics and science was Finland, where all teachers are qualified to at least Masters' level. It would be unfair to describe Balls' idea as simply a piece of policy tourism as it was also clearly a part of Labour's wider programme of transforming the school workforce. The move seemed to have little by way of thoughtful underpinning and careful preparation nor did it recognise the profound cultural and structural differences between England and Finland. The Finnish secondary system is characterised by small state comprehensive schools, for example, and not the highly stratified and diverse system of academies, grammar schools, faith schools and so on that came to characterise Labour's vision for England. Finnish teachers have higher standing in their society than teachers in England and, consequently (rather than the other way around) getting into teaching is a more competitive business than it is in England and it takes rather longer. There are, of course, myriad other differences that might help to explain why Finland does so well in international comparisons.

REFLECTIVE TASK

The Programme for International Student Assessment (PISA) is a project run by the Organisation for Economic Cooperation and Development (OECD). The programme is based on periodic assessments of 15-year-old students in the principal industrialised societies. The question asked is how far the national education systems are preparing young people for full participation in democratic cultures. The results are organised into 'league tables' and have become important touchstones for politicians in the countries involved.

Go to www.pisa.oecd.org. Read the section 'what PISA assesses' and then turn to the most recent results (at the time of writing, 2009). Where is England in the league table? Talk to your tutors, school colleagues and fellow trainees about their reaction to the PISA programme and the most recent results.

As a result of Ed Balls' 2008 speech, the Training and Development Agency for Schools (TDA – now the Teaching Agency) was charged with developing a new Masters' programme for school teachers that would be school-based and organised in partnerships with higher education institutions. The Masters in Teaching and Learning (MTL) was piloted in a number of areas of England with the students funded to complete the course through the TDA. In December 2010, the new Conservative–Liberal Democrat coalition government Education Secretary, Michael Gove, announced that there would no longer be any central government funding for the MTL and so from now on, the MTL will have to compete with other Masters' level courses in education run by universities and colleges on the basis that students fund themselves.

However, most post-baccalaureate teacher education courses in England are now offered at M-level – leading to the award of the Postgraduate Certificate of Education (M-level) or the Professional Graduate Certificate of Education (Honours degree-level). Offering PGCEs at M-level came about as a result of a rather different lever for change – that of a rather esoteric set of arrangements called the Bologna process, whereby academic qualifications in Europe have had to become more comparable and compatible. Any qualification called postgraduate had to be offered at a level above the honours degree (BA/BSc) and therefore contain elements of M-level work. The pioneering work of English universities such as Durham, Reading and the London Institute of Education had long conceptualised teacher education as a continuum and had offered end-on Masters' degrees to its PGCE students. Part of the drive to develop Masters' level qualifications by higher education institutions themselves had been to see teaching as a profession that was responsible for maintaining and enhancing its knowledge-base through active scholarship and research.

Teaching as a profession: accessing and developing professional knowledge

You will find many discussions of 'professional' and 'professionalism', particularly in relation to school teaching. Hoyle and John's (1995) discussion of teaching as a profession is often cited but their main conclusion seems to be that the definition of *profession* is highly contested. Calderhead (1987) refers to professional characteristics such as 'a body of specialised knowledge', the capacity to 'analyse and interpret' complex situations such as classrooms and the exercise of 'judgement' and wisdom (pp. 1–3). Perhaps it is Freidson (2001), a sociologist, who offers the most thorough-going discussion of professions and definitions of professionalism as a 'third logic', separate and necessarily distinct from both consumerism and bureaucracy. The key point for Freidson and those who have followed him is that through their day-to-day work with clients, professionals access and develop the professional knowledge base and they do so on principles of mutuality, collegiality and trust. Now it is fair to say that this is not quite how Labour saw teaching as a profession – preferring to determine the scripts and routines of professional action from the centre and then rely on 'professional' (i.e. efficient) delivery of these in schools. But in order for any profession to remain a profession and to be able to act flexibly, responsibly, ethically and in deeply knowledgeable ways, it is essential that professionals continue to draw on the historically accumulated bodies of professional knowledge and, moreover, essential that they have the responsibility to contribute to these bodies of knowledge. The alternative seems, at least to me, to be an occupational group that just does what it is told efficiently and, even more importantly, actually needs to be told what to do as it has lost the capacity to determine a course of action for itself. That is not a profession.

Ways of accessing and developing the professional knowledge-base

The history of the development of teaching as a profession is closely related to the institutionalisation of mass higher education (Ellis 2007). That is not to say that only universities and colleges have the key role in advancing professional knowledge. It is vital to recognise the day-to-day work that goes on in maintaining one's professional knowledge and in developing professional authority and gaining professional respect. One key expectation is that teachers will be well informed about current affairs and cultural life ('cultural' including science and sport as well as the arts). Membership of teacher unions and subject teaching associations are also vital ways of staying 'plugged in' to what is going on in the educational world by attending conferences, local meetings and reading their publications. In terms of developing the professional knowledge base, there are certain expectations that if we wish to contribute and have our worked judged to be valid and reliable then we will have to show that we have undertaken our developmental work in fairly systematic ways. A key contribution of Masters' level PGCEs and subsequent continuing professional development (CPD) programmes is to show you how to do the developmental work in recognisable systematic ways and this will often come under the headings of 'research' and 'research methods'.

Research means many different things. Some people believe that research can only be undertaken by people who are disinterested and uninvolved in the setting or activity they are researching. Others will argue that in order to make a difference, the only kind of research that matters is that carried out by the practitioners or participants involved. Researchers across the social sciences get involved in 'paradigm wars' or battles over 'methods' and very often these disputes are associated with institutional positioning and perceived intellectual status or reputation. Entering these debates and disputes at this point in the chapter would be meaningless so for my purposes here I am going to refer to 'teacher research' as any kind of knowledge-creating activity undertaken by a teacher practitioner in a systematic and transparent way. The aim of such research might not be to improve practice *per se* (the espoused goals of action research, for example) but to change the teacher's thinking or to clarify the nature of a problem or question.

PRACTICAL TASK PRACTICAL TASK PRACTICAL TASK PRACTICAL TASK PRACTICAL TASK

Have a look at the selection of handbooks and guides to teacher research available in your library or online. A few recommended texts are included at the end of this chapter. Which do you prefer and why? Can you see how different conceptualisations of research inform the books and how this affects what teachers are recommended to do? Talk to your tutors and trainee colleagues about the kinds of 'research' expected of you during your training programme.

In the section that follows, there is an example of how to do teacher-research work in a systematic way – by developing professional knowledge that is useful in learning to be a teacher. It takes as its starting point a common question of interest: the relationship between what students already know and do outside school and what we would like them to know and do in our classrooms.

Developing professional knowledge in practice: understanding young people's cultural worlds

One of the main purposes of the early stages of any teacher education programme is to get you talking to young people in school, to find out about what they do culturally outside school, to take what they say seriously and to begin to speculate on what the potential links might be to what you will be asking them to do in lessons. It is the sort of conversation teachers have informally every day – on the move, in corridors and while doing other things. But sometimes training programmes ask you to have this sort of conversation more systematically; i.e. it becomes the focus for an assignment that will be assessed at M-level.

An assignment about culture and education: preparing the ground

In talking about what young people do culturally we are operating a specific definition of culture, one that is widely known, understood and shared (to greater or lesser degrees) in sociology, psychology, anthropology, political theory and cultural studies. In brief, we are understanding culture as something that is actively made through the joint activities of interested people. The object of cultural activity is to make meanings and to develop the culture as a system of meaning-making. Under this definition, people tend not to use 'sub-culture' to denote 'lesser' (i.e. less intelligent, lower quality, etc.) cultural activity but to take the culture at face value and to try to understand how it works. Key thinkers in this area have included Raymond Williams, whose essay 'Culture is ordinary' (Williams 1958/1989) is often recommended reading, and Brian Street, who coined the phrase 'culture is a verb' (Street 1993).

This theoretical definition of culture also has deep practical (i.e. methodological) implications for you as beginning teachers as well as for researchers and students of the different social science and humanities disciplines. The most obvious practical implication for you as a beginning teacher is that you can't ask for a different group of students if you don't like their cultural activities. You still have to try to understand them, what they do, and to think about how you can build on your recognition to bring them in to working with you in your subject specialism.

So, for M-level assignment purposes, you might look out for a small group of young people to talk to in a systematic way. One way of doing this is to ask teachers if they know who is interested in particular cultural activities and then to follow up these leads individually. Another is to ask teachers if you can make an announcement at the end of the lesson and then ask students to meet you at break time or lunchtime somewhere. In either case, you will need to explain to the students what you are doing and why and ask them explicitly about whether they would like to take part. If they say no, that's it; you can't work with them. If they say yes, great – but you'll need to ensure you don't have too many students to talk to. Setting up these meetings, talking to students and recording or noting the conversation takes time and time is something most trainees don't have much of. You should also ask the students if you can record the conversation – only for you to listen to later and not for public play. And that you will destroy the recording once you've finished with it. If they say yes, great; if they say no, you will have to take notes as they talk.

When you have identified the small group of students, you'll need to work out whether it would be worthwhile and possible to ask to observe them engaging in the cultural activity (on school premises, not elsewhere) so that you can talk about what you see. For example, if students engage with computer games, could they show you how one works at a computer? But this might not be practical, so don't worry if you can't observe. It is the conversation (the interview) that will be important. So, in addition to finding the students, you'll have to use your imagination and empathy, as well as the academic reading you are doing, to come up with questions you'd like to ask them.

So far, this guidance has concerned *sampling* – identifying the people you will talk to. You will be sampling *purposively* if you follow the guidance, i.e. deliberately looking for people who engage in the same activity. This guidance also concerns research *ethics*, i.e. seeking the informed consent of the people you will work with – giving them the right not to take part and to withdraw at any time. Most of the time, you won't have to fill in a formal ethics application as a trainee as trying to understand your classroom and improve your teaching are aspects of professional work teachers can be reasonably be expected to undertake as part of their normal duties; i.e. the assumption is that good teachers talk to students about their subject, observe their students and try to understand their thinking anyway. The guidance here is about doing it systematically.

Generating data: talking to students on the record
So you have identified your focus; you have identified four or so students who have agreed to talk to you (and perhaps agreed to be recorded); you've also planned a day and time and room to have the conversation.

Before you talk to the students, you'll need to make a list of questions. These questions should enable the students to open up to you about the cultural activity; to explain what it is and why they do it; to show you what things mean and how they mean in the culture they're talking about. You'll need to think hard about the questions: you don't want too many and you don't want to ask lots of 'yes/no/dunno' questions. Start with a very general opener – an easy one that invites an easy answer. Perhaps show your genuine ignorance to get them to start from first steps. The final question should end on a nice, positive note. Don't ask superfluous or unnecessary questions. And don't ask leading or judgemental questions (e.g. 'So tell me why you're interested in this vacuous nonsense?')!

Next, check that the questions work as questions (i.e. they make sense and are answerable) by asking them of a friend. Take your friend's feedback and adjust the questions as necessary.

You'll need to make a choice about whether you ask the questions of students individually or in the group. Sometimes asking questions of a group of students makes for a livelier interview – they can have more to say and bounce ideas off each other. They can also disagree with each other, enabling you to form a more complex picture of the cultural activity. But sometimes practical considerations will mean you have to interview the students individually or, at best, in pairs. Whatever happens, usually 30 minutes is enough for this sort of individual interview and 45 minutes for a group interview.

During the interview process, try not to say too much yourself. Limit yourself to the questions and to follow-ups that try to elicit more information. At the end, don't forget to thank the students.

If you have recorded the interview, you can then replay the recording over and over again. Get to know the recording well and begin to make sense of it aurally. Then, when you have a moment, transcribe (i.e. write out) the relevant bits of the interview. Start transcribing just before the relevant section starts and end just after it ends. Relevance means what's useful to your interests.

If you weren't able to record the interview, as soon as it is over, go to a quiet room and add to the notes you were taking while the students talked. Try to reconstruct what the students said as fully as you can. But – just as if you can't make out what was said in the recording – if you can't recall or make out what was said, don't make it up. Just say that that section was inaudible. Type up your interview notes as soon as you can.

Then, whether you recorded and transcribed the interview or whether you wrote notes, you will have data that you can start to analyse.

So, to be clear, in this section, I have covered preparing for and conducting the interview – a *semi-structured interview* (unstructured interviews are really open-ended conversations; structured interviews are the kind that you might be asked to take part in in the street by a market researcher – 'do you prefer a. Daz, b. Persil, c. Ariel? etc.'). You will have developed your *interview schedule* (the list of questions), having first *piloted* it (to pilot something properly, though, you should try it out on the population – but not the specific sample). You will then have *selectively transcribed* the recording of the interview (your selection being made on the basis of relevance to your interests) or reconstructed the interview talk from your field notes.

Working on the data

Once you have your data (selective transcriptions or notes) you can start the messy and time-consuming process of analysis. The first thing to recognise is that transcription and note-taking was the first step: you transcribed or noted things that were important. So why was that? Write down the principles on which you selected elements of the interview.

Then, either by hand (using highlighter pens or by cutting strips with scissors) or on-screen (using the highlighting features of a word processor), mark up your transcripts or notes by identifying important themes. So, for example, if you had interviewed students who made rockets (using fizzy pop and confectionery) in the local park, you might find that a theme is 'shared fear/pleasure' – that is, the young people enjoy making rockets together in a social situation because they enjoy being frightened together – taking a risk (of getting soaked in lemonade) is something they get pleasure from, over and above their responses as individuals. You might identify this theme in what the students say and also in how they say it (i.e. the words and phrases they use). You can use a particular colour to represent this theme and then mark up the transcript/notes with the colour whenever you see the theme emerging.

Once you have finished this process, you will have a very messy or very colourful set of transcripts or notes. You then have to put these themes into some order – do they all make sense? Are they all justifiable with reference to the data? You may find you abandon some or change the way you express the theme. But don't reject anything that simply doesn't fit what you feel you want to say – remember, you're trying to understand other people's experience, not to justify your own preconceptions! It may be that there is a real contradiction in what the young people are saying and that's worth exploring.

So now you will have some notes about why you made the transcriptions you did; you'll have a set of themes attached to quotations from the transcripts/notes; and, of course, you'll have your notes and ideas from the research you've been reading about the particular focus of your interest. You'll have to put the analysis of your data (your themes) next to other people's analyses and theories (from the research you've been reading). Does your data confirm other people's? Or have you found something different?

The final stage in the process of analysis is writing it up. What will you be arguing? What have you found out about these young people's cultural activities? And how can you justify your argument with specific references to your own data (the interview transcripts/notes) and references to other people's research. The most important part of writing the analysis is that you show people why and how you have formed the interpretations you have.

In this section, I have been explaining how to do a simple *content analysis* of interview data, identifying *emerging themes* in the transcripts and notes and using these themes as *codes* with which to mark up the data (the process is known as coding). Once you have written up this analysis – to show what the young people are doing, how they are making meaning, what kinds of expertise they are drawing on – you can then start to think about the final part of the process: the implications for the teaching and learning of your subject in schools.

The exercise of professional creativity: making a curriculum for students you know

The sort of frequently set assignment this guidance refers to asks teachers to undertake something fairly basic (try to find out what students already know and do) but in a systematic way that draws on empirical evidence (transcriptions of students' speech and, perhaps, observation). The final stage in the process asks you to exercise your imagination in the development of professional creativity: to try to work out ways in which the students you have got to know can be brought into the ways of thinking and doing in the subject that you know. It is this creative process of knowing with a practical and future orientation that distinguishes some aspects of the effective teacher and it is in carrying out such thinking and such planning in systematic, transparent and informed ways that teaching as a Masters' level profession might be defined.

FURTHER READING FURTHER READING **FURTHER READING** FURTHER READING

Guides to teacher research

As the chapter makes clear, there are vigorous debates about distinctions within educational research, particularly over the status of the researcher and the position of the researcher as a practitioner investigating her or his own professional practice. For the purposes of this chapter, I have used the categories of *teacher research* or *practitioner research* to indicate the kind of activities in which teachers have and do engage and the kind of activities that are often associated with Masters' level professional qualifications for teachers. The following texts are useful introductory guides.

Lankshear, C. and Knobel, M. (2004) *A Handbook for Teacher Research: From Design to Implementation*. Buckingham. Open University Press. A comprehensive guide to designing and carrying out research projects in schools that is both theoretically informed and methodologically rigorous. A useful reference text for schools.

Somekh, B. (2006) *Action Research: A methodology for change and development*. Buckingham. Open University Press. A classic statement of the principles of the action research paradigm for practitioner research, written by one of its leading exponents. Somekh provides both the principles and rationale and describes some good examples of action research work.

Street, H. and Temperley, J. (eds) (2005) *Improving Schools through Collaborative Inquiry*. London. Continuum. A useful collection of chapters that acknowledges the necessarily collaborative nature of research designed to improve practice and outcomes for students.

Useful guides to data generation strategies

The Scottish Council for Research in Education produced a series of short guides about key data generation strategies aimed specifically at an audience of teachers. These texts are well worth looking for in education libraries and bookstores.

Drever, E. (2003) *Using Semi-structured Interviews in Small-scale Research: A teacher's guide*. Glasgow. SCRE.

In this series there are also guides to using questionnaires and observation. The following more general guide is also extremely useful.

Birmingham, P. and Wilkinson, D. (2003) *Using Research Instruments: A guide for researchers*. London. Routledge.

Some key journals

There are many academic journals publishing educational research, some intended for primarily academic audiences and others for both academic and professional readers. Here is a selection of key journals. If you are registered as a student at a UK higher education institution, you will have electronic access to these journals through your library service databases.

The British Educational Research Journal (BERJ) – the journal of the British Educational Research Association (BERA). BERJ is a high-status international journal that publishes key pieces of research in the field. There are six issues per year.

Educational Action Research – an international journal specialising in reports of action research in educational settings, supported by the well-respected Collaborative Action Research Network (CARN), and published four times a year.

Educational Researcher – a journal of the American Educational Research Association (AERA). *Educational Researcher* publishes articles reporting on empirical and theoretical projects, usually very sharply focused and, although the journal is US-based, the pieces are of international significance. There are nine issues per year.

There are also many subject-specific journals (e.g. for science education, mathematics education, etc.) as well as journals focused on policy analysis and the history of education, etc. Your training programme's librarian can show you how to search educational research databases to identify journal articles relevant to your interests. The Society for Educational Studies (SES) also provides interesting and professionally relevant discussions of research and scholarship in its conferences and its journal, the *British Journal of Educational Studies.*

General reading

A general expectation of advanced professional standing is that a person keeps up to date with general issues in the field and in society. Every year, thousands of educational books are published around the world and it is worth looking out for new or recent publications of interest. Here is a short selection that I have found interesting:

Egan, K. (2008) *The Future of Education: Reimagining our schools from the ground up*. New Haven. Yale University Press. Kieran Egan is one of the most original and engaging contemporary thinkers in the field of education. In this book, he summarises his unique educational philosophy and then builds a series of fictional scenarios outlining how these ideas might be put into practice in the decades ahead.

Claxton, G. (2008) *What's the Point of School? Rediscovering the heart of education*. London. Oneworld Publications. Guy Claxton is one of the UK's most influential educationists and this book dares to ask some very big questions about the school system as a whole – including the very fundamental issue of its compulsory nature. Claxton's writing is distinguished by engagement with current issues such as the information revolution as well as its historical 'long view' and his own personal depth of knowledge and experience.

Furedi, F. (2009) *Wasted: Why education isn't educating*. London. Continuum. Frank Furedi is a sociologist with broad interests who often strays into the educational arena. One of Furedi's themes is that current educational practice is too 'therapeutic' and person-centred and has failed in its core mission of 'imparting' knowledge to young people. Furedi is one of those polemicists with which many teachers might disagree – but it's worth understanding why!

A SUMMARY OF **KEY POINTS**

> **Defining teaching as a Masters' level profession emphasises teachers' responsibilities in relation to the professional knowledge-base.**
> **Teachers therefore should contribute to as well as access this knowledge-base.**
> **Teacher research is characterised by inquiries into practice conducted in systematic and transparent ways.**

MOVING *ON* > > > **> > >** MOVING *ON* > > > **> > >** MOVING *ON*

Following on from your initial training programme, there will be many opportunities for further M-level study as well as non-accredited professional development. Sometimes, providers are able to organise special pathways from PGCEs into their own M-level programmes. Have a look around at the universities and colleges in your local area to see the types of post-PGCE M-level courses on offer and their mode of delivery (part-time, evenings, weekend, etc.). In the future, you might also wish to consider the various professional doctorates (EdD programmes) that are on offer around the country for teachers wishing to develop their expertise as practitioner researchers and pedagogic leaders at doctoral level.

3
Professional values and the teacher
Patrick Fullick with Alaster Douglas

Teachers' Standards

A teacher must

1. Set high expectations which inspire, motivate and challenge pupils

- establish a safe and stimulating environment for pupils, rooted in mutual respect
- set goals that stretch and challenge pupils of all backgrounds, abilities and dispositions
- demonstrate consistently the positive attitudes, values and behaviour which are expected of pupils.

5. Adapt teaching to respond to the strengths and needs of all pupils

- demonstrate an awareness of the physical, social and intellectual development of children, and know how to adapt teaching to support pupils' education at different stages of development
- have a clear understanding of the needs of all pupils, including those with special educational needs; those of high ability; those with English as an additional language; those with disabilities; and be able to use and evaluate distinctive teaching approaches to engage and support them.

8. Fulfil wider professional responsibilities

- make a positive contribution to the wider life and ethos of the school
- develop effective professional relationships with colleagues, knowing how and when to draw on advice and specialist support
- deploy support staff effectively
- take responsibility for improving teaching through appropriate professional development, responding to advice and feedback from colleagues
- communicate effectively with parents with regard to pupils' achievements and well-being.

Part 2:

- Teachers uphold public trust in the profession and maintain high standards of ethics and behaviour, within and outside school, by:
  - treating pupils with dignity, building relationships rooted in mutual respect, and at all times observing proper boundaries appropriate to a teacher's professional position
  - having regard for the need to safeguard pupils' well-being, in accordance with statutory provisions
  - showing tolerance of and respect for the rights of others
  - not undermining fundamental British values, including democracy, the rule of law, individual liberty and mutual respect, and tolerance of those with different faiths and beliefs
  - ensuring that personal beliefs are not expressed in ways which exploit pupils' vulnerability or might lead them to break the law.

- Teachers must have proper and professional regard for the ethos, policies and practices of the school in which they teach, and maintain high standards in their own attendance and punctuality.
- Teachers must have an understanding of, and always act within, the statutory frameworks which set out their professional duties and responsibilities.

What do people think about teachers?

So you've decided that you want to teach. The contributors to this book are very pleased to hear it. But why teaching? It may seem rather strange to suggest to student teachers that they should begin their course by asking themselves this question, but as I hope you'll soon see, there are some very good reasons for doing so. Before we begin the process of reflecting on reasons for wanting to teach, let's look at what some people have said about teachers and teaching.

- *A man who knows a subject thoroughly, a man so soaked in it that he eats it, sleeps it, dreams it, this man can always teach it with success, no matter how little he knows of technical pedagogy.* (H. L. Mencken)
- *For every person wishing to teach, there are 30 not wishing to be taught.* (W. C. Sellar)
- *He who can, does. He who cannot, teaches.* (George Bernard Shaw)
- *It was God who made me beautiful. If I weren't, then I'd be a teacher.* (Linda Evangelista)
- *He was my favourite teacher in the school. If he hadn't been at the school, I don't think I would have been that clever. He's told me everything that I really want to know.* (Training and Development Agency for schools publicity)

PRACTICAL TASK PRACTICAL TASK PRACTICAL TASK PRACTICAL TASK PRACTICAL TASK

Think about each of the statements above. You may be able to add others about teaching that you have come across. Each statement carries a message about teachers and teaching.

- Write down two or three sentences setting out what you think lies behind each statement.
- Now write two or three sentences setting out what these statements say to you about your choice of teaching as a career. A possible starting point for this is to think about what kind of reasoned response you would make to someone who made one of these statements to you.

If you have the opportunity, discuss your reactions to these statements with other beginning teachers, and with experienced teachers too. To what extent do you think stereotypical views of teachers are inevitable? Are such stereotypes a bad thing?

Of course, I have been highly selective in the quotations I have chosen to use – whenever we teach we use quotations and examples that will support the ideas we are trying to convey. But these quotations illustrate a number of things that have been said to me, or to my colleagues and my students, in my years as a teacher educator. The overall gist of these is:

- to be a successful teacher, you've got to know your subject well;
- which will make teaching it pretty easy;
- although you'll still have to deal with a lot of kids who just don't want to know;
- so maybe teaching is something that you do if you haven't got anything better to do;
- although if you're successful, it can be quite a fulfilling job.

If you find these messages about teachers and teaching a bit confusing, then you find yourself in the same position as most seasoned teachers and educators. In my experience, it does not get less confusing when we look outside my (selective) quotations at the messages coming to us from the media, from friends and colleagues – most of these sources provide a great mixture of ideas about what teachers and teaching are all about. Just why this is the case could form the basis of a whole book in its own right. But for the moment I want to encourage you to think about the following points.

- Although adults are often unclear about what they expect of teachers, students are much less so.
- Teachers need to be clear about the expectations that other people have of them in order to behave appropriately.
- Teachers also need to be clear about the expectations they have of themselves as part of the process of deciding how to behave.
- Codes of behaviour and professional standards set out by government and by professional bodies are necessary starting points for deciding on one's own personal, professional standards of behaviour – but they are insufficient on their own.

In thinking about these points, you will not necessarily come to any quick and simple answers, but you will have begun an important process, involving a journey towards a set of personal professional values that are rooted in your own beliefs and values, as well as in what other people require of you.

Expectations – adults vs children

At first sight it seems surprising that there should be so much confusion about people's expectations of teachers. After all, teachers are a set of people of whom we all have experience at some point in our lives, and most people probably feel that they are pretty clear about just what it is that teachers do and how they should behave – their professional ethics. In a review article, Haydon (1996, p. 301) points out that the term 'professional ethics' is *more likely to bring to mind issues about the practice and attitudes of lawyers or doctors than of teachers in schools*, noting that there is *a lack of certainty or clarity about the status of teaching as a profession*. In a lengthy discussion following these points, Haydon compares the activities of teachers with those of other professionals such as doctors and lawyers. What seems to give rise to the confusion about teaching is that, while most people can reasonably readily agree about the 'good ends' that professionals like doctors and lawyers pursue (in the case of doctors, health, and in the case of lawyers, justice), people are generally much less clear about the 'good end' pursued by teachers – education – even though it can be argued that health and justice are not, in themselves, necessarily straight-forward concepts.

Whatever the source of the confusion, at this point in deciding on your own professional values there is little that you can do other than to acknowledge it, and then move on. But while adults as a whole may be unclear about the kind of values they expect teachers to have, there is evidence to suggest that among students there is a fair degree of agreement about the values that teachers should have. In addition, teachers themselves are also in general agreement about these values, while the same evidence also provides some support for the idea that teachers and their students agree quite closely about values; and not only those values that should apply to teachers, but those that should apply to students too.

Research in the area of teachers' values is rather thin on the ground. In those empirical studies that do exist, one interesting strategy employed both with children and with student teachers is the use of drawing. Coming from the field of cultural studies, research methods involving drawing are based on the idea that *writing paints pictures with words, while drawings speak with lines and colours* (Weber and Mitchell 1996, p. 304). Such methods have been widely used by researchers exploring such diverse things as children's images of scientists (Tuckey 1992) and what it means to be healthy (Wetton and McWhirter 1998).

PRACTICAL TASK PRACTICAL TASK PRACTICAL TASK PRACTICAL TASK **PRACTICAL TASK**

Before reading on, take time to think about how you see yourself as a teacher. Now draw a picture to answer the question 'How do you see yourself as a teacher?' (Don't worry about how good your drawing is technically – the ideas it's conveying are the important thing!) If possible, carry out this task among a group of student teachers who are at the same stage of their professional development as you. Share your drawings with one another and discuss what they convey. What similar ideas do you have? What ideas are different?

How do your drawings compare with those in Figures 3.1 and 3.2?

Weber and Mitchell's research was carried out with student teachers on courses in the USA, producing a diversity of images with strong themes of 'nurturing' and 'controlling' running throughout. (See Figures 3.1 and 3.2.) As well as a research tool, Weber and Mitchell see drawing as a means of helping student teachers reflect on and explore their conceptualisation of their developing ideas about how they see themselves as a teacher during their course.

Figure 3.1. A traditional portrayal of a teacher (from Weber and Mitchell 1996, p. 306).

Figure 3.2. A non-traditional portrayal of a teacher (from Weber and Mitchell 1996, p. 306).

Children's drawings of teachers like these share a number of common features (see Figures 3.3 and 3.4), most notably their bright (smart?) clothing and a big smile. For Wetton and McWhirter, the presence of a smile in an image of a person drawn in response to the instruction 'Draw a healthy person' indicates the need for mental health as part of overall healthiness. However, researchers exploring images of teachers are less certain about the meaning of a smile in a drawing of a teacher's face:

Figure 3.3. Mrs Richards by Sophie D, 4R (from Porth Junior School, 2000).

Figure 3.4. Mr Morris by Carys B, 4R (from Porth Junior School, 2000).

What does a smile signify? Surely the female teachers' smiles are intended to indicate good will, a lack of threatening intent. But a smile, as it is often unconsciously practiced [sic] by females, also signifies a lack of threat that may be interpreted as a submissive attitude, a desire to please. Why do the male teachers not need to smile so continuously? Does this reflect male and female socialization, and if so, what does it mean for the role of female teachers both in the classroom and in the larger contexts of school and society?

(Trousdale 1994, quoted in Weber and Mitchell 1996, p. 311)

While draw-a-teacher research provides some insight into teachers' values, text-based research provides insights into the extent to which students and teachers share ideals. Researchers in Finland (Verkasalo et al. 1996) administered a questionnaire to 428 15-year-old students and 134 of their teachers. Analysis of the responses showed that both teachers and pupils were in close agreement as to the values that an ideal teacher should display – especially highly rated were:

- benevolence (incorporating such ideals as loyalty, honesty, helpfulness, responsibility and forgiveness);
- and universalism (broad-mindedness, social justice, equality, world at peace, unity with nature).

There was less agreement about the values held by students. Students were asked to rate the values that they regarded as most important for themselves and for an ideal student. Answers to these questions showed that students felt that values which they regarded as the most important for themselves (true friendship, freedom, meaning in life and sense of belonging) were not the same as the most important values that an ideal student should hold. However, teachers also saw the students' personal values as very important in an ideal student. This means that we have the interesting situation that, while teachers and students are broadly in agreement about the values held by ideal teachers, students do not see their own values as being those of an ideal student, although teachers do ascribe these values to ideal students.

Although this research has not been replicated in the UK, another study with teachers only (Walker and Newman 1995) shows that teachers hold a large number of values in common when asked to rate agreement or disagreement with statements about teaching.

Expectations – what are yours?

We began thinking about developing a set of values to guide you through the early part of your teaching career by posing the question 'What do people think about teachers?'. Having given this some thought, and looked at the kinds of expectations placed on teachers by others (adults and children) and by themselves, as part of the process of clarifying your own values, I should now like to invite you to consider your reasons for wanting to teach.

Why teach?

Whatever your answer to this question, I suggest that it is possible to classify it into one of six different 'teacher portraits', as follows (I am grateful to my colleague Mike Smith for these portraits, and for their descriptions):

- 'it pays the rent/mortgage';
- the missionary;
- the imitator;
- the child;
- the bully;
- the radical.

Let's look at each of these in turn.

It pays the rent
While no one denies a teacher's right to be fairly remunerated, the idea that the job of a teacher can be viewed purely as an economic transaction (labour in exchange for money) is one that is difficult to sustain. Being a professional carries responsibilities, and the role of a teacher is not one that is susceptible to the simple equation x hours of labour = y amount of money. A professional approach to the job is therefore something that must be at the heart of every teacher's set of values.

The missionary
At an early stage in their career, many teachers want to act as a shining example to others, both as a person and as a professional. Yet in the messy world of schools and teaching, many compromises are necessary, which can lead to disillusionment. While initial missionary zeal may not necessarily turn to cynicism in every case, every teacher needs to be able to temper their ideals in the short term in order to achieve what they set out to do in the longer term.

The imitator
As we set out to become teachers nearly all of us will have someone in mind who inspired us in the past. It is all too easy to remember that great teacher who taught us as students and to seek to become 'just like them' – the problem is, you're not them. For one thing, you are working at a different time to them, and almost certainly in a different setting. You have a different set of skills and characteristics to them (no matter how much training you do), and you have a completely different set of experiences.

The child

If we're lucky we have many happy memories of our own childhoods. In order to work with young people effectively we need to move on from childhood and leave childish things behind. The teacher who seeks to relate to children as a friend is on dangerous ground – in more ways than one. Leaving the legal aspects of teacher–student relationships aside, students need a teacher who is able to guide, to offer explanations and to encourage. To do this teachers need to develop a professional relationship with students that is based on respect, but which is not simply a meeting of equals. Never confuse being friendly (good) with being a friend (bad).

The bully

While it is not appropriate here to explore what makes someone a bully, there is a fine line between being assertive and being a bully. There will be many occasions when you will need all your powers of persuasion to convince a class that what you are asking them to do is reasonable – be it to discuss a Shakespearean sonnet on a wet Friday afternoon, or to solve a maths problem for homework. While we may feel that we need to 'bully' children into doing things, we should never do this on the basis of abusing the power that we have as teachers, either as an authority figure or as a person who is older and/or bigger than our students. Any coercion has to be based on our own enthusiasm, to persuade students that they can and should achieve something, and that to do so is both good and desirable, even if it does not seem to be so in the short term.

The radical

While many of us may come into teaching wishing to change the world, there is a world of difference between encouraging discussion and debate among our pupils and fomenting revolution. While all teachers should feel that they have the duty (and not just the right) to encourage debate of controversial issues in their classrooms, to lead that debate by encouraging students to formulate a particular view is something that lies outside the remit of the teacher. Learn to make it clear to students when you are expressing a personal view about something – and to make it clear to them that other people may hold different views. Better still, ensure that they are able to hear more than one side of any argument that may excite particularly strong feelings.

Your reasons for teaching

As you think about these portraits, many of you may find yourselves thinking *but my reasons for teaching are like that...* or something similar. I certainly do not want to argue here that none of these reasons for wanting to teach is valid, or that any of them alone accurately represents a viewpoint that aspiring teachers necessarily hold. However, I do believe that any of these portraits, taken on its own, represents a seriously deficient model for a teacher to have, and encourage you to think more widely. In particular, you should be very clear about your motivation for teaching, whether you see it rooted within your subject, or within a desire to work with young people. Hopefully by this point you are beginning to think in terms of visualising the teacher as someone whose desire to teach comes from both of these sources – you will certainly need a good understanding of your subject to teach it at secondary level, and it will be a difficult job to do if you don't like your students.

Take time to think about your reasons for wanting to teach. No doubt you wrote about this on the form when you applied for your course, and it was certainly explored at interview with your tutors. At some point in your career someone is bound to ask 'what do you teach?' when they find out that you are a secondary teacher. If you reply 'maths' (or whatever your subject is) they might say 'but what about children – don't you care about them?'. On the other hand, if you say 'children' they might say 'but what about your subject – isn't that important to you?'. What will you say?

Professional frameworks

For anyone seeking to be awarded the status of a qualified teacher in England, it is necessary to be able to demonstrate the ability to meet the requirements of the government's Teachers' Standards. See also the other UK frameworks for teaching standards in the appendices to this book. As I hope you will already have gathered, my point to you as a beginning teacher is that you should see the values in the Standards as a statement of what you have to do in order to achieve the Standards rather than a set of values in their own right. I have tried to set out the reason for this in what has gone before in this chapter – that every teacher needs to understand the basis of their own professional values and those of their colleagues, and to have some idea about from where they are derived. This is not to question the values in the Standards document – but we do need to be clear about these values in order to make them our own. It is also important that we do this to ensure that we abide with values in the Standards not just in the detail of what they say but also in the spirit of their meaning.

Other professions have had codes of behaviour for a very long time – most people will be familiar with the Hippocratic Oath of the medical profession, for example. Derived from this oath, the General Medical Council has produced a document called 'The Duties of a Doctor', which is reproduced below. Effectively this is the equivalent of the attributes in the Teachers' Standards.

Good Medical Practice (2006)

The duties of a doctor registered with the General Medical Council

Patients must be able to trust doctors with their lives and health. To justify that trust you must show respect for human life and you must:

- Make the care of your patient your first concern
- Protect and promote the health of patients and the public
- Provide a good standard of practice and care
  - Keep your professional knowledge and skills up to date
  - Recognise and work within the limits of your competence
  - Work with colleagues in the ways that best serve patients' interests
- Treat patients as individuals and respect their dignity
  - Treat patients politely and considerately
  - Respect patients' rights to confidentiality
- Work in partnership with patients
  - Listen to patients and respond to their concerns and preferences
  - Give patients the information they want or need in a way they can understand
  - Respect patients' right to reach decisions with you about their treatment and care
  - Support patients in caring for themselves to improve and maintain their health

---

- Be honest and open and act with integrity
  - Act without delay if you have good reason to believe that you or a colleague may be putting patients at risk
  - Never discriminate unfairly against patients or colleagues
  - Never abuse your patients' trust in you or the public's trust in the profession.

You are personally accountable for your professional practice and must always be prepared to justify your decisions and actions.

www.gmc-uk/org/guidance/good_medical_practice/duties_of_a_doctor.asp

---

PRACTICAL TASK PRACTICAL TASK PRACTICAL TASK PRACTICAL TASK PRACTICAL TASK

Compare the values in the Standards with those in 'The Duties of a Doctor'.

1. Doctors' 'clients' are their patients – who is the 'client' in the case of teachers?
2. Doctors have to respect patients' confidential information – what duties do teachers have in the case of information about students?
3. Patients have rights to be involved in decisions about their care – what rights attach to decisions about students?
4. What other values are present in the Standards, and what are their equivalents for doctors?

While the Teachers' Standards are demanding, I have every confidence that hard work and diligence during your course will mean that you will have no problems in meeting the Standards, and in setting a fine example, both professionally and personally. As you reflect on and evaluate your practice during the course, return to the Standards and to the ideas about your own values that you have thought about as you have read this chapter. Ask yourself *Is this how I would wish others (students, parents, colleagues) to see me, and to think of me?* If the answer is 'yes' – well done! If not – why not – and what will you do about it?

A SUMMARY OF **KEY POINTS**

> Being clear about expectations forms an important part of determining codes of behaviour for professionals.
> Expectations of teachers expressed by teachers, students and others may be at variance – in clarifying expectations it is therefore important to know to whom an expectation belongs.
> Expectations of teachers form the basis for setting professional values for teachers.
> Text and drawings form the basis of two important classes of research tools for clarifying values.
> Beginning teachers must understand their own expectations of what it means to be a teacher in order to begin to build their own value set.
> Meeting the requirements for QTS means that a beginning teacher must be able to demonstrate behaviour consistent with the Teachers' Standards.
> Beginning teachers must build a value set which is consistent with the Teachers' Standards and which is based on a thorough understanding of the role and expectations of a teacher as expressed by all of the stakeholders in education.

MOVING *ON* > > > > > > MOVING *ON* > > > > > > MOVING *ON*

Obtain a copy of the relevant part of each of the professional codes of conduct for teachers, lawyers and doctors. (For example, the part of each code that relates to confidentiality.) Compare the three codes – what do the codes have in common, and where do they differ? What does this comparison tell us about 'profession' as a concept?

FURTHER READING FURTHER READING **FURTHER READING** FURTHER READING

General Medical Council guidance on Good Medical Practice (available from **www.gmc-uk.org/guidance/good_medica_practiceindex.asp**) and Solicitors' Code of Conduct 2007 (available from **www.rules.sra.org.uk**) These two professional codes for doctors and lawyers provide an interesting comparison with the Teachers' Standards.

Koehn, D. (1994) *The Ground of Professional Ethics*. London. Routledge. For anyone wishing to consider professional ethics in more depth, this book provides a good starting point – although it is not for the faint-hearted! Teachers reading this book will find much of interest, although (as Haydon 1996 notes) they will find it necessary to infer what Koehn's arguments mean for teachers, since she refers to teaching only briefly, when discussing practices that might be considered as a profession.

4
Understanding learning
Gary D. Kinchin

Introduction

Learning is clearly central to achieving the aims of education and thus to making a difference in the classroom. As a soon-to-be-qualified teacher or new member of the profession you are also central to raising standards further within the education system and pivotal to some of the key educational reforms, including *The Importance of Teaching* (White Paper, 2010).

The authors of this book hope you will agree that all teachers have a responsibility to know their subject and teach in ways which enable their students to learn. As Pritchard (2005) states: *A basic understanding of processes of learning is essential for those who intend to develop activities that will have the potential to lead to more effective learning in classrooms, that is teachers* (p. 2). *A student learning what was intended* has been identified by some as the basis for describing effective teaching (Kyriacou 1997).

While student learning should be your first consideration in planning and teaching, it is well documented that trainees and early career teachers possess only the beginnings of a knowledge base to achieve this objective and at the same time are more concerned with:

- how they are going to cope with their workload and survive in the teaching environment;
- their classroom management and being regarded as a 'real teacher';
- being liked;
- developing a professional image that is accepted by students (Behets 1990; Fuller 1969; Kyriacou and Stephens 1999; Monk 2001).

These may be anxieties that you have felt yourself.

Whereas the above concerns may not foreground learning or make direct reference to the different ways in which students learn, the promotion of learning will always remain one of the things that a teacher is concerned about across their careers. You will find teaching most enjoyable and satisfying when your students are enthusiastically engaged in their learning and you feel you have got them to the point of the lesson.

Assuming that you are at the initial stages of beginning to understand the nature of learning, learning theories, and how students might prefer to learn, the purpose of this chapter is fourfold.

1. To get you thinking about learning, what it is, and how you might consider it in one classroom and promote it in yours.
2. To provide a description and critique of some of the learning styles which might exist within classrooms.
3. To consider the implications for learning in light of some key reforms in education and in particular the growing interest in personalised learning.
4. To consider some implications of the Teachers' Standards for enabling student learning.

What is learning?

This is indeed a difficult question to answer. Theorists do not all agree what learning is and how it occurs. Learning is a broad concept and perspectives on how learning takes place have been put forward by psychologists, linguists, neurophysiologists and philosophers. There is clear agreement that learning is important. Gredler (2001) has provided some pertinent reasons why the ability to learn is so crucial.

- Learning is important to the individual.
- Learning develops competencies in a variety of school subjects in both childhood and adolescence.
- Learning aids the acquisition of a variety of perspectives, values, and ways to interact with one another.
- Learning enables an individual to carry out a diverse lifestyle.
- Learning develops the capacity for lifelong learning.
- Learning helps to preserve cultural values and traditions.
- Learning aids new discoveries and inventions.

The word 'learning' would seem to imply 'change'. Although learning can occur in both formal and informal settings, Stevenson and Palmer (1994) argue that learning might occur implicitly (without the individual being aware of it) or explicitly (where there is conscious and deliberate effort). Most definitions suggest that learning is an enduring change in an individual as a consequence of an experience in a particular situation (Driscoll 1994). This definition, however, would seem to exclude changes which might occur due to maturation/ growth and development (Long 2000).

As you begin your career in teaching, Kyriacou (1997) offers one of the most helpful definitions of learning, stating *Student learning can be defined as changes in a student's behaviours which take place as a result of being engaged in an educational experience* (p. 22). The changes implied here can span some of the many outcomes possible within a secondary school curriculum, as the following illustrate: greater knowledge of dates in history; having different attitudes towards certain issues or ideas in contexts of personal, social and health education; the improved ability to play a musical instrument; demonstrating an understanding of photosynthesis in science through a group presentation; knowing all major cities in France; or the application of a particular defensive strategy in an invasion game in physical education. Learning here therefore suggests the capacity to do something different to what could be done earlier (Schunk 1996).

Understanding learning: one view from inside the classroom

In an effort to understand learning it is important also to understand the dynamics of classroom life. You and your students will spend considerable time in one another's presence. Creating teaching environments that are both orderly (which we know you are concerned about) and which meet the needs of individual students will be difficult professional work. Your role as a teacher is to enable learning, which could suggest that the direction of influence in class is solely from you to the student in terms of influencing their learning gains. In the dynamics of classroom life this is not always the case, and you may have experienced this. Students can sometimes exert great influence. For example, there may have been times when what is completed and hopefully learned by students feels almost 'negotiated' between you and them, and that they are exploring the boundaries.

Given the current educational climate (explored a little later in this chapter) it is highly likely you will be faced with varying student needs and learning styles and with the expectation that you will begin to personalise learning and teaching, focusing as you will on each child's learning in order to enhance their progress, achievement and participation. Your students are also likely to have varying levels of motivation to be in class and to learn. Being with their friends and fulfilling their own agenda for social interaction (which you might regard as disruptive) may already have competed with your efforts to engage students with the lesson content. Such a situation can impact on learning in the classroom, as an explanation to the following 'model' indicates.

Doyle (1979, 1981) viewed the classroom as an 'ecology'. A brief insight into his model will provide one way of understanding the daily realities of classroom life and the challenges this poses for thinking about and enabling teaching and learning for individual students. Doyle viewed the class in a way that saw the management, instructional, and student social systems interacting and developing around a series of tasks to be completed by students. If the ecological balance between these systems was right in the eyes of students then the instructional element is normally foregrounded and learning tasks and gains become priority. If not, then students may tend to fix the balance in their own way to make the tasks or work they are doing something they can achieve and enjoy, or they may go off-task and do something else which requires you re-establish order and control.

Of relevance to some of the content of this chapter (in particular sections where you are asked to consider some learning theories) Siedentrop and Tannehill (2000) indicate that good teachers tend to be able to promote learning gains by blending the student social system into the instructional system by:

- offering an exciting and relevant curriculum;
- employing strategies such as group work which demand student interaction;
- promoting peer teaching and co-operative learning.

It therefore seems important that we are able to develop students' positive attitudes towards learning, and the use of the above suggestions while acknowledging how Doyle views the classroom may in one way help you see and appreciate the complexities of classroom life.

Theories of learning

As a beginning teacher or new entrant into the profession, do you have your own personal theory or theories of how learning best takes place? Most teachers do, so it is very possible that you do too. You are a learner yourself and have spent many hours observing teachers teaching you in their efforts to enable your learning.

REFLECTIVE TASK

As you ponder over your own personal theory of learning, take a few minutes to consider some of the following questions. What did you learn in and out of school? How did you learn these things? Under what circumstances did you learn best? What circumstances or arrangements tended to impede your learning? How might you use your own experiences as a learner to inform your efforts to enable learning in the classroom?

Your responses to the above task might suggest your learning occurred differently for different tasks (some that were simple, some that were more complex). There may have been things that you learned either in the absence of a teacher (e.g. being with your class-mates) or you felt could only have been learned with a teacher present. You might have recalled examples when class discussions and group work with others helped your learning or when you were required to recite facts successfully from memory alone.

Every intentional teaching/learning experience is built on assumptions about how learning happens, whether this is implicit or explicit (Rink 2001). When these assumptions about learning are formalised or abstracted to a more general level, we call them learning theories. According to Driscoll (1994) a learning theory represents *a set of constructs linking observed changes in performance with what is thought to bring about those changes* (p. 9). In essence, learning theories have attempted to understand how individuals relate to their environment in ways that enhance their ability to use themselves and their environments more efficiently and more effectively.

As you may be aware, writers have put forward a vast number of theories in an effort to explain or describe how learning occurs. Not all theories, however, are applicable to those who work in education but there are some that appear more dominant and have received greater attention in the literature. Child (1986) reminds us that *no one theory has provided all the answers to the kinds of questions of concern to teachers ... no one single theory has yet been formulated which satisfactorily accounts for all the facts* (p. 82).

The following section will set out the main premise of some of the positions/theories of learning. It is not intended that these theoretical perspectives be seen as polarised but that they are available for teachers as fit. The difference between the perspectives involves different ways of focusing on learning but both provide important insights into the processes of effective performance and learning. As Phillips and Soltis (1998) state: *We must be content to deal with a number of theories of learning, each useful perhaps in a different context* (p. 5). Roblyer (1996) also reminds us, and the following section will attest, that there are opposing views as to whether learning should be structured and directed by teachers or that students should take charge of constructing their own knowledge, in essence having more ownership of that learning, but again the situation will dictate. In summary, an awareness of learning theories can be helpful to you in the following ways.

- They can inform your planning and teaching.
- They can help you to evaluate your practice.
- They can assist in the diagnosis of in-class problems.

Some theories of learning

All twentieth-century learning theories can be classified into two broad families: firstly, conditioning theories (behaviourist family), and secondly, interactionist theories (cognitive family). There are differences across these two families, particularly centring upon the behaviourist position that humans are passive beings and therefore react to stimuli while cognitive theorists support the position that learners are interactive. However, no learning theory can ignore the critical nature of the level of student engagement or that motivation is a key factor influencing whether learning does or does not take place. High achievement in learning is more likely when the student is highly motivated as motivation represents a key factor influencing the extent to which students can achieve desirable learning outcomes.

We shall examine perspectives on learning promulgated by theorists within the behaviourist and cognitive families, which some claim to have had the most significant impact upon learning and teaching within schools (Child 1986).

Behaviourist family

If as a teacher on placement you have used immediate praise and positive feedback to students as examples of positive reinforcement or have applied consequences for inappropriate behaviour such as detentions, or you have taught and re-taught with feedback how you want your students to enter and exit the classroom, then you have already incorporated aspects of Skinnerian theory in your teaching. If you are looking to use Skinner's ideas further then as a teacher you will be predominantly concerned with finding ways to get your learners to respond and then reinforce that response. The resultant behaviour should subsequently be reinforced for it is more likely to occur again under similar circumstances.

Skinner

B. F. Skinner (1968), as the founder of the theory of operant conditioning, is considered by some to be the most influential theorist to have impacted on education and learning. Advocates of behaviourism viewed learning as a permanent transformation in behaviour with an emphasis upon measurable changes or outcomes. Learning is seen as a conditioning process concerned with a response to a stimulus. The stimulus is deemed the cause of learning which acts upon the individual, evoking the response or increasing the chances of a response. In the absence of this reinforcement the behaviour is less likely to occur. Learning is therefore interpreted in terms of the strength of the stimulus–response connection. Behaviourists suggest teachers should therefore:

- create environments that enable students to respond properly to stimuli;
- be specific about what are appropriate responses;
- model good behaviour;
- shape appropriate behaviour by rewarding positive responses.

Cognitive family

If during your teaching to date you have:

- provided opportunities for your students to learn in problem-solving settings;
- included content that students are passionate about – that is, you see the importance of making the learning experiences relevant and meaningful for your students with an awareness of the students' current knowledge;
- used teaching which concentrated on the unknown using the known as a basis;

then not only may you see on a practical level elements of Doyle's thinking, but you have already begun to incorporate aspects of cognitive learning theory in your teaching, as the following will explain.

Cognitive theorists have attended to more holistic perspectives on learning with specific interest in the ways learners solve problems. Vygotsky (1962) and Bruner (1966) are considered some of the most influential theorists within this family. According to Bruner (1966) the acquisition of knowledge is an active process. Individuals construct knowledge by connecting the incoming facts to previously acquired knowledge. It is here that the individuals make meaning.

Cognitive theorists typically place action and problem-solving at the centre of learning. Learning is viewed as a process of gaining or changing insights, views or outlooks as individuals make meaning of previously learned facts. Learning is inferred from what people say or do. Thus, the learning process is primarily social and learning occurs through socialisation carried out in a variety of contexts such as the school, the family or peer group. (You will recall within Doyle's model there was a very heavy emphasis upon the social task system and how teachers might develop this to achieve instructional objectives.) The assumption here is that students will learn when placed in these groups – or other interactive settings, as much of what is learned is learned from others (Vygotsky 1962).

Constructivism

According to Marlowe and Page (1998):

> *passively accumulating disconnected knowledge is not learning... To learn a student has to be mentally and often physically active. A student learns when she discovers her own answers, solutions, concepts and relationships and creates her own interpretations.* (p. 12)

The above statement offers one rationale for constructivism as a school of thought on learning. Of late, constructivism and situated learning have become quite popular orientations to teaching and learning as a part of the cognitive family (Rink 2001). The constructivist approach has had a significant impact upon instruction and learning (Kyriacou 1997), and is viewed by some as a component within the cognitive sciences (Terwel 1999) and as a theory about how we learn (Marlowe and Page 1998). Constructivist approaches support the position that learners are not passive recipients of transmitted knowledge. Constructivism emphasises the active role students play in acquiring knowledge personally and socially through engagement with meaningful tasks situated within their immediate environment. Rather than being given specific information on how the task is to be performed, constructivist approaches encourage learners to find their own way through the tasks, developing and creating their own knowledge. Learner autonomy and initiative are accepted and encouraged and knowledge is created by doing, researching and experiencing real-life situations (Roelofs and Terwel 1999). In effect, as the term suggests, learners attempt to 'construct' individual meanings based upon what they currently understand and know. Constructivism assumes that all learners have had different experiences, therefore individual understanding cannot be the same between people.

Constructivist approaches foreground the knowledge structures students currently possess, termed 'conceptions' within the educational literature. Research that originates in cognitive psychology provides considerable support for the presence of students' prior knowledge: that is, students come to every new learning experience with some knowledge about the topic already established (Dodds *et al.* 2001). For learning to take place the student must understand the new material in terms of their existing prior knowledge (Taber 2001). There is a growing literature across a number of the subjects – including science, maths, PE, health, geography, and history – on students' conceptions, that is, what they know and believe about a topic (see Barratt and Hacking 2000; Galili and Bar 1997; Griffin *et al.* 2001; Myhill 2000; Pendry *et al.* 1997; Placek *et al.* 2001). These conceptions have been labelled preconceptions, misconceptions, alternative conceptions, or alternative frameworks. An understanding of alternative conceptions is critical if genuine learning is to occur (Palmer 2001), as it is quite common for learners to enter classrooms with ideas related to topics which are at odds with expert opinion or viewpoints (Taber 2001).

PRACTICAL TASK PRACTICAL TASK **PRACTICAL TASK** PRACTICAL TASK **PRACTICAL TASK**

You are planning to teach a lesson in your subject area. During the closure of the preceding lesson introduce the next topic(s).
- Ask the students to write down what they currently know or believe regarding the topic and what they consider to be some of the sources of their present knowledge.

Collect the written task before you read the responses.
- Predict and write down what you expect your students to possess some prior knowledge of in relation to the topic(s).
- List what might be some possible sources of this knowledge.

Read the responses and attempt to collate them.
- Compare and contrast your predictions with the present knowledge and sources of knowledge among the students. What emerged?
- How did the nature of their knowledge compare with your conceptions of the topic that you are about to teach?
- What are the implications of these findings for enabling learning in your subject?

Marlowe and Page (1998) offer some implications for work in classrooms if teachers wish to move to adopting the constructivist perspective.

- Teachers should emphasise the promotion of learning via questioning and problem-solving.
- Teachers should de-emphasise the 'transmission' of knowledge.
- Work in the classroom should retain the importance of the content to be unearthed and reflected upon.

- Individuals' conceptions of the content are foregrounded to help learners decide between the relevant/ meaningful and the irrelevant.

In summary:

- learners construct knowledge actively and socially;
- learners already possess ideas about the learning situation;
- learners take greater responsibility for and ownership of their learning.

If you take account of what you currently do in your teaching and consider some of your most recent experiences with your classes, it may be quite possible that you have used some activities/tasks which illustrate the above positions on learning. If you can associate yourself with some of the activities below then you could well have incorporated some elements of them in your classrooms already. Have you:

- asked your students in their groups to predict the outcome of a science experiment before they begin?
- used punishment to discourage certain types of activities?
- developed an interactive multimedia presentation to make a topic more interesting in geography?
- asked students to count to 50 in French and then praised them for this?
- allowed your students in your class to set their own personal targets in physical education when fulfilling a role of their choice (e.g. team leader)?
- structured an environment in a citizenship session where your students engaged in critical thinking?
- used a reward to encourage your students to complete a task in history?
- played background music to encourage a mood or stimulate a group routine within dance?
- provided your students with the materials to create their own presentations in IT?

At the surface you may not realise that the fundamental underpinnings across these tasks are quite different, but part of becoming an effective teacher will be your ability to quite skilfully blend these different approaches and positions on learning for different classroom-based situations.

Learning styles

There is a large body of research on learning styles or preferences for learning new information and then connecting this information to something that is already known. Specifically, research on learning styles has attended to efforts to define learning styles and has documented elaborate attempts to understand and categorise elements that make up different learning styles. While writers have put forward multiple definitions (Cano-Garcia and Hughes 2001), throughout educational research the idea of 'learning style' typically refers to how people prefer to learn (Heffler 2001; Kolb 1984; Sternberg 1997) and thus access and process ideas and new information.

You may have been informed as part of your training that one reason why learning may not take place is a possible mismatch between a student's preferred learning style and the learning opportunities and tasks they face. Indeed this is often true. As Fleming and Baume (2006) state: *Teaching often reflects the teacher's preferred style, rather than the student's preferred learning styles* (p. 5).

There is general agreement that individuals do indeed differ in their preferences for gathering and processing information. Like adults, children and students learn in different ways. Felder and Silverman (1988) and Barbe and Malone (1981) claim students and young people could be considered hear-learners, see-learners or do-learners. Individuals will rely upon a consistent set of behaviours or approaches to learning and seeking meaning (Van

Zwanenberg *et al.* 2000) which are determined by a combination of hereditary and environmental factors, and the demands of the present environment.

Research on teaching to different learning styles is not conclusive with reference to the impact upon students' academic achievement (Muijs and Reynolds 2001) and as will be seen later, there are some who have questioned the use of learning styles. Regardless, a number of writers have attempted to 'catalogue' a range of learning styles that appear to exist across individuals or have produced inventories to enable learners to self-report their preferences. An extensive review of the learning style literature is not appropriate here. The reader is encouraged to consult Riding and Raynor (1998) and Honey and Mumford (1982). For the purposes of this chapter the work of Kolb (1976, 1984, 1985), and Honey and Mumford (1982) in the area of learning styles will be discussed followed by some attention to Gardner's theory of multiple intelligences.

Kolb: Learning Styles Inventory (LSI)

One of the most noted writers in the area of learning styles is Kolb. Kolb's LSI is arguably the most widely documented instrument for measuring and analysing learning styles (Kolb 1984). Kolb (1976) identified four adaptive learning modes, which are summarised in Table 4.1.

Table 4.1: Summary of Kolb's learning modes and associated characteristics

Learning mode	Unique characteristics
Concrete experience	Responds to kinaesthetic elements of the experience
Reflective observation	Learns by introspection and reflection
Abstract concept	Comprehends information conceptually
Active experimentation	Learns by environmental manipulation

The construct of learning style as identified by Kolb included two dimensions. Firstly, perceiving, which describes the concrete and abstract thinker, and secondly, processing, which describes the active or reflective processing ability. When these dimensions were integrated by Kolb, some alternative ways of relating to the world were expressed as four types of learning styles.

1. Divergers: who learn by personal experience gathered from feelings.
2. Assimilators: experience is grasped through abstract comprehension.
3. Convergers: use abstract reflection.
4. Accommodators: process information concretely and actively.

Kolb (1984) offered a conceptualisation of learning through the 'experiential learning cycle'. This model described learning as a continuous cyclical process of experience, reflection, theory and preparation. The ability to learn, according to Kolb, can commence at any point in the cycle. The individual elements of the sequence are described as follows.

- Experience: represents an active experience where new information is fed in.
- Reflection: process of learning change, the individual now passively thinks about what has just happened.
- Theory: the individual thinks about the new information and now contrasts this with other ideas and theories.
- Preparation: this is where the learner considers what to do next.

Honey and Mumford

Honey and Mumford (1982) applied Kolb's experiential cycle to produce a learning styles model that consisted of four descriptions of individuals who prefer to learn at the respective stages of the Kolb cycle. Their 20-item questionnaire enables the individual to locate their preferred learning style. Cotton (1995) offers a useful summary of the characteristics of each learning style, which has been outlined in Table 4.2.

Table 4.2: Summary of Honey and Mumford's learning styles with associated characteristics

Style	Stage of Kolb's Experiential Learning Cycle	Characteristics
Active learners	Experience	Welcome new experiences, rush into new experiences, take centre stage, easily bored, happy to combine with others, and like opportunities for problem-solving. **Activists** are individuals who learn by doing, enjoy novel experiences, and generally dislike structured situations
Reflective learners	Reflection	Are cautious, tend to take a back seat, are calm, prefer to take their time, generally have a low profile and are more disposed to observational experiences. **Reflectors** are individuals who learn through feelings and experience, enjoy asking questions and try to predict outcomes
Theorists	Theory	Learn by investigation, carry out tasks in logical steps, and think through application of general rules. **Theorists** are individuals who learn through observation and investigation and tend to focus upon logic and systematic planning
Pragmatists	Preparation	Tend to try out ideas in practice, want to get on with things, and thrive on direct work experience. **Pragmatists** are individuals who learn by thinking and engaging in problem-solving and role playing

Multiple intelligences

Gardner

As we have seen, many learning styles can be found within one classroom. The intellectual strengths and weaknesses each student possesses will determine how easy or difficult it is for this individual to learn the subject matter presented in a particular way by the teacher. As an attempt to recognise the different abilities and talents of students, Howard Gardner (1983) proposed a new concept of intelligence and formulated a list of seven intelligences.

1. Logical-mathematical intelligence: logical thinking, deductive reasoning (mathematical and scientific thinking).
2. Linguistic intelligence: mastery of language to remember information.
3. Spatial intelligence: development of mental images to solve problems.
4. Musical intelligence: recognition of musical tones, pitches and rhythms.
5. Bodily-kinaesthetic intelligence: mental ability is used to co-ordinate bodily movement.
6/7. Personal intelligences: include interpersonal feelings of others, and intrapersonal intelligence, which is the ability to understand one's own feelings and motives.

Gardner claimed the intelligences are needed for productive functioning in our society, that they rarely operate alone, but are used concurrently when facing problems or acquiring skills.

Gardner suggests some implications for teachers.

- Think of all the intelligences as equally important.
- Present material which attends to most if not all the intelligences.
- Use knowledge of the intelligences to reinforce the subject matter in multiple ways.
- Implement different assessment techniques to enable learners to show what they know, understand and can do (journals, portfolios, creative tasks).

Guidance on the teaching with multiple intelligences is available, such as Jasmine (1996).

PRACTICAL TASK PRACTICAL TASK PRACTICAL TASK PRACTICAL TASK PRACTICAL TASK

Select a topic/concept. Using your understanding of Gardner's multiple intelligences plan and teach a lesson where you aim to address most if not all of these intelligences. What different ways will the material be presented which attends to these intelligences? What alternative evaluation practices might you use? What do you notice about the level of participation within the class and the work the students produce?

As a beginning teacher, do you sense that some of your students might prefer structure, or some might prefer learning on their own, or with others in groups? Are there some students who seem to prefer situations when the room is silent or there is noise? Do you recognise these seven intelligences within the classes you teach?

Learning styles: a critique

As was intimated earlier within this chapter, the notion of learning styles has been challenged by some. Fleming and Baume (2006) offer the following possible reason: *This is probably because it is very difficult to measure learning (in) part because it is difficult to define learning in useful way(s), especially if one wants to know when learning happened or to what it can be ascribed* (p. 7). Other scholars are of the view that most learning style models have limited efficacy and that more work must be undertaken to validate these theories through research, as there seems to be some variability in the evidence (Demos 2005). Readers are encouraged to consult the following sources for a useful critique of learning styles and a discussion of the theoretical base upon which they rest: Coffield *et al.* (2004); Franklin (2006); Demos (2005).

A trend towards personalisation of learning

Some writers have deemed the use of learning styles as 'superficial quick fixes, that do not lead to sustainable personalisation of learning' (Aspect 2006). As has been mentioned in this chapter, the present educational climate, in part, speaks to a long-term, learner-focused provision designed to meet the needs of students and which teaches learners how to learn. The development of the personalisation agenda within public policy is concerned with meeting the individual needs of children and young people in an effort to maximise their individual achievements and standards. It also sets the agenda for learners to have far greater involvement in the ways in which they are taught. Specifically, the Gilbert review included within its main points that: *every secondary student has a learning guide who will meet with them at least once every half-term, monitor their progress and act as their advocate in the school* (*Times Educational Supplement* 2007, p. 1).

In 2004, a speech by David Miliband (former Labour Minister of State for School Standards) first identified five components to the then government's conception of personalised learning (Milliband 2004). These were: 1) Assessment for learning, 2) Effective teaching and learning, 3) Curriculum entitlement and choice, 4) Organising the school, 5) Supported by effective teaching and learning strategies. Personalised learning requires teachers, in conjunction with a range of other adults, to develop knowledge of a student's strengths and weaknesses using feedback that is provided to and obtained from students to inform their planning. The teacher's role is to develop the confidence and competence of each student using appropriate teaching strategies that aim to build upon individual needs, including information and communications technology (ICT) and being aware of the various student intelligences.

Catering for such an array of individual needs will be a challenging task for trainees and newly qualified teachers when interacting with large groups of learners. However, it is important that beginning teachers are aware of the different learning styles that might exist in their classes and what might be some characteristics of individual learning preferences. Such information will inform how you organise the curriculum, select appropriate teaching strategies and their accompanying learning experiences or tasks to enable access to the content for all students.

The Teachers' Standards: implications for student learning

What might be some implications for trainees in enabling student learning in light of the language and intent of the Teachers' Standards? In this section, attention is drawn to some aspects of the Standards that appear most relevant for enabling learning.

Mention was made earlier in the chapter of the typical concerns/fears which are apparent in most inexperienced teachers during the very early stages of their development and training, which could limit the range of teaching approaches which are adopted. New in-service teachers will also experience a range of stressors during a period which Katz (1972) referred to as 'survival' and which is a time when the teacher is coping on a daily basis, and may be questioning their ability to teach. Acknowledging Fuller's three-stage model of teacher development (Fuller 1969), moving from (1) concerns about self, to (2) concerns about tasks, to (3) concerns about students and the impact of teaching, seems pertinent here and leads us to ask whether trainee teachers are capable of achieving such a focus upon outcome rather than on self so early in their development as teachers.

The Standards also emphasise the need to support and guide students to reflect upon the progress they have made as part of an ongoing dialogue and collaboration with them. The ability of students to talk about their experiences and make adults aware of their views is a key issue in personalisation. Consulting students about teaching and learning, as one aspect of 'student voice', has received considerable attention within the literature (Cullingford 2006; McIntyre *et al*. 2005; Thomson and Gunter 2006). Engaging in dialogue with students will, in part, help you as a teacher become better informed about how and when they learn.

It has been documented that inexperienced teachers tend to adopt more direct forms of instruction that both lead to less developed independent learning skills among students (Gipps and McGilchrist 1999) and do not 'connect material' (Muijs and Reynolds 2001, p. 15). Indeed, in some subject areas Ofsted (1995) have highlighted that experienced teachers have tended to use more command styles of instruction. Attention to some of the personalisation literature foregrounds group work as one instructional approach considered significant in the shift towards personalisation (TLRP 2004). Many have advocated the benefits of groupwork (e.g. Cohen 1994) and the educationally worthwhile outcomes that group work can promote including enhanced student motivation, developing social communication, and better relationships with students. If indeed there are commonly used pedagogies that fit within the more teacher-directed mode, then this trend would seem to be a little counterproductive to enabling a more learner-focused provision. Student teachers will be expected, within the context of the current reforms in education, to have good subject knowledge and to be able to contribute to the workforce via contact with a range of support staff, other professionals and parents. Beyond this, can we indeed expect trainees to have sufficient pedagogical knowledge to provide, monitor, and manage learner-centred environments (couched within cognitive/constructivist schools of thought) when they are typically 'getting to grips' with subject and curricular knowledge? If we aim to develop the very best teachers then the answer to the above question has to be yes. However, all of us involved in initial teacher education realise the difficulty and complexity inherent in this process and one of the primary functions of any teacher education programme has to be the provision of support in the achievement of this goal. It is perhaps timely to heed Kyriacou and Stephens' (1999) remark in their study of Postgraduate Certificate of Education students:

> *If student teachers believe that students should be occupied principally to keep bad behaviour at bay, future generations of teachers are going to be more preoccupied with the management of 'order' than the cultivation of learning.* (p. 28)

A SUMMARY OF **KEY POINTS**

This chapter has offered a very brief insight into the nature of learning and learning styles. The key points of this chapter are as follows.

> **Student learning should be the first consideration in teaching a lesson.**

> **Learning theories typically fall within one of two umbrellas (behaviourist and cognitive), should be applied as the situation demands, and critically examined within the dynamics of classroom life.**

> **Learning styles refer to how individuals prefer to learn. Several learning styles and their associated characteristics have been identified by researchers (Kolb, Honey and Mumford) and that children possess different abilities (see Gardner).**

> **Individuals with different learning styles possess some unique characteristics.**

> **Constructivism represents a dominant school of thought on learning. An understanding of students' prior conceptions is critical to helping them connect new learning with established knowledge structures.**

> **The concept of personalised learning puts forth a system where the child is at the centre and where teachers engage in dialogue with children so their voices are heard.**

FURTHER READING FURTHER READING **FURTHER READING** FURTHER READING

Aspect (2006) *Personalised Learning: From Blueprint to Practice*. Wakefield. Aspect.

Bleach, K. (2000) *The Newly Qualified Secondary Teacher's Handbook*. London. David Fulton Publishers.

Coffield, D., Mosely, D., Hall, K., and Ecclestone, E. (2004) *Should We Be Using Learning Styles: What research has to say on practice*. London. Learning and Skills Research Centre.

Cohen, E. (1994) *Designing Groupwork: Strategies for the Heterogeneous Classroom*. New York. Teachers College Press.

Cullingford, C. (2006) Children's own vision of schooling. *Education 3–13*, 34(3), 211–221.

Demos (2005) About Learning: Report from the Learning Working Group. London. Demos.

DfE (2010) *The Importance of Teaching – the Schools White Paper 2010*. London. DfE.

DFES (2003) *Every Child Matters*. London. DfES.

DFES (2004) *Five Year Strategy for Children and Learners*. London. DfES.

DFES (2005) *Higher Standards: Better Schools for All*. London. DfES.

Fleming, N. and Baume, D. (2006) *Learning Styles Again: VARKing up the right tree.* Educational Developments, SEDA Ltd 7(4), 4–7

Franklin, S. (2006) VAKing out learning styles – why the notion of 'learning styles' is unhelpful to teachers. *Education 3-13,* 34(1), 81–87.

Kyriacou, C. (1997) *Effective Teaching in Schools: Theory and Practice (2nd edn).* Cheltenham. Nelson Thornes Ltd.

Milliband, D. (2004) Personalised learning: building a new relationship with schools. Speech made to the North of England Education Conference, 8 January 2004, Belfast.

McIntyre, D., Pedder, D. and Rudduck, J. (2005) Student Voice: Comfortable and uncomfortable learnings for teachers. *Research Papers in Education.* 20 (2):149–168.

Pritchard, A. (2005) *Ways of Learning: Learning Theories and Learning Styles in the Classroom.* London. David Fulton Publishers.

Thomson, P., and Gunter, H. (2006) From consulting students to students as researchers. *British Educational Research Journal,* 32(6), 830–856.

Times Educational Supplement (2007, January 5) Students' personal advisers, p.1.

Tirosh, D. (2000) Enhancing prospective teachers' knowledge of children's conceptions: The case of divisions of fractions. *Journal of Research in Mathematics Education*, 31(1), 5–25.

TLRP (Teaching and Learning Research Programme) (2004) Personalised learning: A commentary by the teaching and learning research programme. ESRC.

PART 2
PROFESSIONAL SKILLS:
PLANNING AND ASSESSING LEARNING

5
Planning for learning
Charlotte Wright, Miranda Peverett and Viv Ellis

Teachers' Standards

A teacher must

4. Plan and teach well structured lessons

- impart knowledge and develop understanding through effective use of lesson time
- promote a love of learning and children's intellectual curiosity
- set homework and plan other out-of-class activities to consolidate and extend the knowledge and understanding pupils have acquired
- reflect systematically on the effectiveness of lessons and approaches to teaching
- contribute to the design and provision of an engaging curriculum within the relevant subject area(s).

5. Adapt teaching to respond to the strengths and needs of all pupils

- know when and how to differentiate appropriately, using approaches which enable pupils to be taught effectively
- have a secure understanding of how a range of factors can inhibit pupils' ability to learn, and how best to overcome these
- demonstrate an awareness of the physical, social and intellectual development of children, and know how to adapt teaching to support pupils' education at different stages of development
- have a clear understanding of the needs of all pupils, including those with special educational needs; those of high ability; those with English as an additional language; those with disabilities; and be able to use and evaluate distinctive teaching approaches to engage and support them.

Introduction

This chapter addresses the key issues of teacher preparation and planning for learning. It follows on from the themes of Chapter 4, with its overview of theories of learning and learning styles, and anticipates those of Chapter 6, a chapter concerned with the vitally important and inseparable issue of assessment of – and for – learning. Underlying this chapter as a whole is the assumption that the processes of teaching and learning are inextricably bound up with domains of knowledge, that teachers and students are dealing with what is often referred to as 'content' and that – in the UK context – this is often specified by the National Curriculum, National Strategies or examination syllabuses. But Herbert Kohl (1986) reminds us to give equal attention to the interpersonal dimension of teaching as an activity – interacting with students and contributing positively to the development of learners' identities:

Teaching . . . involves helping students acquire understanding, knowledge, and skills they didn't previously have. To do this, it is essential to enable students to feel good about themselves as learners and to create an atmosphere that enables them to focus energy on learning.

(Kohl 1986, p. 90)

Curriculum and learning

The word 'curriculum' means a course of study or a set of ideas (to be taught and developed). In England and Wales, the first ever National Curriculum was implemented in 1989 (Scotland and Northern Ireland have never had a National Curriculum).This was the first time that a range of subject knowledge, understanding and skills had been specified across the 5 to 16 age range. The National Curriculum became a statutory instrument and its implementation has been monitored ever since through the inspection system. These new arrangements supplemented the syllabuses for 16+ and 18+ national examinations with which secondary teachers have worked for a very long time. Since September 2001, secondary schools have also been asked to work with the Key Stage 3 Strategy (subsequently, the Secondary National Strategy). This non-statutory but recommended initiative has been designed to address the difficulties many students experience on transition from the primary phase in accessing the secondary curriculum and also the problem of student regression (in terms of attainment) between Key Stage 2 and the early years of Key Stage 3.

REFLECTIVE TASK

In your school (and preferably in your own subject department), find a teacher who was teaching prior to the introduction of the National Curriculum in 1989. How did this teacher design a course of study – a curriculum – for students then? What are the differences now? What are the benefits and drawbacks (for individual students, teachers and society) of a National Curriculum?

The activity of teacher planning, then, has become more complex over the last 20 years as more detailed curriculum prescription in terms of 'content' – combined with a more recent emphasis on recommended teaching methods and strategies – means that individual teachers (through their work in subject departments) have had to 'map' their curriculum against national frameworks as well as examination syllabuses. This complexity arises from the obvious requirement to consider the children to be taught first (their needs, interests and ways of learning), the available resources (physical, including the classroom, sports equipment, textbooks, musical instruments, computers, library stock, etc.; and human, including classroom assistants and teacher expertise) and the students' entitlement to the National Curriculum, and what is generally referred to as the ideal of a 'broad and balanced curriculum'. Complex planning at this level is discussed later in this chapter but, as a trainee, you will need to develop an awareness of how your work – and that of your department – relates to the rest of a student's experience of the secondary curriculum.

Different traditions in planning for learning

One of the most influential models of teacher planning and preparation was that of Tyler (1949). Tyler's original theories of instructional design were based on rational, behaviourist approaches to learning. The psychologist Jerome Bruner (1966) later expounded rather different theories of teaching and learning that were focused on the processes of mental growth and the teacher's role in facilitating this. Glaser (1976, 1984) critiqued what he saw as 'process-based' approaches to instruction but proposed a 'knowledge-based' or 'competency' model that to some extent reflected Bruner's notion of 'optimal structures' of knowledge:

> . . . a theory of instruction must specify the ways in which a body of knowledge should be structured so that it can be most readily grasped by the learner. 'Optimal structure' refers to a set of propositions from which a larger body of knowledge can be generated . . . since the merit of a structure depends upon its power for simplifying information, for generating new propositions, *and for* increasing the manipulability of a body of knowledge, *structure must always be related to the status and gifts of the learner. Viewed in this way, the optimal structure of a body of knowledge is not absolute but relative.*
>
> (Bruner 1966, p. 41; emphasis in original)

Inspection evidence from Ofsted (2002) suggests that effective departments in secondary schools do not necessarily have more detailed or especially long schemes of work but that what exists clearly specifies what knowledge, skills and understanding should be developed with a class and how students can make progress.

For many beginning teachers, this is one of the most difficult aspects of planning. How do you represent ideas or model skills that you have developed at the graduate level to, say, a bottom set Year 9 last thing on a Friday afternoon during a force eight gale? The Teachers' Standards – and this book – assume that much of your training will concern the principles of developing 'optimal structures' in your own specialist subject and providing you with opportunities to practise this development in classrooms.

The question of teacher knowledge

The Teachers' Standards specify that you should understand the subject knowledge requirements of your own specialist subject. The transformation of your subject knowledge in the context of the secondary classroom will be an important part of your training.

When discussing teaching strategies, Kohl drew our attention to the importance of the teacher's knowledge of the subject:

> There are many other modes of explanation, such as drawing diagrams, providing examples, or even improvising a dramatic presentation of an idea. All these techniques require a mastery of the content you are teaching so that you are free to play with it.
>
> (Kohl 1986, p. 102)

In other words, in order to teach effectively, matching 'content' and method to the particular children's needs – and to analyse what the children have learned – teachers need to be able to reshape ideas, to represent knowledge in different ways. This is only possible if teachers have confidence in their own knowledge, and thus the process of training will continue throughout each teacher's career. Good teaching is born out of a recurring process: successful teachers continually update their own understanding, reflect upon the process of learning that they themselves are constantly undertaking, and then use that subject and pedagogic knowledge in their planning for students' learning.

Planning for learning over time

Teaching is sometimes described as a cycle of planning, transaction and evaluation (Figure 5.1).

Figure 5.1. Teaching cycle

Simply put, planning goes on before teaching; transaction is what happens in the classroom with students; and evaluation occurs after teaching. However, the reality is much more complex.

The planning stage includes a consideration of aims, justifications, concepts, strategies, assessment and resources. It is ongoing and plans are adjusted based on assessment information.

The transaction stage is the execution of the plans made earlier (although in practice the transaction may involve changes of plan in response to the emerging and unforeseeable responses of the learners). Simultaneous evaluation of the transaction can lead to changes in planning. Transaction – implying, as it does, interaction and interplay – is a term that is used in preference to 'delivery'. Deliveries can be made while the intended recipients are 'out'.

The evaluation stage includes a comparison of the learners' achievements in the lesson with the teacher's plans; and an evaluation of the effectiveness of the teaching strategies and resources used. The evaluation is the start of the planning stage for the next and subsequent teaching activities/lessons.

But why bother writing lesson plans?
It is worth stating explicitly here that your initial training's emphasis upon careful and thorough planning, and reflective, critical evaluation, is to ensure high standards of teaching and learning (the 'transaction') through which your students will make progress. Planning and evaluation are not simply administrative requirements. There are at least two main reasons why trainees are asked to plan carefully and thoroughly.

1. For new teachers without substantial classroom experience, the planning process is often difficult. In trying to plan teaching that is successful for you and your students and draws upon your own strengths (rather than simply trying to copy successful lessons you have observed), you will need to spend time thinking about what you want the students to learn and how you will help them to achieve this. The very process of trying to write a plan – including the inevitable redrafting and revisions – will help you to develop planning skills. There is a body of research that views writing as a mode of learning (see, for example, Emig 1977) and so writing lesson plans can be seen as being useful to you, the trainee.

2. As a trainee, you will need to demonstrate – consistently and over a period of time – certain skills and attributes, including those contained within the Teachers' Standards. You will need to evidence your achievement of these Standards to a variety of people to whom you are accountable: your mentor and tutor, an external examiner and, perhaps, an inspector during an inspection of your training course or school. The evidential requirements for trainee teachers are sometimes seen as greater than for fully qualified teachers. This shouldn't be surprising. That said, qualified teachers seeking threshold payments or applying for Advanced Skills status (or indeed going through Ofsted inspection or post-Ofsted special measures) all have to produce detailed plans and records as part of portfolios of evidence.

Nevertheless, you will be aware that experienced teachers do not appear to 'need to plan' as much as you do. This doesn't mean that experienced teachers' plans aren't as detailed as yours; rather that *experienced teachers more often rely on their extensive experience to form a mental framework of how they want the lesson to proceed* and that their plans and their ability to adjust them to the specific needs of each class *have become internalised through repetition* (Kyriacou 1991, p. 17).

Long-term planning: schemes of work or key stage plans

A scheme of work is a description of the work planned for pupils over a specific period. Sometimes, they are known as key stage plans if they relate to the groupings of National Curriculum years. The planning of these is the responsibility of the whole subject department in a secondary school, co-ordinated by the head of department with all members of staff contributing to the planning process. It is at this level that the links between planning and teacher development become clear: different teachers with differing strengths contribute to the design of a curriculum for students in which teacher expertise is shared.

Long-term plans usually give an overview of the year or key stage. At departmental level, a scheme of work is made up from a series of units of work which describe:

- how a school's curriculum policy is to be translated into effective teaching;
- how the curriculum will be implemented;
- how human and material resources will be used efficiently.

To develop a scheme of work, departments will need to decide on an overall programme with regard to the range and depth of experiences/topics/activities they teach and ensure progression and continuity of student learning. The National Curriculum and the relevant national priorities and examination syllabuses will inform this process, which is sometimes called 'curriculum mapping'.

Talk to your mentor about your subject department's approach to longer-term planning. How does the department go about planning at this level and reviewing their plans? What kinds of long-term planning records are kept?

The cover sheet to one department's key stage plan is reproduced as Figure 5.2. It is not intended to be exemplary and we would need to see the detailed (medium-term) planning that followed it. It does, however, give us the opportunity to see how one secondary department (in this case, English) represents its Key Stage 3 programme on one side of A4.

Medium-term planning: units of work/sequences of lessons

These are the plans for the teaching of one of the components of the scheme of work, i.e. a topic, text or activity, which will involve a series of lessons, perhaps over a five- or six-week period (one-half of an average term). The planning of these is sometimes the responsibility of individual teachers, although departments often collaborate in this process. In some cases, the unit of work is detailed to the level of content of individual lessons. As a beginning trainee, you will not normally be asked to design an entire unit of work straight away but, instead, you are likely to be given specific content and asked to plan an individual lesson. As you progress, however, you will be given increasing responsibility for designing your own units of work.

An effective medium-term plan shows how lessons fit together, indicates the progress expected and is a way of identifying targets for progression that apply to groups rather than individual students. An effective medium-term plan should:

- identify what pupils will learn over a half-term/term;
- be based on assessments of what students already know, understand and can do;
- show evidence of progression, in line with the department's scheme of work or key stage plan; this may be in the form of differentiated expectations (see below);
- give recommendations for teaching and learning approaches;
- identify opportunities for assessment.

An example of a medium-term plan (unit of work) proforma used by one training provider is given in Figure 5.3. It is not presented as an example of good practice. As a guiding principle, we should recognise that different secondary specialist subjects will have different planning requirements and that any generic proforma is meant to be adapted or used in the development of personalised planning formats.

Medium-term planning will ideally start at the bottom of the proforma, with the expectations and differentiated outcomes. This should then inform the sequencing of tasks/activities so that cumulative and directional learning can take place.

You will notice that a good deal of information is required on this plan and that some of it will require considerable thought. Remember that some departments' units of work may not be as detailed but, in the context of your training, a proforma like this gives you the opportunity to demonstrate your understanding (briefly and meaningfully) of a number of key areas

Key Stage 3 Plan for English		

7

Induction unit: making a student prospectus; – writing non-fiction	writing/telling autobiography – differences between speech and writing	class novel study *Holes* by Louis Sachar – language awareness – social variation
extended simulation activity – *Escape from Kraznir* – – drama (role-play, writing in role, etc.)	expressive arts project – based on the *Beowulf* story – – ICT focus (multimedia)	diaries – integrated project – *Diary of a Survivor* – pre-1914 non-fiction

8

Individual poetry anthology – writing poetry – using quotation	the language of advertising (media focus) – media languages – audiences	drama text for class study – *Frankenstein* – (inc. comparison with Mary Shelley's novel)
class novel study – choice of Anne Fine texts	individual/group extended narrative – – narrative POV	Introduction to media studies – media technologies

9

presenting a written argument – response to non-literary texts – – persuasion	forms of poetry – ballads and sonnets –	class novel study – theme: different generations – choice of Robert Westall or Aidan Chambers texts
drama text as class study – Shakespeare –	control of narrative – twist in the tale –	newspapers – their production and impact – ICT focus

– independent reading programme
– literacy skills programme   KS3 starter activity units – word and sentence
level)
– ICT available – limited but systems
  in place for use
– information skills (Year 7)
– storytelling (Year 8)   } cross-curricular projects

Figure 5.2. Key Stage 3 diagram

related to planning such as the cross-curricular learning specified at the beginning of each National Curriculum document.

Assessing Pupils' Progress (APP)

APP was introduced by the former Qualifications and Curriculum Development Authority (QCDA) and has been implemented in fairly patchy ways across England. The purpose of APP was two-fold: first, to monitor curriculum coverage against the National Curriculum programmes of study (and former National Strategies objectives); second, to help teachers plan for 'progression' in pupils' learning. In practice, teachers have been encouraged to use the APP Assessment Focuses (AFs) to build 'learning ladders' for pupils – a staged progression of objectives that can be shared with the learners and that builds incrementally on previous stages. Some schools have adopted APP as an approach very consistently and this is reflected in their medium-term planning. Other schools have not adopted APP at all; at a recent meeting, we heard one teacher say 'APP hasn't arrived in Putney yet!'

At the level of principle, APP lays out the pathways through the curriculum for every learner in the published documentation and the networks and 'ladders' of AFs. Some schools adopt a different principle which is that they want their teachers to determine these pathways for the specific learners they are teaching and to do that in very individualised or personalised ways. Either way, the relationship to planning sequences of lessons (units or schemes of work) is vital.

Learning across the curriculum

All teachers have responsibility to develop their students' capacities in a number of areas. The National Curriculum specifies a number of general teaching requirements (including the use of language, ICT and citizenship across the curriculum) and aspects of cross-curricular learning.

As an individual trainee, you shouldn't feel obliged to take full responsibility for all aspects of students' learning across the curriculum. This responsibility can only be assumed by the school and planned for collaboratively across departments and pastoral areas. You should, however, be interested in whether your specialist subject can make a contribution and be aware of how your own teaching might contribute. The sections on the unit of work proforma concerned with key skills and spiritual, moral, social and cultural development/ other learning across the curriculum would only be completed if there were obvious ways in which the unit contributed to the development of students' capacities in these areas. For examples of how secondary subjects can contribute to these areas of cross-curricular learning, go to: **www.nc.uk.net/** and follow the link for 'Learning across the curriculum'.

General teaching requirements: health and safety

One of the general teaching requirements specified by the National Curriculum is that of ensuring the health and safety of students. This requirement applies particularly to teachers of design technology, art and design, physical education, science and ICT. Training in these specialist subjects will include attention to this important aspect of planning and teaching. On a medium-term plan, it is useful to draw attention to particular health and safety issues associated with the topic or activities so that a more detailed risk assessment can be made. On the generic proforma, health and safety issues can be identified underneath a list of any particular resources needed for the unit.

| Secondary ITE **Unit of work** | Year Group: | Date developed: |
| | | Date revised: |

Unit title:	The rationale for this unit:
Focus:	
Aims:	Potential outcomes for summative assessment purposes:
Particular resources:	Opportunities to develop cross-curricular dimensions:
Health and safety issues:	Links to previous work:

Personal, learning and thinking skills:

Independent enquirers
Creative thinkers
Reflective learners
Team workers
Self-managers
Effective participants

Tasks/Activities	NC Programmes of Study/ APP AFs/A-Level AOs	Teaching approaches (including use of ICT)

Differentiated expectations:	AT and NC Level, APP AFs or exam criterion and grade, etc.:
1. After completing the unit, **most** students will have:	
2. After completing the unit, **some** students will **not have made as much progress** and will:	
3. After completing the unit, **some** students will **have progressed further** and will:	

Figure 5.3. Unit of work proforma

Differentiated expectations

In this section of the proforma, you would briefly indicate the level of attainment (expressed as a National Curriculum level or examination grade) you expect of the different groups within your class. In this way, you are setting targets for groups of students based upon your knowledge of class. The (three) groups are broken down in the following terms.

1. 'After completing the unit, **most** students will have ...': this is what you expect of the majority of the class; the core, the key concepts and basic skills related to an appropriate level of attainment.
2. 'After completing the unit, **some students will not have made as much progress** and will ...': this is where you indicate the level at which you expect the lowest attaining in the class to achieve; this may arise out of a different task for these students.
3. 'After completing the unit, **some students will have progressed further** and will ...': this is where you indicate what you expect the highest attaining students to achieve; this may arise out of a different task or extension work with additional content.

Teaching approaches

This column on the unit of work proforma provides some information about teaching strategies that have proved or will prove to be effective. For example, in relation to a particular activity or task, it may be that teacher modelling of a particular skill will be most effective; or perhaps the use of ICT would effectively consolidate children's understanding. The teaching strategies necessary to include all members of the teaching group should also be mentioned here.

PRACTICAL TASK PRACTICAL TASK PRACTICAL TASK PRACTICAL TASK PRACTICAL TASK

Use this medium-term planning proforma in the development of a unit of work you are going to teach. What are the strengths and weaknesses of this format and of using proformas in general?

Short-term planning: lessons

You will probably begin to develop lesson plans fairly early in your training. Two definitions are useful here.

- A lesson is a 'period for teaching something; an experience from which to learn'.
- A plan is an 'arrangement for carrying out future activity; an arrangement of parts in a system'.

We have already made the obvious point that you – the teacher – are going to teach something that the students will learn. In this context, 'experience' refers to the methods or strategies that you use to connect what you want the students to learn to your assessment of that learning. The word 'arrangement' draws attention to the need to think carefully about the parts of a lesson: in what order do you put the experiences? How does the order influence the students' learning? In turn, that starts to take you back to the medium-term plan (unit of work) because a lesson plan comes from within this overview plan. A lesson plan is part of a sequence.

Although each lesson plan must be related to what has gone before and show how it is related to what is to come, it can appear to stand by itself. But it is a plan, not a script: it is something you work from and not to. There is the danger of planning too much and too little: too much detail can lead to you telling rather than teaching; too little can lead to a lack of focus in the teaching and to under-developing what it is you want the students to learn.

An effective short-term (lesson) plan should:

- identify in detail what pupils should learn (the objectives or learning intentions);
- identify how you will know that progress has been made (the outcomes);
- identify opportunities and strategies for assessing the learning outcomes;
- show how lessons will start, end and continue;
- outline activities which show what pupils will do, how they will be grouped and what resources will be used;
- identify key teaching points and key questions;
- show how students' learning can be supported or extended (differentiation);
- note how any support staff will be deployed.

Once again, this probably sounds like a daunting and unrealistically detailed list. In the example of lesson planning that comes at the end of this chapter, you will see how these requirements can be met manageably and meaningfully. At the moment, please remember that a lesson plan isn't a script nor is it an essay. It must be useful to you and allow an outside observer or examiner understand what – and how – you have been teaching.

PRACTICAL TASK PRACTICAL TASK PRACTICAL TASK **PRACTICAL TASK**

Referring to the checklist above, use ICT to prepare a lesson plan format that you would find useful in your specialist subject.

Differentiation

This aspect of planning involves matching your tasks or activities and your teaching approaches to the needs and preferred learning styles of the children in your classroom. For a more detailed discussion of differentiation and inclusion, please see Chapter 13. At this point, however, it will be useful to note some principles of differentiation as they would impact upon a lesson plan.

In planning lessons as in planning units, it is useful to think about a core of learning that you will plan for all students in a class. This would consist of the key concepts and basic skills. Based upon your assessment of all students' likely progress against this 'core', you may also plan for two eventualities.

1. A 'support loop' that could involve a different task or activity, a different teaching approach or the support of another adult for those who may have difficulties; it is essential that any other adults are aware of your plans before the lesson and what you see as their role in supporting an individual or small group.
2. Extension activities for those who will be able to progress further, which may involve additional content of greater challenge, more independent research or the development of higher-order skills such as synthesis, evaluation or application to different situations.

On lesson plans, these strategies can be related to individual students by name. If a student has been assessed at Stage 2 or above of the Code of Practice for Special Educational Needs, you will need to refer to their Individual Education Plan (IEP) when planning differentiated work (see Chapter 13 for more information on planning for students with special educational needs).

Assessment

You will need to give some details of the assessment opportunities (what and who?) and the assessment strategies (how?) employed during the lesson. Assessment strategies could take the form of monitoring a few individuals and discussing their contributions to a whole-class discussion, observing a specific student at work, a question and answer session with a small group, reading any written work produced during the lesson or marking homework or classwork after the class. You will also need to be aware of the record-keeping requirements of your department and how your ongoing assessment of students' progress will need to be recorded. The next chapter in this book deals with assessment of – and for – learning in some detail but for the moment, the key questions to address in lesson planning are:

- who will your assessment activities focus on?
- what aspect of their work will you be assessing?
- how do you intend to achieve this?

Managing the lesson

An important aspect of planning a lesson involves thinking about the various stages or elements in the lesson's structure and the transitions between them. This will include the organisation of students (how they are grouped) and resources. The most common structure to lessons in secondary schools (especially at Key Stage 3) has three parts.

In the introduction (which may include a starter activity), the teacher:

- provides a clear, brisk start to the lesson;
- makes the purpose of the lesson and your expectations clear (very often, especially at Key Stage 3, this will involve sharing the objectives with the class explicitly);
- recaps on previous work;
- has strategies for ensuring all students take part;
- introduces key ideas through exposition, modelling, example, etc.;
- makes a smooth transition to the main part of the lesson.

During the development/main activity, the teacher:

- ensures students know what they are to learn;
- gives students a deadline for completion of work;
- ensures students know where to obtain resources, get help or receive further work;
- maintains pace by motivating students and keeping them on task;
- concludes the main activity smoothly and moves to the conclusion/plenary.

In the conclusion or plenary, the teacher:

- summarises important facts or key ideas;
- identifies what needs to be remembered for the next lesson.

A plenary may also involve the teacher managing:

- students presenting and explaining their work;

- students generalising a rule from a number of examples;
- students reflecting on and evaluating how they have been working;
- the setting of homework.

Managing behaviour

The justifiable assumption of this book is that if the teacher matches tasks or activities and teaching approaches to the needs and preferred learning styles of his or her students, then the potential for off-task or disruptive behaviour can be minimised. This applies to both 'ends' of the ability scale and the bored and unchallenged 'able' children pose just as great a disruptive threat as the confused and frustrated 'less able'. Further guidance on managing challenging behaviour in the classroom is the focus of Chapter 7 of this book.

Evaluation

Evaluations of learners' progress and your own effectiveness as a teacher will form the basis of written evaluations of your lessons. 'Good' lesson evaluations are honest and constructive and draw upon the student assessment information you have gathered during the lesson. The two most important evaluative questions that should be answered at the end of every lesson are:

1. To what extent were the learning objectives achieved?
2. Based on your assessment, what needs to be planned/taught next and why?

Your answers to these questions will have a direct influence on your planning for the next lesson and, indeed, for the remaining lessons in the series. This link between assessment and planning is discussed in detail in Chapter 6. The process of reflection and adjustment in response to your findings is crucial, and will need to be ongoing: analysis of the actual outcomes of the lesson in comparison with the planned outcomes will help you to consider what the students are trying to tell you about their own learning.

Sometimes, trainees are asked to complete a more detailed evaluation of their teaching on a weekly basis that will be used in meetings with their mentor or tutor to set targets. An example of such an extended evaluation form from one training provider is reproduced in Figure 5.4.

PRACTICAL TASK   PRACTICAL TASK   **PRACTICAL TASK**   PRACTICAL TASK   **PRACTICAL TASK**

Complete the evaluation proforma in Figure 5.4 yourself at the end of a week's teaching. Use your evaluation as the basis of a meeting with your mentor. What aspects of teaching and learning will you focus on next week (e.g. structure, timing and pace, or assessment opportunities)?

IN THE CLASSROOM: THE LESSON-PLANNING PROCESS

The following account of the lesson planning process was given by a PGCE English trainee (Miranda) near the end of her first block school experience.

Lesson commentary

Context:

This was a lesson given towards the end of my first school experience placement at an 11–18 technology college. The class was a Year 9 mixed-ability class of 22 students with attainment levels ranging from two to six. Eleven students were on the SEN

Secondary ITE Weekly Evaluation

Trainee's name:	Classes taught:

1. Planning and preparation
Did my lesson planning adequately cater for the activities and content of the lessons? How effective was my preparation?

2. Planned learning objectives and outcomes
How realistic were they? To what extent were they achieved?

3. Teaching and learning methods
How effective were my teaching methods in bringing about student learning?

4. Structure, timing and pacing
How effective were these?

5. Management and resources
How effective was my classroom management and the use of resources?

6. Students' tasks
Did I introduce points clearly? To what extent did students understand them? Did I provide opportunities for students to contribute to discussion?

7. Behaviour management
How effective was it? To what extent was I able to motivate the students?

8. Use of Information and Communication Technology
Did I exploit the available opportunities to enhance students' learning through the appropriate use of ICT? Did I exploit the potential of ICT to help me in planning, preparation, recording and presenting information?

9. Assessment opportunities
Did I share the criteria for assessment with the students? How did I provide feedback to students on the quality of work? Did I encourage student self-evaluation?

10. Individual student/students
Comment as appropriate on the progress of individual students

11. Future planning
What implications does this evaluation have for my future planning? What will be my focus for the next set of lessons?

Figure 5.4. Evaluation proforma

register. One student was on a part-time timetable. In this lesson, there would be one teaching assistant.

I had been teaching this class throughout my placement, and by this stage, I felt I knew them well. The class had spent the past four weeks studying *Macbeth* in preparation for the Shakespeare section of the End of Key Stage 3 tests. This was the final lesson of a four-lesson scheme of work that I had developed independently to prepare the class for questions on dramatic interpretation of the play. In the previous three lessons, we had compared some versions of the play, and I had introduced the notion of dramatic interpretation while watching sections of a modernised film version (*Macbeth on the Estate*). The class were becoming more familiar with how actors and directors had achieved different effects on stage or screen; now I wanted to use this final lesson to encourage students to complete creative work on their own interpretations.

Planning the lesson

My first step in planning the lesson was to develop the learning objectives and outcomes. I made the objectives student-friendly by turning them into 'key questions' to be written into student planners at the start of the lesson. I then considered the assessment opportunities I would have in the lesson.

In planning the activities, I considered the class's degree of prior knowledge about the topic. In preparation for the main activity, I had set a homework in the previous lesson where students were required to write down some ideas about where, when and how they would set the play if they were a director. I needed a contingency plan in case there were students who had been away, or had not done the homework, so I planned a starter activity to help students to revisit their own ideas and opinions about different versions of *Macbeth*, and to remind them of the previous work we had done on the film version. A simple matching activity would hopefully build confidence.

The range of abilities in the class made differentiation essential. I spent time considering how to explain the main task, and prepared an example of how to tackle it for weaker students. We were to watch the end of the film, but this still needed a focus for learning, so I planned questions to help students remember this scene clearly when designing their own staging of it. For more able students there would be an extension activity to allow them to develop their ideas about staging independently. I also needed to take into account those students with special educational needs. One student was not taking the same end of key stage test, and so was undertaking an individual project on *Macbeth* while the rest of the class did the more focused work for the tests. I therefore needed to plan one part of the lesson to allow him to participate, and one part when he would continue with his project.

I then considered how the teaching assistant could help with each activity, which students she would work with, what information she would need. Finally, I prepared my lesson resources.

As I made progress in my PGCE course, I found that time spent developing clear and detailed learning objectives and outcomes made planning the details of the teaching much easier. Having learning objectives clearly shared with students as 'key questions' also helped me to reinforce learning and assess progress during the plenary. I have experimented with a number of different planning formats to help me remember all the pieces of the jigsaw, but it has really been active experience that has caused all the elements to start to fall into place for me.

Evaluation of learning achieved

Most of the learning outcomes were met. However, we spent longer than anticipated on the first two activities, so there was less time for the main activity. The students showed secure knowledge of the events in the scene, and were able to make creative choices about the staging. Most could articulate why they had made these decisions by writing on the sheet, but some had more difficulty with this. I realised that all students would have benefited from more time to develop their ideas. Only a few students had time to move on to a more detailed set or costume design, and many needed more help to enable them to articulate and write down why they had made their staging decisions with reference to the play.

Class: 9	Date: **Thurs P2**	Scheme of work: **SATS, Macbeth, Dramatic interpretation**	Lesson 4

Learning objectives		Learning outcomes
Kn/U: Understand that the words of a play can be interpreted in different ways. Know the variety of aspects to be considered when staging a scene. See the events of *Macbeth* scene 5.5 as open to different staging possibilities. **Skills**: Explain decisions about staging with reference to the play. Visualisation of written text. **Values**: Appreciate their *own* ability to affect meaning through staging decisions – existing directors do not hold a monopoly!		*All* will make decisions about staging the scene that are appropriate and can be justified with reference to the play. *All* will consolidate their knowledge of the events in scene 5.5. *Most* will show creativity and originality in their choices about how to stage the scene. *Some* will be able to articulate the impact of staging choices on the audience. *Some* will extend their ideas through costume or stage designs.

Key questions:		Resources: Starter sheet x15, A3 direct the scene
How would you direct scene 5.5 of *Macbeth*? What should a director consider to make their interpretation convincing?		sheets x27, video of *Macbeth on the Estate*. Coloured pens, blu-tac.

Activities	Teacher	Students
Starter: Pictures of different film versions of *Macbeth*. 5 min	Explain L.O. and sheet. Explain purpose is to recognise the possible variety of interpretations.	Write L.O. – Emphasise that students may be asked to write an exam response as if 'directing' a scene in the SATS. Match a picture on the starter sheet to direction descriptions. Which one sounds the most interesting to you?

Main activity
Watch *Macbeth on the Estate*, and fill in chart of what is different to the Polanski film version.
20 min
	Prompt at key moments to make notes.
	Check understanding and last boxes on sheet filled in.
		Follow film, and fill in chart to show how the film is different to the play.
		Focus on how Macbeth reacts after Lady Macbeth dies.
		After watching, consider: What do you think will happen to Malcolm, now that he is leader?
		  Daniel: watch and follow the sheet.
		  (Differentiated version)

Annotate a picture to show how you would direct the scene. (5.5)
20 min
	Remind of the scene. Explain task.
	Model an example. Emphasise need to explain *why* as well as *what*.
		Remember what happens in Act 5 Scene 5.
		Answer questions in the box first – about setting and the feeling of Macbeth.
		Then draw Macbeth as you want him to look.
		Annotate with details about position on stage, gestures, costumes etc.
		Explain *why* you chose to do each thing.
		  Extension: begin costume or stage designs on the back.
		  Daniel: continue with Macbeth summary

Plenary Look at different 'Macbeths' on show.	How can the effect of a particular line be changed by the way it is staged?	picture book. Students to write their names on sheet and blu-tac to the board. Students to nominate a poster to be read out. Share good practice.

Assessment	Homework: none set in	Key words
Notes on picture/chart. Q&A, talking with groups and individuals.	this lesson.	Interpretation, direction, scene, stage, lighting, costumes, gestures, expression, voice position.

Figure 5.5. Macbeth lesson plan

I do think the lesson was successful and caught the imagination of the class. In future planning, I would extend this scheme of work to allow another lesson for students to complete their designs and do a related practice question. I would also plan more time to teach students how to explain and justify their decisions, and to allow them to practise this.

Commentary on the lesson planning

This is a very detailed lesson plan that uses a format developed to meet the needs of a secondary English trainee. The evaluation at the end of the plan begins to address the two key, evaluative questions discussed earlier. The trainee's mentor or tutor would want to gather the following additional information when making any judgement about achieving the Teachers' Standards.

- When will the trainee take the assessment opportunities mentioned (at what point in the lesson) and who (which students) will be her focus?
- The evaluation indicates that the starter overran. Were students given enough time to develop their own responses before the plenary?
- The evaluation also indicates that some students had difficulty with the worksheet. What adjustments would allow for more successful completion of this section of the lesson?
- The lesson was described as the final lesson in a sequence. How might the knowledge, understanding and skills fostered here be kept visible and current during further study of the play, and how might they be consolidated in terms of the department's longer-term plan for Year 9?

This information would be gathered through lesson observation, discussions with the trainee and students, and an examination of both the resources designed by the trainee and samples of work actually completed in the lesson. Judgements about the effectiveness of resources and planning should not be reached without examination of actual outcomes.

Overall, it is clear that this trainee was beginning to consider the myriad aspects of planning for learning and beginning to integrate these in her lesson plans without undue anxiety or the production of over-detailed scripts.

PRACTICAL TASK PRACTICAL TASK PRACTICAL TASK PRACTICAL TASK PRACTICAL TASK

Work with your mentor as she or he plans a lesson in the format you devised earlier for your own lesson planning. Ask your mentor questions about the decisions they are making. This will help them to complete an activity that they will find fairly difficult (having already internalised a planning structure) and will help you to understand the planning process.

Then, observe the lesson being taught and notice how your mentor adapts the plan during the transaction of the lesson. Make notes about the adaptations and changes and speculate on the reasons for them. After the lesson, discuss your notes with your mentor.

A SUMMARY OF **KEY POINTS**

> **Effective planning builds on high expectations of students informed by a knowledge of their past and current achievements.**
> **Effective planning clearly identifies what is to be learned and the teaching strategies by which this will be achieved.**

> > Effective planning identifies the means by which learning will be assessed.
> > Trainees need a good knowledge of their specialist subject so that they can plan over the long, medium and short term, ensuring student progression.
> > Trainees need to be able to demonstrate the ability to plan for the development of students' learning across the curriculum and promote active and independent learning.

MOVING *ON* > > > > > > MOVING *ON* > > > > > > MOVING *ON*

As your experience of planning progresses, consider how you might foster a greater degree of independence in your students. Don't neglect the importance of pursuing the students' perspectives. What can the (apparently) least motivated student in the class tell you in response to the question: *What would you like me to do to help you learn more effectively?*

FURTHER READING FURTHER READING **FURTHER READING** FURTHER READING

Kyriacou, C. (1998) *Essential Teaching Skills (2nd edn)*. The second edition of this popular book covers a wide range of topics, including planning and managing lessons; classroom climate and discipline; streaming and setting; assessment, and continuing professional development.

Ofsted (2002) *Good Teaching, Effective Departments*. This report presents the findings from an HMI survey of subject teaching in secondary schools during 2000–2001. There are many practical implications for trainees and mentors arising out of this report, including comments on planning for learning and managing teaching time.

6
Assessment for learning
Jane Briggs and Viv Ellis

Teachers' Standards

A teacher must

6. Make accurate and productive use of assessment

- know and understand how to assess the relevant subject and curriculum areas, including statutory assessment requirements
- make use of formative and summative assessment to secure pupils' progress
- use relevant data to monitor progress, set targets, and plan subsequent lessons
- give pupils regular feedback, both orally and through accurate marking, and encourage pupils to respond to the feedback.

What do we mean by assessment?

Assessment is the process by which teachers analyse students' learning. It is central to the activity of teaching. In 1988, a group of experts given the task of devising an assessment framework for what was to become the first National Curriculum, put it this way:

> The assessment process itself should not determine what is to be taught and learned. It should be the servant, not the master, of the curriculum. Yet it should not simply be a bolt-on addition at the end. Rather, it should be an integral part of the education process, continually providing both 'feedback' and 'feedforward'. It therefore needs to be incorporated systematically into teaching strategies and practices at all levels. Since the results of assessment can serve a number of different purposes, these purposes have to be kept in mind when the arrangements for assessment are designed.
>
> (TGAT 1988, p. 4)

You will see this quotation in a good deal of writing about assessment. To an extent, it has become a definitive statement. Often, however, its meaning and its importance are not immediately grasped by trainee teachers. Assessment has come to mean all sorts of things. Perhaps, most commonly, the term is used to describe the practices of awarding marks or grades to students' work and recording these. Assessment in its full sense, however, is so much more. The purpose of this chapter is to familiarise you with the various aspects of educational assessment and to demonstrate the relationship between assessment and the processes of teaching and learning.

The various aspects of assessment

What follows is a brief overview of the various aspects of assessment that have come to be included in this umbrella term. There are suggestions for further reading about key aspects of assessment at the end of this chapter.

Teacher assessment

In its general sense, this is the ongoing analysis of students' learning that is the day-to-day life-blood of good teaching. By observing, reading, questioning and interpreting students' comments and actions, teachers learn whether students are learning what they had intended them to learn. This process is constantly influencing an effective teacher's interventions in the classroom with students and this is how a teacher's lesson plans are adapted as those lessons are being taught.

Teacher assessment is a term that is also used to refer to the judgements teachers make about students' attainment in National Curriculum levels at the end of Key Stage 3 and is contrasted with and reported separately from the levels students are awarded through the externally marked national tests.

Student self-assessment

This term refers to students' involvement in the assessment process. It begins with students understanding the learning intentions or objectives for the particular lesson and the success criteria for the specific task or activity. It develops into students' awareness of their own strengths and weaknesses in a particular subject (and as a learner in general) and the ability to identify their own 'next steps' or targets. It may include a formal review of the students' work over a period of time – perhaps using a target-setting or progress review document – at which teacher and student identify progress, negotiate future targets and then report these to parents or carers.

Formal tests

There is no shortage of formal tests or examinations in the secondary phase. The formal tests you may encounter in schools may include:

- standardised tests such as CATS (Cognitive Abilities Tests) or tests of reading and spelling ability;
- school (internal) examinations such as end-of-unit tests or annual end-of-year examinations;
- optional 'Progress' tests for Year 7 in literacy and numeracy;
- controlled assessments – set and marked by the teacher but taken in examination conditions;
- GCSE and other 'intermediate' national examinations taken at the end of Key Stage 4 that lead to certification;
- the multiplicity of vocational and post-16 examinations.

For further information on the examination system from 14 to 19, see Chapter 11.

Record-keeping

Teachers are required to keep records of students' progress and attainment in school subjects. At the very least, this will probably take the form of recording whether a significant activity or task has been undertaken and the level of attainment. Some schools may issue teachers with customised documents or portable electronic devices in which to keep assessment records and marks; teachers in other schools may rely on their own mark books or 'teacher's planner'. You will need to find out about the expectations and requirements of your school. Assessment records should also provide teachers with information that can be used in their own forward planning or in planning that takes place in departments across year groups.

Target-setting

There are several different layers to target-setting, all of which are designed to make the action required to raise standards explicit, to designate who is responsible for the action and the date by which progress will be reviewed.

- Local Authority (LA) targets are determined by local education officers as a means of monitoring and raising standards of achievement across groups of schools and may be expressed as the number of students expected to achieve a particular level in an end of key stage test by a particular date.
- School targets are negotiated between the LA and the school's management team and, once again, may be expressed in terms of the percentage of a year group achieving five or more GCSEs at grade C or above.
- Curriculum targets are negotiated between a school's management team and a head of department or curriculum manager and would take into account past performance, student ability and the school's own targets.
- Student targets are negotiated between teacher and child following a review of the child's work; the student should be able to monitor their own progress and identify areas for future development; this is an aspect of student self-assessment mentioned earlier.

Assessing Pupils' Progress (APP)

As discussed in the last chapter, APP was designed to monitor curriculum coverage and progression. APP encourages teachers to use Assessment Focuses (AFs) to set targets for children's learning.

Reporting

You can probably remember your own school reports and may be surprised at how much they have changed over the last few years. Annual reports to parents and carers (including, for example, the End of Key Stage 3 test and teacher assessment results) now also detail strengths and areas for improvement in addition to the standards achieved.

Use of comparative data

'Data' means information and includes national and local test/examination results so that comparisons can be made between LEAs and between schools. Within school, the data can be used to identify trends with a view to setting curriculum and teaching targets; this will be increasingly important as you develop your career in schools.

At the moment, however, your first priority as a trainee is to develop the ability to analyse students' learning and to use the information you gather to inform your planning and teaching. By regarding assessment as an integral part of teaching you will be able to provide the continuous 'feedback' and 'feedforward' that are essential for effective student learning.

Why and how do teachers assess?

To take learning forward

There is a firm body of evidence that formative assessment is an essential feature of classroom work and that development of it can raise standards.

(Black and Wiliam 1998, p. 19)

As an integral part of the process of teaching and learning, assessment that is used to take students' learning forward can be described as 'formative assessment'. Teachers assess students' learning on a daily basis in order to be able to respond appropriately to their learning needs. Formative assessment is concerned with analysing students' comments and their answers to questions. It is concerned with listening to what students have to say and the way in which they go about a task. It is concerned with really looking at tangible end-products to find out what students know, understand and can do. It involves responding to information gained about students' learning during the course of teaching and afterwards to inform future teaching. Formative assessment means analysing, reflecting and acting in ways which will take students' learning forward. Formative assessment is an integral part of the interaction between teacher and students, informs future planning and teaching and provides information which enables the quality of teaching and learning to be evaluated.

We can, therefore, consider formative assessment as being:

- the analysis of students' learning and appropriate response during the course of teaching;
- the analysis of students' learning and appropriate response after the teaching episode.

The analysis of students' learning and appropriate response during the course of teaching

During teaching, you will be assessing students' learning continuously. Shipman describes this as:

> *the thinking-on-the-feet that is one of the main skills of teaching.*
>
> (Shipman 1983, p. 12)

While teaching, you will be interpreting what the students say and do in order to make judgements about their achievements. The ability to analyse the students' learning is vital if you are to make appropriate teaching points which help the students develop their knowledge and/or competence. You will be using your subject knowledge to help you identify what to look for and where to take the student next. You will need to listen, observe and question in ways which will enable you to give appropriate feedback or further instruction. It is crucial that feedback to students is explicit and indicates to them what they have achieved and how they can progress further. It is also crucial that you are able to interact with students in ways which enable them to take risks: you will discover much from students' errors and misconceptions. The ability to respond immediately, providing appropriate feedback and further teaching, can be much more meaningful for that child than waiting to the next day when the moment has passed. This is sometimes referred to as monitoring or 'monitoring and assessment'.

Black and Wiliam (1998) highlight the importance of assessment being used to enhance teaching and therefore to raise standards. They argue that the real way to raise standards is to improve the quality of teaching by enhancing teachers' ability to use formative assessment in the classroom. The Assessment Reform Group explores these issues further in *Assessment for Learning: Beyond the Black Box* (1999), including discussions about the involvement of students within the assessment process and the impact this can have on their motivation and self-esteem. They also stress the importance of teachers asking the right questions in order to analyse effectively. The work of the Assessment Reform Group (King's College) underpins approaches to assessment for learning within the Secondary National Strategy.

IN THE CLASSROOM

In a Year 7 maths lesson, the teacher was revising area and perimeter. The students were asked to find the measurement in centimetres of one side of a rectangle. They were shown a diagram of the rectangle on which the area had been written in (10cm squared) and the height (2cm). The students were asked to write their answers on their individual whiteboards and hold them up for the teacher to see. One child had written '3cm'. The teacher asked: 'Explain to me how you got that answer. How did you work it out?' The child explained: 'I added 2cm and 2cm to get 4cm. Then I took 4cm away from 10cm which left 6cm. Then I divided 6cm by 2 which gave me 3.' From this the teacher clearly realised that the child was confusing perimeter and area.

She then explained to the child what she thought he had done – that he had thought the perimeter was 10cm and used that information to work out the length of the rectangle. She repeatedly asked questions such as: 'Is that what you were thinking?' and 'Is that right?'. She then explained that 10cm squared was the area, drawing the cm squares onto the diagram to illustrate her teaching point. She demonstrated how to work out the length of the rectangle by counting the cm squares. Next, she asked the child: 'Can you explain to me the difference between perimeter and area?' He was able to explain that one was 'the total distance around the outside edge of the shape' and the other was 'the surface of the shape', pointing at the diagram appropriately as he spoke.

The teacher then demonstrated how to work out the area of the shape by multiplying the length by the height, writing on the board: 5cm x 2cm = $10cm^2$. She then reminded the student of the inverse operation: 10 divided by 2 = 5 and explained how to use the information about the area of an rectangle to find out details of the length of the sides. She carried out two more similar examples with the whole class, checking that everyone, and particularly that one boy, had the correct answer.

This example demonstrates how teachers need to ask the right questions in order to analyse students' misconceptions and errors. By using the whiteboard the teacher could see the child's error and respond immediately to rectify the misunderstanding rather than the child completing several examples incorrectly during the lesson and not learning of the mistake until the work had been marked and returned at a later stage. The teacher was able to make appropriate teaching points based on her analysis of the student's response to the task. In this, her questioning was vital.

The analysis of students' learning and appropriate response after the teaching episode

In order to evaluate your teaching and to make decisions about what to teach next and how, you will need to reflect upon the students' learning and make judgements about their attainment. Analysis after teaching will include looking at samples of the students' work, reflecting on their comments and actions and may also involve discussions with colleagues. It may be that you need to amend your plans to clarify misconceptions or to raise the level of challenge. It may be that you need to develop your own subject knowledge further in order to enhance the quality of experience offered to the students. You will need to think about the feedback which you will give to the students and how this can motivate them to further their own achievements. Assessment knowledge will, therefore, be used to inform future teaching and, if used effectively, should enhance future learning.

Formative assessment, then, can be defined as the process by which teachers make judgements about students' attainment and use this information to inform teaching and learning and planning in order to take students' learning forward. Involving students is a key element of formative assessment. Explicit feedback enables students to recognise what is required of them and how they can progress. They need to have ownership of their own learning and need to be able to identify their successes and areas for development. Students need to engage in meaningful dialogue with their teachers to reflect upon their learning and to work together effectively.

IN THE CLASSROOM

During a Year 7 unit of work on poetry, an English trainee had been working on the production of individual poetry anthologies with the class. He used the marking of these anthologies to inform his teaching in the remainder of the unit and to give positive and constructive feedback to the students that could inform the extended piece of writing they would prepare towards the end of the unit. His marking appears below.

Jane, your work was perfectly presented. I like the way you chose appropriate colours for each poem, eg, seaweed green near the lines about the stomach!

In your comments on the poems, your ideas are first-rate. I particularly liked your comparison of the sea to a 'plaything' for a child and where you examined how this brought to mind ideas of 'harmlessness' – why not think a little more about this idea by considering the question mark that comes after it? What effect does the poet achieve by placing the question mark here?

Although I thought you'd completed the difficult part of this task well, I don't think you were as successful with the easier part. When you are expressing your opinions about poetry, a good way of justifying these to a reader is by using quotations from the poem (as we discussed). So, although you say the writer compares the sea to beautiful things, you don't say that the phrase 'it runs in beads on their jackets' made you think this. We will work on this in readiness for the final piece of writing in the unit.

The trainee's marking is specific and focused on the student's work. It identifies positive achievements and demonstrates to the student that he has read and engaged with her work. The trainee has also identified an important skill that the student will need to develop and how this relates to what he plans to teach next.

In his marking of the completed individual poetry anthology, the trainee is beginning to engage in a dialogue with his students. This dialogue was developed during part of a lesson when the trainee worked with groups of students to review their marked work while the remainder of the class worked on an independent activity. Over a period of three lessons, the trainee had seen all the students about their work and used the marking as the basis for a dialogue about improvement.

REFLECTIVE TASK

From a lesson or lessons you have taught, identify examples of:

(a) your analysis of students' learning and your appropriate response during teaching; consider your use of questioning, explaining, demonstration, etc.;

(b) your analysis of students' learning and appropriate response after teaching; consider how assessment influenced your future teaching and was reflected in your plans.

In both cases, how did your assessment enhance your teaching and what impact did it have on the students' learning?

To make judgements about standards

Summative assessment is more commonly associated with testing or making judgements about students' overall achievement at the end of a period of time. It requires students to demonstrate their knowledge, skill or understanding as a means of what Harlen, Gipps, Broadfoot and Nuttall (1994) describe as 'summing up and checking up'. They describe the former as:

> *a picture of current achievements derived from information gathered over a period of time in order to set future targets.*
>
> (Harlen *et al.* 1994, p. 223)

This picture of student achievement can be used to inform students of progress and to set future targets. It can also be used by teachers to reflect upon the quality of teaching and to inform future planning. Since the introduction of the National Curriculum and its assessment, teachers have increasingly been required to make judgements about standards of attainment within a criterion-referenced system. Barrs (1990) highlights the impact this can have when teachers' assessment practice becomes that of measuring attainment of previously identified criteria rather than considered analysis of students' learning.

With the current emphasis on national test results forming a key part of political agendas, the judgement of standards is more commonly linked to the evaluation of teaching performance. National test results are used as an indicator of school effectiveness and teacher performance. LA and school targets influence the expectation of student attainment.

Information about standards of attainment can be considered from the key perspectives:

- measuring progress and attainment;
- evaluating the effectiveness of schools.

Measuring progress and attainment

Your judgements about students' attainment over a period of time will enable you to consider whether progress has been made and to identify future learning targets. You will need to look closely at students' work to identify what improvements there have been: this will require you to draw on your subject knowledge. You will also need to develop your ability to identify the National Curriculum levels at which the students are operating. Your record-keeping should enable you to consider what progress students have made and should help you identify ways forward for individuals. It is important that your record-keeping system is manageable and that you can use it to further your understanding of students' progress and attainment.

REFLECTIVE TASK

Examine examples of teachers' record-keeping in your department. Consider the following.

- How 'learning-specific' are they? What do they tell you about the students' knowledge, skills and/or understanding?

- How would these records enable you to take the students' learning forward? What information do they contain that could inform future teaching and planning?
- How would these records support reporting to parents/carers (in writing and orally)?

The use of comparative data can help you identify trends and patterns in student attainment but you will need to consider the data carefully as they can be limited. Teachers are now expected to be aware of students' attainment in national tests and to use comparative data across key stages to monitor progress. Clearly, only that which has been tested can be considered and teachers need to be aware of the limitations of testing and the reliability and validity of the data provided.

Evaluating the effectiveness of schools

Teachers are accountable to their students, their parents and carers, the school, the LA and the wider community. Scrutiny of the standards of student attainment and their performance in national tests and examinations are key features of Ofsted inspections. This leads into an evaluation of the effectiveness of the school. Making simplistic comparisons between the examination results of different schools serving very different communities and with very different resources does not allow us to make valid judgements about the effectiveness of the teaching in those schools. For example, comparing the GCSE results of a selective grammar school in an affluent suburb with the results of a comprehensive school in a city where many students enter late in Key Stage 3 without fluency in English will not tell us much about the work that goes on in classrooms. To try to quantify the 'difference' made by teachers in schools, the notion of 'value-added' was developed whereby the effectiveness of teaching in a school is judged partly by the progress made by its students from a baseline assessment on entry to the school. Increasingly, school examination result league tables – and Ofsted inspections – are building in elements of 'value-added' assessment.

So what do trainee teachers need?

The Teachers' Standards set out the minimum that you must demonstrate as a student teacher and teacher. Assessment is given prominence in the Standards by being one of only eight Standards but it is important to remember that assessment is present implicitly throughout all the other Standards too. For example, assessment helps us to understand how students learn and how to plan lessons. It is in this spirit, therefore, that we offer the following list of skills and attributes that you will develop as an effective, beginning teacher.

- The ability to interpret students' learning using a variety of strategies appropriate to your subject.
- A confident knowledge of your specialist subject in which you take delight and pleasure so that you can re-formulate lesson ideas, answer questions and represent concepts in a way that is appropriate to the needs of the learners in your classroom.
- The ability to make assessment a continuous and integral part of your teaching so that the information gathered has an immediate effect upon your interventions in students' learning as well as informing future planning.
- The ability to ask the 'right' questions that check understanding rather than simple recall and probe misconceptions.
- The ability to implement a record-keeping system that is manageable and meaningful to yourself, other members of your department and school and that is open to parents and carers.
- An awareness of the implications of formal, national tests for curriculum planning and your own professional development.

- An awareness of the use of comparative data in setting targets and understanding how your students' performance compares with those in other classes and other schools.

A SUMMARY OF **KEY POINTS**

> **Assessment is an integral part of teaching and learning.**

> **It is a process by which we make judgements about students' learning.**

> **Effective formative assessment (including student self-assessment) is a key part of raising standards of attainment.**

> **Summative assessment is used to measure students' progress and attainment, but also school effectiveness.**

> **Trainee teachers need to be able to use their analysis of students' learning in a dialogue with parents, carers and others involved in the education of students.**

MOVING *ON* > > > > > > MOVING *ON* > > > > > > MOVING *ON*

The Assessment for Reform Group define assessment for learning as:

> *The process of seeking and interpreting evidence for use by learners and their teachers to decide where the learners are in their learning, where they need to go next and how best to get there.*
>
> (Assessment Reform Group 2002)

Look at the Department for Education (DfE) website and search for guidance on 'assessment for learning' (AFL) and formative assessment.

FURTHER READING FURTHER READING **FURTHER READING** FURTHER READING

Black, P. and Wiliam, D. (1998) *Inside the Black Box: Raising Standards Through Classroom Assessment.* London. King's College. This short pamphlet offers a review of research into the ways in which formative assessment can have an impact on the quality of teaching and learning in classrooms. The authors put forward an argument for the improvement of formative assessment in order to raise standards.

Gipps, C. and Stobart, G. (1997) *Assessment: A Teacher's Guide to the Issues*. London. Hodder and Stoughton. This well-respected guide is available in most education libraries and is written in a lively and accessible way. It covers a wide range of assessment issues, including fairness and validity in assessments, baseline and value-added measures, and the National Curriculum.

7
Managing behaviour for learning
Alan J. Child with Lynne Parsons and Alaster Douglas

Introduction

This chapter title is an important emphasis in its own right because it is a natural instinct for a trainee teacher to seek to manage students' behaviour and then to focus on their learning. The key message is that the appropriate use of the knowledge and skills discussed in Chapters 4, 5 and 6 will enable the teacher to create a classroom climate in which the students' right to learn is matched by the teacher's right to teach.

Hardly a day passes without some horror story appearing in the press about the unacceptable behaviour of students in secondary schools. These headlines do not, of course, capture the reality in the vast majority of schools where students engage in learning and a culture of mutual respect exists. David Bell, former Her Majesty's Chief Inspector of Schools, said:

> *Behaviour was found to be at least satisfactory in the majority of schools. The proportion where behaviour was good or better was greater than in the schools inspected in 2003/04, and the proportion where it was unsatisfactory was a little lower. However, generally across Key Stages 3 and 4, small numbers of pupils fail to respond appropriately when admonished and low level disruption interrupts teaching and learning. Even a small number of pupils of this kind have a disproportionate detrimental effect on learning; this can become a major problem.*
>
> (HMCI Annual Report 2004/05)

In surveys conducted by the Training and Development Agency for Schools (TDA) among newly qualified teachers (NQTs), 50 per cent of respondents maintain that the training they received in behaviour management was inadequate to meet their needs in the first year of teaching. Some 45 per cent of teachers who decide to leave the profession cite student indiscipline and lack of respect for the teacher as major reasons for their decision to pursue an alternative career. So, quite clearly, if you have early concerns about how you will manage students' behaviour for learning, you are certainly not alone in experiencing some genuine uncertainty and perhaps a little trepidation at the prospect of working with a lively group of Year 11 students on a Friday afternoon.

All the analysis and research into effective teaching emphasises that unacceptable behaviour is likely to be minimised when the teacher:

- aims to personalise the learning for each student and identifies the most appropriate learning style;
- supports and challenges students as well as planning activities and content which are interesting;
- monitors and recognises progress based on well-developed assessment strategies.

In addition to these pedagogical principles, effective teachers employ a range of techniques to encourage students who are disengaging from the learning to re-engage and be 'on task'; the very best classroom practitioners anticipate students' 'off-task' behaviour and take pre-emptive action. If you have observed an experienced and effective teacher at work with a demanding class you might have had a mixed reaction: sheer admiration as you watched this paragon manage the learning of 30 Year 9 students with good humour, effortless transitions from activity to activity and real pace and momentum; some despair as you reflect that such multi-skilled, multi-tasked teaching is beyond you – an impossible dream.

In 2005 the report of the Practitioners' Group on School Behaviour and Discipline was published (Steer Report). The group focused on identifying practical solutions to a range of behavioural issues that most schools are dealing with on a day-to-day basis. The report is based on six core beliefs.

1. The quality of learning, teaching and behaviour in schools are inseparable issues and the responsibility of all staff.
2. Poor behaviour cannot be tolerated as it is the denial of the right of pupils to learn and teachers to teach. To enable learning to take place preventative action is most effective, but where this fails, schools must have clear, firm and intelligent strategies in place to help pupils manage their behaviour.
3. There is no single solution to the problem of poor behaviour, but all schools have the potential to raise standards if they are consistent in implementing good practice in learning, teaching and behaviour management.
4. Respect has to be given in order to be received. Parents and carers, pupils and teachers all need to operate in a culture of mutual respect.
5. The support of parents is essential for the maintenance of good behaviour. Parents and schools each need to have a clear understanding of their rights and responsibilities.
6. School leaders have a critical role in establishing high standards of learning, teaching and behaviour.

(DfES 2005)

As you continue to read this chapter it is important that you reflect on how the strategies and techniques that are described are aligned to the core beliefs of the Steer Report.

REFLECTIVE TASK

In a school where you are working keep a diary to see if any of these core beliefs inform everyday practice. Where they are well established, how does this impact on student behaviour? What happens when positive beliefs do not inform practice sufficiently well? Share your reflections with your school mentor or your college tutor. If you know of other trainees who are undertaking a similar task, share your reflections with one another. Remember to respect the school in which you are working. Try not to present your findings as a negative list. Emphasise the positive and offer ideas to improve the situation. This may well include good ideas picked up from trainee colleagues.

Every teacher, at some point in their career, experiences challenging student behaviours. Often, factors are at play which relate to the student's home circumstances or with social groupings and influences outside the school environment. Although teachers so readily accept responsibility and endure intense reflection wondering how this awful moment could have been avoided, you will also no doubt meet some cynical staffroom commentary which alludes to the past ('things were better then'), falling standards ('we used to have a discipline policy here'), and the decline in family and society values ('what do you expect when programmes like *Footballers' Wives* are on TV?'). You might also be tempted by the quick fix ostensibly offered by some of the burgeoning catalogue of classroom management textbooks. The idea of tips for teachers needs to be dispelled as, at best, they are a short-term strategy. You can gain from reading around the subject of behaviour management but success in the classroom is not predicated simply on the deployment of techniques.

Praise

There is ample evidence to support the effectiveness of teacher praise in creating a positive classroom environment and in motivating students into behaviour for learning. This is not to say that the teacher who uses praise in a cosmetic, artificial way will be successful. Praise used in the appropriate way is indeed a powerful force; praise used insincerely will undermine relationships and learning.

There are three important aspects to consider.

Personal: praise should be given to the individual or group so that it resonates personally. The most obvious thing to do is to name the students and to ensure that they receive the praise in a direct way with, for example, positive non-verbal signals like a smile.

Specific: praise should be firmly grounded in a particular achievement or attainment which is clearly referred to. For example, if a student has finished a task which has previously caused difficulty, the teacher's compliment should specify that the praise is for finishing the task and for the effort to overcome the particular problem.

Genuine: praise must always be given to students who have really achieved something. The careless, repetitive use of praise will undermine the value of other praise you want to give. Imagine how you have felt when in the presence of someone who overuses the words 'thank you': in a short time they no longer ring true and can, indeed, become irritating.

Praise which is offered in close proximity to the achievement or attainment is usually the most well received and the most powerful in motivating students.

You might need to consider some less public ways to praise senior students. Year 10 and 11 students may not welcome the embarrassment of public acclaim in front of their classmates.

Imagine that a student in your Year 10 group who has been an inconsistent performer achieves really well in a particular lesson, making useful contributions during small group discussion with four other students. You are delighted to witness this quality of work and engagement and you can see that the student has been motivated by the task. You also know that he has a reputation as 'one of the lads' and know that any public acknowledgement will not go down well and might even provoke disengagement in subsequent lessons.

Think of five ways you can privately praise a Key Stage 4 student and still follow the three key principles of making the praise personal, specific and genuine (and in his case, private).

Rules and routines

It is increasingly common in a school to find that not only has it a behaviour management policy but also some clearly specified classroom rules prominently displayed on notice-boards. Additionally you may come across other documentation (probably in the staff handbook) which advises on anti-bullying, anti-racism, attendance, school uniform regulations and even a code of conduct or key principles. This material can be quite daunting and far from easy to absorb. It is important, however, to do some research and reading about the school's key policies and practice as you are working in a context and need to be in tune with its key concepts and the practicalities. For example, a school might have a sophisticated system to manage challenging student behaviours like an on-call scheme involving the support of senior staff; or it might have access to a facility like a Learning Support Unit (LSU); or it might employ a school counsellor.

PRACTICAL TASK PRACTICAL TASK PRACTICAL TASK PRACTICAL TASK

In the school where you are working collect all the printed and published information relating to the management of student behaviour. Examine (trace) the links between the school's mission statement/ school development plan and the rules and routines which operate on a daily basis: the school aspires to be a community which respects the environment and its members, but do staff and students work together to minimise litter? Do you see common courtesies exchanged between staff and students (a good place to observe is doorways and staircases)? Are the rules and routines followed and are they reinforced by staff? When you have gathered this data you might want to share your reflections with your school mentor or your college tutor. Do remember to respect the organisation in which you are training; it may feel defensive if you simply list the aspects in a purely negative way. A fruitful approach is to see if you can offer some ideas to improve the situation. A group of trainees can work as a 'think tank' and offer a joint analysis and action plan.

It can be a very reassuring and supportive environment if you undertake some of your training in a school which has very clearly expressed values, rules and routines. It can be very helpful if you work in a school where the staff have good relationships with students and can offer you insights into the effective management of behaviour for learning. You might, however, feel that the environment is so supportive that you are not actually developing your own skills but simply adopting the good practice of others. At the other end of the spectrum where you are left largely to your own devices, the challenge may be far too great and you may feel daunted and confused as you try to establish your classroom rules and routines.

Students do need the freedom to work within constraints. Classroom rules are an effective way to establish and develop the climate for learning. The general wisdom pertaining to classroom rules is that they should be:

- developed and owned by the students and the teacher;
- few in number;
- expressed in positive language;
- about improving learning;
- reinforced and reviewed regularly.

A classroom behaviour plan

You might find it useful to think about an overall approach for your classroom under several headings:.

1. Movement.
2. Learning.
3. Communication.
4. Mutual respect.
5. Safety.
6. Problem-solving.

If you do this you will think about how students enter and leave your classroom, how they will work in groups, noise levels, common courtesies, using equipment and how to deal with challenges.

PRACTICAL TASK PRACTICAL TASK **PRACTICAL TASK** PRACTICAL TASK **PRACTICAL TASK**

Working with another trainee, develop five 'golden rules' for the classroom. Remember to phrase them positively and to produce rules which encourage behaviour for learning. Why not share these with other members of your group?

You might like to compare your proposals with those you have seen published in your placement schools.

Consequences

In most schools, unacceptable student behaviour incurs a consequence. Commonly, schools operate reward strategies and a hierarchical set of sanctions. As a trainee it can be rather disconcerting to find yourself working in a school without a full appreciation of the systems. If you act idiosyncratically, the students will undoubtedly react, or possibly over-react, to your sanctions. Therefore, it is essential to know and follow the school's protocols. This can be a source of some tension if you find yourself working within a system that does not attune with your own values and beliefs. As you become more skilled in managing behaviour for learning you might feel that the school's approach is undermining your teaching style, or you might feel that the system offers insufficient support, or that you are not given sufficient independence by your mentor. Any one of these reactions is understandable but the school is a community in which you are a privileged guest and you should seek to integrate as fully as possible with its *modus operandi*. However, your own professional development can certainly be enhanced by careful reflection on the contexts in which you are working and perhaps through discussion with other trainees and your college tutor. Good teachers give students choices and make clear to students the consequences of the choices they make. In an ideal world you would hope that the use of sanctions would be a small part of your work but there will be several occasions when you feel that a student is deserving of some consequence. The purpose of your intervention is to manage behaviour for learning so you need to think very carefully about the actions you take.

PRACTICAL TASK PRACTICAL TASK **PRACTICAL TASK** PRACTICAL TASK **PRACTICAL TASK**

In the table (Figure 7.1) below there is a list of sanctions which are typically deployed in schools. For each one, identify the student behaviour that could invoke it and then consider the possible advantages and disadvantages of the teacher's action. Some commentary has been added to encourage your thinking.

Sanction	Student behaviour	Possible advantage/disadvantage
'See me at the end of the lesson.'		
Work to be repeated to a higher standard		
Verbal warning/ reprimand		
Written report to Head of Year		
Contact with parent/ carer		
Detention		Detentions at break, lunchtimes and after school are commonly used in schools. They are highly inconvenient to staff and often require considerable administration. What is the intended outcome?
Exclusion from the classroom		This should be a very rare event and in many schools is discouraged and only acceptable in extreme situations to avoid confrontation in front of the whole class.
Withdrawal of privileges		
Stern/disapproving look		Effective teachers are skilled at using non-verbal techniques. Sometimes the eyes can work wonders and get a student back on task without a word being spoken.
Moving student to another desk		
Issuing a bad conduct mark		

Figure 7.1. List of sanctions

Teacher techniques

As a trainee teacher you are expected to know some of the techniques for managing behaviour for learning. You will learn these in a variety of ways: from your own reading, in workshops and by the careful observation of effective teachers. There are some techniques which have been identified by several researchers into effective teaching. They have been extensively written about, feature in many INSET sessions and form part of the ever-expanding literature on behaviour management. You may try some of these and find no or little success; others may work beautifully. The techniques themselves work best when other key aspects of pedagogy are present. But the classroom is above all else an environment where interpersonal relationships have pride of place. Students recognise when a teacher is knowledgeable, well prepared, the lesson has a clear learning focus and shared objectives and the teacher cares: they respond positively to a climate of learning. The techniques discussed in the next few paragraphs are certainly field-tested and effective but only if the foundations of good teaching are well established.

- Tactical ignoring: sometimes as a teacher you have to ignore some students' behaviour because if you respond then the flow of the lesson will be interrupted and your intervention will be more disruptive than the student's behaviour. This is never an easy judgement to make. Nor does it mean that you cannot speak to the offending student at a later stage.
- Thank you: acknowledging those who are on task can often encourage those who are still thinking about getting down to work to follow suit.
- Redirecting: rather than pointing out to students what they are not doing, you can simply reassert what 'we' are doing. 'Ismael and Alice, we are looking at the diagram on page 3, OK?'
- Room to change: it is often useful to draw a student's attention to what you would like them to do, then move away saying you'll check in a minute or two to see if they are on task. This gives the student a chance and room to do it without a stand-off or confrontation developing.
- Location: if you always teach from the front of the room you are wasting opportunities. Move around the room. Often, your proximity to a student or a group can encourage on-task behaviour and you don't need to say a word. (In taking different perspectives you also scan the room and may see things which were not visible in teaching from the front.)
- Non-verbal signals: effective teachers use a wide range of strategies which you may not be aware of as you observe them working with a group of students. You may be amazed at how a teacher uses eye contact to attract a student's attention or with a gentle smile indicates approval. Students are receptive to body language so you need to adopt a positive but not overbearing posture which exudes confidence. The appropriate use of a 'thumbs up' can send a strong message of approval as can a subtle nod; or the symbolic shaking of the head to indicate unacceptability. Sometimes to gain the attention of a whole class teachers can use signals to gain listening order: for example, standing at the front of the classroom with an outstretched arm pointing to the whiteboard can indicate your readiness to move to another activity. Some teachers count down from five to one (the five is loudly issued but not shouted and the following numbers are spoken with decreasing volume) and teach the class that at number one there is a listening silence.

Personal feelings

It is a cliché to observe that people have different reactions to different experiences. It can be quite challenging as a teacher when things do not go according to plan or when a student speaks to, or behaves towards, you in a manner which you find totally unacceptable. For some it could mean a really tearful moment; for others it could mean a groundswell of anger and frustration. And on a daily basis, of course, we have days when we feel a bit under the weather or the journey to work has been a stressful one with heavy traffic and delays. Teachers need to have a good sense of themselves and have to work hard at managing their emotional state so that it does not interfere with the business of teaching and learning. This is not to suggest that teachers are automata without feelings, delivering some sterile, bland curriculum in a highly prescriptive way, but you do need to look hard at yourself and use your 'emotional intelligence'.

Confrontation/challenging behaviours

These words evoke some of the horror images referred to in the introduction but you probably do want some advice on this area. One thing to bear in mind is the very language we use when we talk about student behaviour. It is important to agree definitions. For example, some writers talk about unacceptable behaviour, some use the phrase challenging behaviour and some refer to confrontational behaviour. There is, of course, a sliding scale from a student's refusal to follow a simple instruction to threatening the teacher's physical well-being (a very rare event indeed).

As teachers we cannot control all the frustrations and pent-up emotions of our students, but we can try to equip them with the skills to express their anger effectively. If you encounter an angry student try these ideas.

- Don't match the student's anger with your own. This leads to escalation. The student needs you to be calm as a palliative to their own anger.
- Be consistent in your response: express that you are not happy at being shouted at, respond to the behaviour and be specific.
- Offer the student a chance to talk about how they are feeling. You might suggest a cooling off period before they tell you more. Offer to be a listener; do not be judgemental.
- Point out the positives in their behaviour which you have seen previously: use this as a way to give genuine praise and work towards a resolution.
- Give space and room: do not invade the personal space of the challenging student.
- Speak calmly, clearly and ask questions which show a genuine wish to understand the problem.
- Deal with the behaviour and not the student.
- Remember that the challenge is probably not directed at you personally.
- Assistance should be available from other staff in the school. (Note: as a trainee you are under the supervision of a designated mentor who is legally responsible for your welfare. Technically, you are never responsible for the students in your classroom; that responsibility lies with the school that is hosting your training.)

Being able to recognise and understand your reaction to unacceptable behaviour enables you to be more objective, respond appropriately and use one or more of the techniques already discussed to redirect students and avoid confrontation. If this is an area where you feel you need further ideas, you will find some useful material in Paul Blum's *The Teacher's Guide to Anger Management* and in Michelle MacGrath's *The Art of Teaching Peacefully*.

It is important in these challenging moments to be able to control your own emotions so that they do not impede your ability to act professionally. This is easier said than done of course because the 'moment' is highly charged. Different actions trigger different responses in people, as you well know, but you should begin to think through your own sensitivities so that you can manage them accordingly. Are you likely to overreact to a student who fails to extend the common courtesy of using 'Sir' or 'Miss'? Would a student ostentatiously chewing in your lesson invoke a major incident? Would you be very offended if you overheard a student using offensive language to their neighbour? How would you react if a student commented on your hairstyle or your clothing? Would you 'lecture' a student you found smoking because you are a non-smoker yourself? Would you be affronted if a student asked about your family or made a so-called witty comment about your ancient car?

IN THE CLASSROOM

A trainee teacher is having considerable difficulty with a Year 10 Set 1 English group who are studying *Othello* for GCSE. The students are enjoying the play, and were particularly attentive while watching extracts from a film version starring Lawrence Fishburne. As soon as the trainee teacher tries to lead a whole-class discussion, the students disregard the classroom conventions (and school policy) of orderly response. Students shout out answers and comments without waiting for permission. The trainee is unsure how to recover the situation without destroying the students' enthusiasm and obvious engagement with the text. There is nothing malicious in the students' behaviour but the trainee feels that there is a distinct lack of order: the students are manipulative but never rude.

Understandably, the trainee decides that the next lesson will be more orderly and decides that the discussion about the film will continue but it will be done differently. In fact, the trainee decides that the classroom rule of students seeking permission to speak by raising their hands will be strictly followed. The trainee rightly plans to limit the discussion (it will only last for 20 minutes) and decides that the students will be told that a written task will follow the discussion.

Unfortunately, and rather predictably, the next lesson does not go as anticipated because the students simply refuse to accept the classroom rule about raising their hands and the trainee becomes increasingly wearied and irritated. The discussion becomes fragmented and disjointed because the trainee spends time and verbal energy trying to establish the 'new order'. Eventually, the trainee moves to the written task to restore acceptable levels of behaviour and tells students that they can expect more writing in future lessons unless their attitude and behaviour improve. The students do engage in the written task and the quality is good.

REFLECTIVE TASK
REFLECTIVE TASK

Referring to the classroom story, try the 'miracle question' technique. Imagine a fairy godmother is able to grant one wish to the trainee who is working with this Year 10 group! What would the trainee ask for?

To frame the question for the fairy godmother, the trainee needs to think carefully about the desired outcomes. There are some suggestions below.

Desired outcomes:

- the students will answer questions and join in the discussion in an orderly way which gives everyone a chance to make a contribution;
- the students will listen carefully and politely to the contributions from others and learn from them;
- the students will respect the teacher's role in structuring the discussion and follow the established protocols;

- the discussion will enable the students to learn through reflection and debate;
- the students will be able to accept different views and opinions;
- the discussion will last long enough for key learning objectives to be achieved.

The idea of the miracle question technique is to enable a problem to be changed into an achievable goal. Often, because of the intensity of the classroom with so many things happening simultaneously and a steady stream of interactions, the trainee may not be able to analyse the problem beyond the immediacy, for example, of irritation and disappointment with the non-cooperative students. The miracle question is a chance for fresh thinking and an opportunity to see a positive future. From this vision, it is possible to derive the possibilities and also to really see what the problem is.

So, what wish should this trainee put to the fairy godmother?

Scaling

Another way to address classroom management issues which are causing you concern is to use a scaling technique. The trainee with the Year 10 English group might feel that chaos was the key feature of the lesson and that their authority has been undermined. Worse still, they might have genuine dread at the thought of the next lesson: how can I restore my professional credibility? The truth is often hard to see when you are overwhelmed by emotions. It can be really helpful to analyse the situation, perhaps with the help of a mentor. Scaling is a simple strategy. Think of a scale of 1 to 10 with 1 representing the lowest point and with 10 representing the highest point. You then attach a brief description to each point on the scale, decide where you are on that scale and consider steps to move you gradually up the scale: you are not trying to make a giant leap but small manageable steps towards a better situation. This is a really positive way to address concerns and helps you to see the wood for the trees.

PRACTICAL TASK   PRACTICAL TASK   **PRACTICAL TASK**   PRACTICAL TASK   **PRACTICAL TASK**

Refer again to the classroom story about teaching *Othello*.

There are three stages to this task.

(a) Look at the following scale which has been part completed. Can you attach descriptions to points 7, 8 and 9?

(b) Now consider where on the scale you would place this Year 10 English class.

(c) Then, working with a mentor or another trainee, suggest one or two strategies which could be attempted to move the class one point up the scale in the conduct of whole class discussion.

Point 10 is of course the ideal, but no teacher can move a class from point 1 to point 10 in some great miraculous leap.

1. The students shout out, don't listen and much of the talk is irrelevant and designed to upset the teacher and prevent learning.
2. The teacher tries to follow the classroom rules but the students ignore them.
3. The teacher keeps having to stop the discussion to remind students about the rules for discussion; occasionally they are followed.
4. The students know the rules but break them because they want to be talking; the teacher has to be very firm on the rules and is unhappy that students are not learning and using them.

5. The students engage well with the topic and make lively contributions but it is rather chaotic, and certain students are dominating the discussion.

6. The teacher is taking a back seat for parts of the discussion because students are talking to/with each other in a fairly sensible way.

... 7, 8, 9 – Describe these points on the scale.

10. The class discuss the film in a mature way following all the conventions of debate and verbal exchange; the teacher is able to take a back seat and only occasionally intervene as a facilitator to move the discussion forward.

Every Child Matters

The Children Act 2004 had, at its heart, five outcomes to ensure the health and well-being of all children. The five outcomes were:

1. be healthy;
2. stay safe;
3. enjoy and achieve;
4. make a positive contribution;
5. achieve economic well-being.

Everyone in all settings (including the trainee) must consider how the activities of their classroom, their attention to good relationships and their development of a positive classroom climate contribute to securing these five outcomes.

Promoting positive behaviour for learning and creating a climate for purposeful learning touch, to a greater or lesser degree, on each of the five outcomes.

Consider the chart in Figure 7.2, which has been adapted from the grade descriptions for evaluating *Every Child Matters* (ECM) outcomes (Ofsted 2005).

Be healthy	Students are able to recognise what situations contribute to their personal stress levels and are beginning to develop an understanding about how to deal with this
Stay safe	Students feel safe from bullying, racism and other types of discrimination. They are able to demonstrate concern for the safety and well-being of others, both other students and staff
Enjoy and achieve	Students are well motivated and engage well with the learning process. They attend school regularly and are punctual for lessons. Students understand rule reminders and respond positively to requests and gentle reprimands
Make a positive contribution	Students understand the importance of good personal relationships. They understand that with rights come responsibilities and they are able to apply this to their work in the classroom
Achieve economic well-being	Students have enough self-confidence to be independent learners yet are still able to work co-operatively in a team. Students are able to cope with change and are actively engaged with the learning process. They are beginning to develop problem-solving skills

Figure 7.2. *Every Child Matters*

REFLECTIVE TASK
REFLECTIVE TASK

Read through this chapter again in relation to Figure 7.2.

Consider which of the strategies and techniques that have been described will support you in securing one or more of the five outcomes. For example, praise that is personal, specific and genuine might contribute to being healthy, enjoying and achieving and making a positive contribution.

Think 'outside the box' in terms of your personal feelings and the way in which you model behaviour for students.

What other strategies and techniques might you need to develop and employ to ensure that you contribute to securing the five ECM outcomes?

This chapter has attempted to offer some guidance and support. There will be days when you feel that your best plans for learning have fallen foul of things beyond your control, whether that be inclement weather or the distraction of a false fire alarm. Other days, your students will be responsive and engaged, you will see real progress and you will gain those rather intangible benefits ascribed to the 'buzz' of the successful classroom. As your competence and confidence grow, you will become less conscious of managing behaviour for learning and the skilful blending of pedagogy and student and classroom management will be achieved almost without your knowing it. Good teachers, like good poets, borrow from one another: do not be afraid to try new ideas and new techniques acquired from other teachers or your own reading; do not be disappointed if what works one day is less effective on another. The successful teacher is innovative; the effective teacher is reflective and the very best make mistakes and learn from them.

A SUMMARY OF **KEY POINTS**

> The management of behaviour is not a separate set of skills to be applied to students but an integral part of the teacher's role in enabling students to learn. That is why the chapter is entitled 'Managing behaviour for learning'.

> The climate of the classroom depends on key values and beliefs: paramount is that of mutual respect.

> Techniques and tips are part of the effective teacher's repertoire but in themselves will not deliver effective teaching and learning.

> Through reading, observation, discussion and practice your skills will develop.

> Students will occasionally exhibit really challenging behaviours and as a trainee you need to be confident not only to use your skills but also to call on the support of the school's staff and procedures.

> Everyone has a responsibility to contribute to securing the five outcomes of Every Child Matters.

MOVING *ON* > > > > > > MOVING *ON* > > > > > > MOVING *ON*

The next step is to consider how you might measure the impact of your behavioural interventions, and the kind of qualitative and quantitative data you can collect. You might need to do this to demonstrate that the strategies you are using are having an impact not only on students' levels of confidence and their developing social, emotional and behavioural skills but also on their academic progress. This form of measurement is particularly important at the school level.

FURTHER READING FURTHER READING FURTHER READING FURTHER READING

Blum, P. (2001) *A Teacher's Guide to Anger Management*. London. RoutledgeFalmer. This book offers a range of tips, techniques and strategies and is written by a successful practitioner.

Cowley, S. (2001) *Getting the Buggers to Behave*. London. Continuum. This book is a bestseller and attracted considerable attention when it received a very positive endorsement from Tim Brighouse. It has spawned a series of books for teachers.

DfES (2005) *Learning Behaviour. The Report of the Practitioners' Group on School Behaviour and Discipline*.

MacGrath, M. (1998) *The Art of Teaching Peacefully.* London. David Fulton.

Marland, M. (2002) *The Craft of the Classroom*. 3rd ed. London. Heinemann Educational Books. This book is a very accessible and practical survival guide with ideas which are still applicable today.

Rogers, B. (1997) *You Know the Fair Rule*. London. Prentice Hall. This book contains lots of good advice and strategies for making management easier and also good fun.

Watkins, C. and Wagner, P. (2000) *Improving School Behaviour*. London. Paul Chapman. This book is based on detailed research and offers insights and ideas in a very readable style.

PART 3
PROFESSIONAL KNOWLEDGE:
ACROSS THE CURRICULUM

8
Teaching literacy across the curriculum
Rob Batho with Alaster Douglas

Introduction

Anyone who is reading this book is likely to have sophisticated literacy skills but may not know how they acquired them or be able to identify them in order to teach them to others. This lack of understanding is not unusual and is not confined to literacy. Think of riding a bike or swimming. Imagine how difficult it would be to explain how to do one of those activities, for which you have tacit understanding, to someone who hasn't a clue. Part of the difficulty is remembering how you acquired those skills in the first place. More than likely you would have had some tuition and, most importantly, support and advice as you practised, spluttered or wobbled your way to success. To attempt to achieve such success and learn those skills only through trial and error and immersion in experience, without tuition, guidance or support can often lead to failure and an unwillingness in the learner to try again. The same can be said for literacy; all of its skills can be taught and can lead to more effective and efficient learning. As a good reader yourself (and probably writer and speaker too), you may not realise how important it is for weaker readers to be taught and given support in developing their reading skills and strategies, and that the same applies to writing and speaking and listening.

The purpose of this chapter on literacy across the curriculum is to encourage you, as a beginning teacher, to be alert to the specific literacy demands and skills of your subject so that you are in a position to support students in your class to develop their own literacy skills and by so doing improve their ability to understand your subject and to communicate that understanding to others. The Teachers' Standards include mention of early reading. This is applicable to all teachers in a secondary school setting working with students whose level of attainment is that expected of a child working at Key Stage 1. These may be students with special educational needs or students who have English as an additional language. Having a clear understanding of systematic synthetic phonics and using them with students to support their development is a government expectation expressed through the Teachers' Standards.

The chapter will consider briefly the nature of and the context and reasons for literacy across the curriculum in secondary schools before focusing on strategies, supported by evidence from research, which can assist teachers in improving the literacy skills of students in all subjects. It will also offer practical tasks to help improve your understanding of literacy within the school context, and finally, summarise the key points of the chapter and suggest further reading.

The context

In 1998 the National Literacy Strategy and the National Numeracy Strategy were introduced to improve standards of literacy and numeracy in primary schools. These initiatives were built on and developed into the Key Stage 3 National Strategy with the introduction of the English and mathematics strands in 2001 and science, foundation subjects, ICT and behaviour and attendance in subsequent years. In 2005 the Key Stage 3 National Strategy was renamed the Secondary National Strategy to reflect its worth across Key Stages 3 and 4 becoming part of the National Strategies.

The need to improve literacy in schools arose out of evidence indicating poor standards of literacy in England and Wales. For example, the DfEE report *A Fresh Start* (1999) reports that:

- an estimated seven million adults in England cannot locate the page reference for plumbers in the *Yellow Pages;*
- of the 12 OEDC nations surveyed in 1997 for levels of adult literacy, only Poland and Ireland emerged with a lower level than Britain.

Although contracts for the primary and secondary strategies have not been renewed, expectations are that you demonstrate through your teaching that you can teach aspects of literacy as befits the literacy demands of your specialist subject.

What is literacy?

Before going any further, it is important to define the boundaries of what is meant by literacy in the context of literacy across the curriculum. Until the latter part of the twentieth century, literacy was defined as simply reading and writing, but since the late 1980s it has been argued (Graff 1987; Meek 1991; Cairney 1995) that there is a plurality of literacies which includes such areas of knowledge as the visual arts and the media. While accepting that argument, in this chapter literacy is defined as reading, writing and speaking and listening to maintain parity with the National Curriculum (DfEE/QCA 2000) and the *Framework for Secondary English*. Moreover, David Wray (2001), when writing about literacy in the secondary curriculum, gives a definition of literacy which suits the purpose of this chapter:

> *Literacy is the ability to read and use written information and to write appropriately for a range of purposes. It also involves the integration of speaking, listening and critical thinking with reading and writing and includes the knowledge which enables a speaker, reader or writer to recognise and use language appropriate to different social occasions.*

> (Wray 2001, p. 12)

Literacy is not being viewed as a mere set of basic, functional skills to meet societal demands such as filling in forms or reading newspaper headlines; it is rather seen as a means to enable individuals to apply their literacy skills, knowledge and strategies to a range of texts and situations and, as Eve Bearne (1999, p. 202) puts it, *being able to read the small print as well as read between the lines*.

Literacy and subjects

The view that language and literacy are the responsibility of all subject teachers is one which is advocated in the expectations of the National Curriculum:

> *Pupils should be taught in all subjects to express themselves correctly and appropriately and to read accurately and with understanding.*

> *Pupils should be taught the technical and specialist vocabulary of subjects and how to use and spell these words. They should also be taught to use the patterns of language vital to understanding and expression in different subjects. These include the construction of sentences, paragraphs and texts that are often used in a subject.*

> (DfEE/QCA 2000, p. 40)

In the rationale to the *Framework for Teaching English* (DfEE 2001a) (renewed as *The Framework for Secondary English* (2008)), literacy and language are also viewed as the responsibility of all subject areas:

> *Language is the principal medium of learning in a school, and every teacher needs to cultivate it as a tool for learning. Teachers have a genuine stake in strong language skills because language enables thought.*
>
> (DfEE 2001a, p.15)

It will make more sense to students if they consider specific literacy matters within the context of the subject where it naturally occurs (e.g. a science report in science, an historical enquiry in history). Each subject, in the way it is structured and formulated, will make certain and specific literacy demands on students beyond some that may be common to most or all subjects (and which the English department may well attend to). As Christine Counsell (2001) explains:

> *A subject ... is a way of working with certain kinds of information in order to answer certain kinds of questions. A subject is not 'information'; it is knowledge. Any knowledge has a structure ... The way a subject uses words, sentences and texts will be dominated not just by its types of information but by the questions and issues that each subject confronts.*
>
> (Counsell 2001)

Sheeran and Barnes (1991), when discussing writing in subject areas, take much the same view:

> *Cognitive and communicative ground rules are the essential definers of any discipline ... Specialist subjects consist of both implicit and explicit rules and organising principles governing both academic cognition and the social presentation of knowledge in the form of writing.*
>
> (Sheeran and Barnes 1991, pp. 55 and 101)

The Qualifications and Curriculum Authority (QCA 2001) in their publication *Language at Work in Lessons: Literacy Across the Curriculum at Key Stage 3*, underline the importance of all subject teachers being in involved in language work because teachers who currently incorporate a focus for language in their subject believe that it will:

- help pupils manage their learning in a subject more confidently and effectively;
- enable pupils to make good progress with the subject's increasing conceptual complexity and the specialist language involved;
- give pupils the tools to articulate, explain and justify their ideas and understanding;
- enhance pupils' achievements overall.

(QCA 2001, p. 5)

Having established the need for literacy teaching in all subjects, what then of the approaches and strategies which you could adopt to assist students' literacy development?

Approaches and strategies for teaching literacy across the curriculum

Research suggests that there are many such strategies and there is not the space here to detail them all. Neither is it the intention to consider separately reading, writing and speaking and listening, mainly because a number of the strategies require all four aspects of literacy to combine in support of one another. For instance, speaking and listening are essential to the discussion of reading and the sharing and planning of writing; and writing a specific text type for the first time is best promoted through the initial exploration through reading of the conventions and patterns of such a text. However, what can be done is to approach and group the strategies in a way that should help teachers who are planning for literacy in their lessons. The approach to be adopted is an active one. It will also be expressed chronologically in terms of the cyclical sequence for teaching from the planning stage, through the lesson introduction, the main part of the lesson, the plenary and the ensuing evaluation and assessment which feed back into future planning (see Figure 8.1).

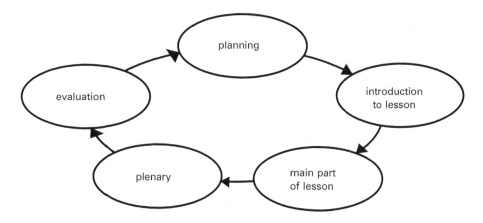

Figure 8.1. The teaching cycle

Wray (2001), when discussing literacy in relation to teaching and learning, makes the point that:

> *It is useful for secondary teachers to recognise that many of the processes involved in supporting literacy are also involved in developing learning.*

(Wray 2001, p. 50)

Planning

In planning for literacy, you first of all need to identify and select which aspect of literacy needs developing, and in many subject department schemes or units of work that selection will already have been done, very often where the objectives for learning have been adapted or taken from *The Framework for Secondary English* (2008). Departments might also have adapted their schemes of work to include literacy using the QCA's schemes of work in combination with their publications *Language for Learning* (QCA 2000) and *Language at Work in Lessons* (QCA 2001) which demonstrate, through worked examples, how literacy objectives (taken from the Strategy's *Framework*) can be employed effectively in planning and classroom practice. Once the literacy objective has been identified, then you can consider the strategies which you think will most help students meet that objective in the lesson. That range of strategies will be explored in the sections to follow.

Think of a Year 7, 8 or 9 lesson in your subject which you have recently seen taught, and ask yourself what was the main literacy demand of that lesson. Did it concern reading, writing or speaking and listening?

Lesson introduction

During the introduction you should clearly state and explain to students what the literacy objective for the lesson is in order that they can know what is to be expected of them. Wray (2001) emphasises the importance of teachers setting clear literacy objectives in contributing to high-quality teaching:

> *High quality teaching can be characterised by several factors, one of which is clarity of purpose. Making the literacy objective of a lesson explicit helps do this.*
>
> (Wray 2001, p. 50)

A further strategy which is often introduced at this stage, but which should also precede most tasks, whether they be to do with literacy or not, is the activation of prior knowledge. Langer (1981), following her development of a method for identifying and classifying prior knowledge in students, found that, when reading, those students who engaged in activating their prior knowledge learned and retained more than those who did not. She argued that activating prior knowledge helps students make new learning more meaningful. Activating prior knowledge can provide students with a bridge between their existing knowledge and the new and it can also assist the teacher in early assessment of students' knowledge as a basis for further planning. If this activation does not happen then, as Wray (1999) points out, learning is: *rote only, and is soon forgotten once deliberate attempts to remember it have stopped* (p. 54). Practical activities which activate prior knowledge can range straightforwardly from you asking the students what they know, to:

- brainstorming around the subject to be focused on;
- predicting what might happen next, building on previous knowledge and/or experience;
- word association from key word, picture or artefact from the subject to be focused on;
- filling in a mind-map, or grids (further details later).

Main part of the lesson

What is important in the main part of the lesson is that wherever possible it should be directly and explicitly linked to the introduction. The teaching process should generally follow a movement which begins with teacher explication and demonstration to the whole class, through a series of activities which are often collaborative to support students' learning, to students working independently. This teaching process owes much to the ideas of Vygotsky (1962), who suggested that learners learn best when they start learning with an expert (could be teacher, parent, other adult or peer), who they first watch and observe, before gradually, under the guiding hand and eye of the expert, they take over some parts of the work, and then as confidence and competence grow, they take over more and more until they finally take over the task completely and work unaided. Lewis and Wray (2000), in their work on literacy in the secondary school, have translated this process into four distinct stages.

1. Demonstration.
2. Joint activity.
3. Supported activity.
4. Individual activity.

Demonstration

Particularly if this task is to involve a new type of writing or the reading of a text not met before, it often helps students if you speak aloud your thoughts so that they can gain an insight into the mental processes. Bereiter and Scardamalia (1987), who researched the writing process and composition, emphasise the importance of the teacher modelling writing composition:

> *The thinking that goes on in composition needs to be modelled by the teacher, who can thereby show the problem-solving and planning processes that... pupils are often unaware of... and so that they can benefit from observing and discussing each other's mental efforts.*
>
> (Bereiter and Scardamalia 1987, p. 174)

Similarly when students are expected to read an unfamiliar text (a subject textbook, a reference text [which could be electronic], a pamphlet, etc.) you could use an enlarged version (via OHT) of part of the text and demonstrate the reading skills needed.

Joint activity

This is where *The expert and the learner share the activity* (Lewis and Wray 2000, p. 27), and in terms of the writing and reading activities referred to above, it could be where, having demonstrated the writing of the first couple of sentences of a type of writing, you ask students to suggest the next sentence or so and discuss the suggestions as you write them on the board. Or, with reading, having demonstrated certain skills, you ask students to offer their readings.

Supported activity

In this stage of the process you, the teacher as expert, should maintain careful observation of the students and a readiness to assist but ask the students to work on the activity, sometimes with a partner or as part of a small group or with other support (writing frames, diagrams, instructions, etc.). It can also be the stage, again for reading or writing, where you work closely with one particular group of students in order to support and monitor their progress.

Individual activity

Some students may attain this stage earlier than others. You need to be sensitive to students' progress and needs in the early stages of support.

PRACTICAL TASK   PRACTICAL TASK   PRACTICAL TASK   PRACTICAL TASK

GROUP TALK
Think back over some lessons you have observed recently and jot down the different types of student groupings (paired, small group [4–6], large group [6+], mixed ability, etc.) you observed. How were the groups organised? What would you say was the function and purpose of such groupings?

Plenary

The plenary is a vital stage in the lesson. It is the point where you and the students can reflect upon, review and consolidate what has been learnt so far; a point where the learning objectives for literacy, stated at the opening of the lesson, can be revisited. This is a time which can develop a student's metacognitive intelligence (one of seven different intelligences identified by Howard Gardner [1993]), the ability to reflect upon and take control of one's learning. (For more information on multiple intelligences see Chapter 4, pp. 36–7.)

Evaluation and assessment

This is another important area, where you need both to evaluate the effectiveness of the lesson on students' literacy development in order to inform future lesson planning, and to assess individual students' literacy learning so that class and individual literacy targets can be reviewed and set. You can achieve this informally, during (through talking with, listening to and observing students) and after the lesson (through reading and marking students' work).

A word or two on marking written work for literacy. When you set a piece of written work, indicate which aspects of literacy will be commented on or 'marked'. This requires you to prioritise and be selective. For example, if one of the objectives for the lesson has been to learn and spell key vocabulary, it would be appropriate to tell students that those key words will be assessed both for understanding and spelling (rather than marking every spelling mistake). Similarly, if the literacy objective had been understanding how to introduce paragraphs in a particular type of writing in a subject, comments on the success or otherwise of the paragraph opening would also be appropriate. An important element to consider when responding to students' work is that of praise and positive reinforcement. On this subject, Lewis and Wray (2001, p. 51) make the point that low levels of literacy are often associated with poor self-esteem and advocate teachers giving positive rather than negative feedback to students on their reading, writing and speaking and listening. Debra Myhill, in her book *Better Writing* (2001), which is based on the research she carried out into writing in schools, gives the advice to teachers when assessing writing to *isolate and praise what is effective as well as weaknesses* (p. 98).

The EXIT model and further strategies

The EXIT model

The EXIT model (Extending Interactions with Texts) grew out of the work of David Wray and Maureen Lewis on the Nuffield Extending Literacy (EXEL) Project. The purpose of the EXIT model was to present a *description of the processes involved in learning with texts* (Lewis and Wray 2000) and thereby to suggest certain strategies which are directly linked to the model. Lewis and Wray identified ten mental activities involved in learning with texts and devised a ten-stage process as follows.

1. Elicitation of previous knowledge.
2. Establishing purposes.
3. Locating information.
4. Adopting an appropriate strategy.
5. Interacting with text.
6. Monitoring understanding.
7. Making a record.
8. Evaluating information.
9. Assisting memory.
10. Communicating information.

(Lewis and Wray 2000)

As can be seen, the sequence complements in part the sequence for teaching from the earlier part of this chapter, with its allusions to activating prior knowledge, stating the learning objective and evaluating the learning. Each part of the sequence can be linked to certain strategies. As mentioned earlier, there are far too many to be listed here but it is worth referring to a few.

One particularly effective group of strategies which would appear within 'Interacting with text' in Lewis and Wray's EXIT model and which has been in use in schools for many years is termed DARTS.

DARTS

DARTS stands for Directed Activities Related to Texts and they were activities first devised in 1984 by Lunzer and Gardner to further and encourage active approaches to reading. Since the inception of DARTS, teachers have added to and amended activities, but helpfully, Geoff Dean (2000, pp. 110–111), following many others, has categorised them into:

- reconstructive activities;
- processing activities.

With reconstructive activities, the text has been altered in some way and the students have to reconstruct it and it includes such activities as cloze procedure, which involves students filling in words which have been deleted from a text; sequencing, where the text has been cut up into segments and the students have to reorganise them and give a reason for their decisions; or prediction, where students are given a text where the ending of it or the ending of a section is missing and they have to predict the next part based upon their reading and understanding of their reading so far.

Processing activities require the students to work with unamended texts and include such activities as text marking, where students are asked to apply a specific focus or question to the text and to respond by highlighting or annotating the parts of the text that refer to the focus or question; and questioning, where they are asked to generate questions about the text being studied for others to attempt to answer.

Most DARTS activities lend themselves to collaborative work, where students work in pairs or groups, and can be seen as especially useful in supported activity in the main part of a lesson.

Another effective strategy for use with texts can be the use of grids to help in terms of activating prior knowledge, establishing a purpose and making a record. Lewis and Wray advocate the use of two in particular: the KWL grid and the QUADS grid (Lewis and Wray 2000).

KWL grid

What do I *know* about this topic?	What do I *want* to know about it?	What have I *learnt* about it?

It can be seen that this grid helps the students to organise their approach and to record their findings and is based on *three cognitive steps – accessing prior knowledge, determining what needs to be learnt, recalling what has been learnt* (Lewis and Wray 2000).

QUADS grid

Question	Answer	Details	Source

This grid acts in a similar way to the KWL without so much emphasis on the activation of prior knowledge but with more emphasis on recording information. Students are required initially to formulate a question about the topic they are exploring, to find (via books, internet, etc.) and record the answer, but also to record any relevant details connected with their research question as well as the source of the information.

Writing frames

It was through the EXIT project that Lewis and Wray suggested that the use of 'frames' could act as a support for students when they are engaged in writing (particularly non-fiction) in any subject. A 'frame' in this context is simply a bare outline of a text such as the one in Figure 8.2 (Lewis and Wray 2000, p. 93).

UK and Kenya – a comparison

Although .... and .... are different they are alike in some interesting ways.

For example they both ....

....

They are also similar in ....

....

They also have the same ....

....

Figure 8.2. Example of a writing frame

Writing frames are helpful in structuring text, providing examples of ways to begin both whole texts and paragraphs and how to connect the different parts of a text, but, as Roger Beard points out:

> *they are intended to be used as a kind of prompt, eventually to be dispensed with, as children begin to adopt the features of the genre for themselves.*

(Beard 2000, p. 113)

Spelling

The ability to spell is not innate; it is a skill which can be learned. There are various strategies which can be employed to help students improve their spelling. It is first of all important to recognise that there are three basic reasons why students may be poor at spelling.

1. They have underdeveloped visual memory – they can't remember how words look.
2. They have underdeveloped auditory analysis – they have poor awareness of the constituent sounds of words (phonological awareness).
3. They have underdeveloped intellectual awareness – they lack the understanding or ability to use knowledge of the way words are derived or structured or follow spelling conventions.

It follows that the spelling strategies which you advocate for your students (individual and whole class) should attempt to address these weaknesses singly or together, as does the popular 'look – cover – say – write – check' method.

Make spelling active. When a student asks you for a spelling, you should resist the temptation to give the spelling immediately but instead ask the student to try spelling it.

IN THE CLASSROOM

In Jane Marston's science class one student, Alex, put up his hand and asked her how to spell immediately. Jane asked Alex to try spelling it.

'I-M-E-D-I-A-T-E-L-Y,' Alex uttered.

'Very good, Alex,' responded the teacher, 'You have ten out of the eleven letters right. There's one missing; what d'you think it might be?'

'Is it another M, Miss?'

'It is Alex, well done.'

The lesson in this story is that even if the student doesn't get the whole word right, you should give praise for the number of correct letters before asking or indicating where the error lies. You should ask the class how to spell words which are vital to the subject they are addressing in the lesson, and you should encourage students to keep a spelling log book which contains words which are important in their subject and which they can easily refer to.

PRACTICAL TASK   PRACTICAL TASK   PRACTICAL TASK   PRACTICAL TASK

VOCABULARY

Find out and make a list of the key vocabulary for your subject in Year 7 and see how you might incorporate some of those words into a scheme of work for that year.

Using the teaching environment to support literacy

Medwell (Medwell *et al.* 1998 in Lewis and Wray 2001, p. 49), in the *Effective Teachers of Literacy* project, found that it was important to create 'literate environments' in the classroom. It is yet another way for the teachers in the school to show how valued literacy is in that community. The teaching environment could be any site in the secondary school where teaching and learning take place, including classrooms, IT suites, gymnasia and drama studios, but also other sites such as the school's entrance hall and corridors. All are sites which teachers could use to support and emphasise literacy within and across subjects. You, as an individual subject teacher, could ensure for instance that wall displays are changed regularly to coincide with current literacy objectives for different classes (e.g. key terminology and vocabulary); or that good examples of students' writing are displayed attractively and effectively; that key books are displayed and that literacy materials and resources such as dictionaries are easily accessible by students.

PRACTICAL TASK PRACTICAL TASK **PRACTICAL TASK** PRACTICAL TASK **PRACTICAL TASK**

LITERACY WALK

During a break, take a walk around the school and look to see how the school environment (classrooms, corridors, reception areas, halls, etc.) supports students' literacy development. Make a note of good examples and practice in your school and be prepared to share these with others. For example:

- in which areas are there examples of advice for students as to how to improve an aspect of their literacy?
- in which areas are there good displays of books?
- in which areas are there good displays of recent students' written work?

Literacy and students with English as an additional language (EAL)

The inclusion of students learning English as an additional language is a key principle of the National Curriculum 2000. Literacy competence and confidence are essential for students with EAL if they are to access all subjects in the curriculum. Virtually all of the strategies for developing literacy outlined above will be helpful to those students because they encourage teacher support, scaffolded activities, collaborative working, the activation of prior knowledge and planning for talk. In order to be of greatest assistance to your students you will, in addition, need to know the language and literacy background and identity as well as their previous educational experiences. You should also have high expectations of your students and plan for them all to be involved. (For more information on teaching students with English as an additional language, see Chapter 14.)

Literacy across the curriculum and the role of the English teacher

If your subject is English, all that has been discussed so far in terms of strategies and approaches will apply to your classroom practice, but it is not your responsibility to teach all aspects of literacy that will be covered across the curriculum. I hope that it is now clear that each subject has a responsibility for identifying its own literacy demands and teaching those accordingly. With English as your subject, what you can do to help support literacy across the curriculum is to teach some of those generic aspects of literacy which will support students' literacy in other subjects. For instance you can teach pupils many of the conventions of English spelling; strategies for spelling; paragraphing; punctuation; understanding and writing the main text types; reading strategies; the roles and skills of group discussion; etc.

A SUMMARY OF **KEY POINTS**

The foregrounding and teaching of literacy are an essential responsibility of all teachers, whatever their subject, if they are to fully develop and sustain the learning of all their students. The following are, I believe, the key points from the chapter which will lead to your success in improving the literacy skills of the students you teach.

> **Understand the literacy demands of your subject.**

> **Plan your lessons to include literacy objectives and the development of students' literacy.**

> **Teach literacy skills. Don't assume that their literacy will automatically improve by simply doing more reading or writing.**

> **Model and demonstrate good literacy practice.**

> **Provide support and guidance for students' reading, writing and speaking and listening.**

> **Respond constructively to students' literacy in their reading, writing and speaking and listening.**

MOVING *ON* > > > > > > MOVING *ON* > > > > > > MOVING *ON*

In your subject, which aspects of literacy, reading, writing or speaking and listening do you think give your students the most difficulty? Ask some of your students and your subject colleagues for their views. Now decide what seems to be the single most important aspect, and with a colleague consider how you might address the problem in your planning and teaching with a particular class that you teach.

FURTHER READING FURTHER READING **FURTHER READING** FURTHER READING

DfEE (2001a) *Framework for Teaching English: Years 7, 8 and 9.* London. DfEE. The document which contains all of the objectives for literacy for Key Stage 3 as well as advice on planning and guidance on inclusion.

DfEE (2001b) *Literacy Across the Curriculum.* London. DfEE. This is the training folder for all subjects at Key Stage 3 and it contains discussions and teaching advice on all aspects of literacy from writing non-fiction to spelling and from active reading to managing group talk.

DfES (2002) *Literacy in...* series. A series of booklets and video extracts exemplifying good practice in literacy teaching in art, PE, MFL, design and technology, history, geography, music, RE, citizenship and careers.

DfES (2004) *Literacy and learning*. London. DfES. A further series of subject-specific booklets and CD-ROMs which incorporate the Literacy Across the Curriculum materials and give practical ideas on how to devise effective objective-led teaching which focuses on learning through talk, from text and through writing.

Lewis, M. and Wray, D. (2000) *Literacy in the Secondary School*. London. David Fulton. This contains information on the EXEL project together with discussion and advice on teaching strategies to improve students' literacy.

Myhill, D. (2001) *Better Writing*. Westley. Courseware Publications. Good advice on teaching writing based on recent research.

QCA (2000) *Language for Learning in Key Stage 3*. London. QCA. Useful advice on mapping the objectives in the QCA schemes of work for various subjects.

9
Teaching numeracy across the curriculum
Kate Mackrell with Alaster Douglas

Introduction

When the first edition of this book was being written in 2002, the Key Stage 3 strategy was very new, and an important part of that strategy was the Numeracy across the Curriculum initiative. This initiative has now been implemented, with each school expected to have a numeracy policy and subject departments expected to collaborate in enhancing student numeracy both for its own sake and as a contribution to other subjects. The focus of attention at Key Stage 3 has hence shifted away from numeracy as other initiatives are being developed. However, the Teachers' Standards include a phrase *early mathematics*. This should not be overlooked by secondary teachers as it refers to all students working at a level of attainment equivalent to the expected level of a primary school child up to Year 6. So, students working below expectation in Years 7 and 8 (and beyond) will fall into this category. Therefore, numeracy continues to be critically important to students at Key Stage 3, and, particularly for trainees who teach subjects such as science, geography or design technology in which mathematics is used extensively, must be taken seriously.

The aim of this chapter is hence:

- to help trainees whose main subject is not mathematics to successfully incorporate the mathematics necessary to their subject in their teaching;
- to encourage those trainees whose main subject is not mathematics to see the development of student numeracy as enhancing both their subject and the development of other cross-curricular skills;
- to help mathematics trainees to be aware of the issues faced by non-mathematics teachers in incorporating numeracy in lessons and to begin to distinguish their own role in encouraging numeracy across the curriculum.

In this chapter, the following questions will be considered.

- What is numeracy?
- Why focus on numeracy across the curriculum?
- What are the objectives of numeracy across the curriculum?
- What maths is relevant to your specialist subject?
- How can you make sure you know the maths you need?
- How can you plan to incorporate numeracy in your lessons?
- What's important in delivering such a lesson?

What is numeracy?

Numeracy is not just about being able to do calculations: it is about being able to use mathematics effectively outside the mathematics classroom. This includes for example the ability to use simple formulae, understand basic probability and create and interpret graphs.

It is probably more useful to think of numeracy skills as being mathematical skills used in a real context rather than as a particular group of mathematical skills, as it can be argued that numeracy encompasses all of the mathematics at Key Stage 3 (Perks and Prestage 2001).

Why focus on numeracy across the curriculum?

Do you feel bogged down at the thought of including numeracy in your subject teaching? Surely teacher training is tough enough without throwing maths into it!

REFLECTIVE TASK

Spend some time writing about how you feel about mathematics. Do you enjoy it? Have you found it hard? Boring? How confident are you with everyday maths? How do you feel about incorporating mathematics into your subject teaching?

You have probably just pinpointed a major problem with numeracy: many people dislike maths, become anxious when required to do any maths and lack confidence in their ability. Many people also have very negative images of mathematicians and these likewise (and perhaps particularly for girls) can get in the way of learning. Here are some common misconceptions.

- Maths doesn't involve creativity.
- Maths is about rules to be memorised.
- Boys are better at maths than girls.
- Some people can do maths but some can't.

Also, being 'innumerate' is socially acceptable in a way that being 'illiterate' isn't. Hence there can be little incentive to become competent at mathematics.

Does this matter? I get very anxious about the idea of diving off a board 20 feet above the water and hence I avoid having to do it and have not developed the skills needed to do it successfully. Impact on my life? Negligible.

The effects of maths avoidance and lack of skill are not negligible. Mathematical skills are increasingly needed in employment: research has shown that poor numeracy skills have more impact on employment prospects than poor literacy skills (Basic Skills Agency 1997).

Why can't problems with numeracy be solved in mathematics classrooms?

Mathematics classrooms have indeed changed considerably: concerns about both adult numeracy and the relatively poor performance of English students in international studies of mathematics achievement led to the introduction of the National Numeracy Strategy at Key Stage 1/Key Stage 2 in 1998 and the Key Stage 3 Framework for Teaching Mathematics in 2001 becoming part of the National Strategies. This involved the introduction of a detailed programme of study for each year and a change in teaching strategies, with emphasis on reasoning and questioning and a high proportion of oral and mental work.

Contracts for the primary and secondary material strategies have not been renewed. Nevertheless, numeracy remains an important topic for secondary school teachers.

All learning is situated in a context (Lave 1988): in mathematics classrooms students learn how to do mathematics in mathematics classrooms. They do not and cannot learn how to do mathematics in other settings until they are in that setting. For example, students who are competent at drawing graphs in a maths lesson may not be able to draw similar graphs in a geography lesson, despite the fact that their mathematics teacher has taken care to introduce graphs taken from many different contexts. This can lead to a great deal of frustration on the part of teachers of other subjects: it is easy to assume that the students are unintelligent or that their mathematics teaching is poor.

In order for students to make the links between the mathematics of the mathematics classroom and the mathematics required in other subjects it is important that teachers of other subjects are also involved in the mathematical development of the students.

The Numeracy across the Curriculum initiative

The Numeracy across the Curriculum initiative, initiated in secondary schools in 2001, had the aim of addressing this problem. The main focus of this initiative was to set up collaboration between mathematics and other subject departments to enable teachers to make explicit links with mathematics in different subject areas and to achieve consistency in approaches and expectations.

The fundamental objective was that standards in numeracy should be raised and learning in other subjects enhanced.

The priorities identified were:

- to improve accuracy, particularly in calculation, measurement and graphical work;
- to improve interpretation and presentation of graphs, charts and diagrams;
- to improve reasoning and problem-solving.

In order to achieve these objectives, schools designated a numeracy co-ordinator and ideally, the curriculum for mathematics and other subjects began to be organised so that topics required for other subjects were first taught by the mathematics department. Schools had to develop a numeracy policy which:

- set out an agreed approach to:
  - the teaching of agreed numeracy skills;
  - vocabulary, notation and units to be used;
  - use of calculators and other ICT;
  - methods for calculation;
  - algebraic techniques;
  - the representation of graphs;
- indicated areas of collaboration between subjects and processes for facilitating collaboration;
- gave links with using and applying mathematics;
- gave advice from the mathematics department on common difficulties, errors and misconceptions.

PRACTICAL TASK PRACTICAL TASK **PRACTICAL TASK** PRACTICAL TASK **PRACTICAL TASK**

Find out from the numeracy co-ordinator in your school how the Numeracy across the Curriculum initiative was implemented. What type of collaboration occurred between departments?

What maths is relevant to your specialist subject?

The maths necessary to different subjects will vary: geography, science and design technology rely on mathematics extensively (for example, can you imagine design technology without measurement, or science and geography without graphs?), whereas there are no specific demands for mathematical skills in studying English.

Mathematics which is not strictly required can also be used to enrich subject teaching. A good example is found in the excerpt from the history lesson on the NAC video, where pie charts are used to enhance student learning about the daily life of a monk.

Here are some further enrichment examples from English and modern foreign languages (MFL).

- Exploring the metrical pattern of poetry when using a poem as a model for writing.

- Exploring average sentence length in samples of various newspapers' front pages over time and considering whether any generalisations can be made.
- Number games such as *Countdown* conducted in the target language.
- Looking at the structure of the number system via the different words used for number in different languages.
- Money: conversations around shopping and internet shopping, currency conversions.
- Conducting surveys and presenting data in the target language, interpreting data from the target language country.
- Using mathematical language (e.g. square, rectangular) in describing objects.

REFLECTIVE TASK

Identify the mathematical content necessary to your subject and begin to identify areas where maths could enrich your subject. Some sources of information are listed below.

- Your subject department.
- The Mathematics Association publication *Numeracy across the Curriculum*.
- A search on the internet on your subject and mathematics.

As well as identifying mathematics content (such as percentages), improving reasoning and problem-solving will require you to identify the relationship between your subject and mathematical thinking skills (which are the sorts of skills you used in creating maths GCSE coursework). Thinking skills in mathematics in the National Curriculum are known as 'using and applying' and are categorised as:

- problem-solving (making decisions about problems and methods and monitoring decision-making);
- communication (formulating, discussing, interpreting and presenting findings);
- reasoning (finding solutions and giving justifications).

How can you make sure you know the maths you need?

You can't. As an experienced mathematics teacher, I still sometimes get asked questions that I can't immediately answer. What matters is that I have the confidence and the resources to go away and come back with an answer – or to open out the question so that the class can explore it and we can all learn something new. You need to ensure that you are confident with the specific mathematics that you need in a lesson, but be prepared for unexpected questions to arise that you may not be able to respond to immediately. You can set an excellent model for students in your handling of unexpected difficulties if you openly discuss the issue and plan strategies to find out the mathematics needed.

What may be more important than knowing the mathematics in great detail is to check whether or not you have any misconceptions about maths. All of the statements below are true – some may surprise you.

Misconceptions in maths are common: even if you feel confident about mathematics you may find you have some. It's very important that you don't pass these on to students.

- Multiplying doesn't always make numbers bigger.
- Putting a nought on the end of a number to multiply it by ten doesn't always work.
- Sometimes adding two numbers can give a bigger result than multiplying them.

- To convert square metres to square centimetres you don't multiply by 100.
- If the price of an item is increased by 5 per cent and then reduced by 5 per cent the final price will not be the same as the original price.
- On the other hand, if the price of an item is reduced by a certain percentage and then VAT is added, the result will be the same as if the VAT is added before the price is reduced.
- If a set of data is grouped into five class intervals, the mean could fall into any one of the intervals.
- If you toss a coin twice, the probability of throwing two heads is not 1/3.
- Two cuboids with the same volume will not always have the same surface area.
- If you double the lengths of a shape you will not double the area and the volume.
- Division sometimes makes numbers larger.
- When the area of a shape increases, the perimeter can sometimes decrease.
- Dividing any number by zero does not give zero.
- The order in which you combine numbers using +, -, x or ÷ sometimes matters.
- There are nine times as many students as teachers in a school. P represents the number of students and T represents the number of teachers in the school. Hence $9T = P$.

(Adapted from Pope and Sharma 2001)

Detailed explanations of a variety of misconceptions may be found at **www.cimt. plymouth.ac.uk/resources/help/miscon.htm**

How can you plan to incorporate numeracy in your lessons?

PRACTICAL TASK PRACTICAL TASK PRACTICAL TASK PRACTICAL TASK PRACTICAL TASK

Observe a mathematics lesson, ideally one in which mathematics relevant to your subject is being taught. Make notes of the teaching strategies used, in particular the use of questioning and mental and oral work and of the students' responses. Now observe a lesson in your subject in which mathematics is used. Contrast the teaching strategies and pupil responses with those in the mathematics lesson.

1. Identify prior learning

This is quite important in mathematics teaching: you need to ensure that you are building upon mathematics with which the students feel confident. Information about what mathematics the students have been exposed to should be in the mathematics departmental schemes of work. Mathematical exposure is not the same as mathematical learning, however: find out as much as you can about the mathematical attainment of individual students. In particular you need to identify students who have particular difficulty with maths: they may not be the same students as the ones who find your subject difficult.

2. Decide on learning objectives

You may find at this point that there is a mismatch between the mathematics required and the students' prior learning. The mismatch between required mathematical skills in other subjects and prior learning in mathematics should be minimised so that you do not need ever to introduce new mathematical techniques for the first time to a class: your objectives will normally involve using mathematics in the context of your subject. If the mismatch is too great, you will need to revise your plans to include mathematics which is more appropriate to the students' prior learning.

You may find it difficult to break a piece of mathematics down into measurable objectives or to see what would be an appropriate progression. Your objectives will normally involve consolidation of mathematical skills and application of these skills within your subject.

Remember that cross-curricular priorities focus on accuracy, interpretation and presentation and reasoning and problem-solving. Do your learning objectives relate to these priorities?

3. Decide on teaching strategies

There can be an emphasis on questioning: the students may never be told what to do or how to do it, but are asked to reflect on their knowledge of mathematics in order to decide for themselves. Mental calculations may be required and students asked to explain how they worked out particular answers.

Discussion and questioning are key teaching strategies: students can be asked how they worked out their answers, whether or not their answers are reasonable and why they have chosen their methods or reached their conclusions. Students can be encouraged to discuss their strategies and share ideas.

It's important to use the same approach as the maths department in dealing with specific topics. A temptation is to show the students a shortcut, as illustrated in the following story.

IN THE CLASSROOM

As part of their study of rivers, students in a geography lesson were converting some numbers from fractions to percentages. The teacher noticed that the students were using a variety of methods, most of which were unfamiliar to him and many of which did not seem very efficient. The teacher decided to address the class about this and said 'I know a better method for doing this – first you ... and then you ...' The students left the class feeling confused: though able to use the shortcut in that particular lesson, none of them understood why it worked or when it could be used. The consequence was, as noted in subsequent mathematics lessons, that their basic understanding of percentages deteriorated. It would have been better for the teacher to have listened to them explaining their methods.

A major consideration will be the approach you use to calculation: you need to consider whether to use mental, written or calculator methods and plan accordingly. Note that students may well be much better at mental arithmetic than you expect: by Year 7 students are expected to add and subtract two-digit numbers such as 73 and 49 mentally. If students can reasonably be expected to work out calculations mentally, telling them to use a calculator may deprive them of an opportunity to practise their skills in mental calculation. On the other hand, if the required calculations are lengthy and difficult, students may lose track of the purpose of the lesson by focusing on calculation alone. See units 5 and 6 of NAC for a consideration of calculations and calculator use.

4. Decide on assessment strategies

Appropriate assessment will enable you to gauge whether or not you have met your learning objectives and will also provide feedback which enables students to improve. Much of this you will achieve through observation and questioning during the course of your lesson. It is usually not appropriate to set a series of problems (even well-related to your subject) which you can tick, cross and give a mark out of 20. While you should point out and comment on issues to do with accuracy and errors in mathematical techniques, much as you would point out spelling errors in student work, the focus of your assessment should be on how well the mathematics has been used in the context of your subject. It's important to remember the general research findings about formative assessment (Black and Wiliam, 1998): students make better progress if they are aware of your assessment objectives and if you give feedback only with no mark. (For further information on formative assessment see Chapter 6.)

What's important in teaching a lesson involving numeracy?

We're going to come back to your attitude to mathematics, because at this stage it's critical. It's easy to let your dislike, lack of confidence, or prejudices show: consider the message you are giving if you get flustered when you make an arithmetic mistake, or your voice becomes more lively when you finish the maths and can get on to the 'important' stuff in your subject or you say *Here's an easy question, so let's hear from one of the girls* (I've heard this said!). It's crucial to convey that mathematics is an important part of your subject, and an aspect of your subject that all students can participate in: remember that much of the problem with numeracy is not just lack of attainment but negative attitudes.

IN THE CLASSROOM

A drama teacher was working with a group to stage a play, and they were discussing how to design the set. A student, remembering maths homework in which they'd drawn scale drawings of their rooms, suggested they could make a scale drawing. Should the teacher respond with:

No, let's do something a bit more imaginative, and anyway you can't expect me to do anything like that – I'm not a maths teacher.

Mmm, has anyone got any other ideas?

Good idea. How could we start?

Your lack of confidence with mathematics is likely to be the biggest issue. Hopefully you will have gained some confidence through ensuring that you can in fact deal with the maths and that you have planned appropriately, but you may still be fearful of making a mistake, or feel daunted that some students will be better at maths than you are.

IN THE CLASSROOM

A science teacher had been transposing a formula on the board, and a student pointed out that he had made a mistake. Which do you think would be the most helpful response?

No, I haven't.

Oh, uh, well it was deliberate, uh, just testing you, uh – time to set the homework!

Yes, I might have. Let's check it through. How did you spot it – and well done!

Many students will be better at mental arithmetic than you are: can you add and subtract two-digit numbers in your head? Remember that what you have to offer is your understanding of how maths is going to enhance your subject – and let them teach you some of their strategies.

Another issue is that of creating a supportive atmosphere. All students should feel that their contribution is of value and should not worry about making mistakes. Notice that in the geography lesson when a student gives an incorrect answer the teacher indicates that it is almost right and invites other students to correct it.

IN THE CLASSROOM

In comparing the proportions of various pictures an art teacher asked the class for their measurements. One student gave a measurement that was, to the teacher, obviously inaccurate. Which response will be most helpful?

No, that's wrong. Go and do it again.

I'm not sure that that's quite accurate. How did you get it?

Students should also not be put under pressure to do mathematics that they find too difficult. If you see any signs of anxiety, such as a lack of response when you ask questions, or a deterioration in behaviour, it's best to back off and do something else. Talk to someone in the mathematics department about what you observed and, with their help, plan a different strategy. On the other hand it's important that students are challenged. With reflection on your experience you will begin to achieve this balance.

For the mathematics trainee

Your responsibilities with regard to numeracy across the curriculum are rather different: it's expected that almost everything that you do as a teacher will be enhancing pupil numeracy.

There are two aspects of numeracy across the curriculum which should inform your teaching, however. First, you should bring in contexts from across the curriculum and make explicit the links between mathematics and other subjects: you might for example talk about the way in which scale drawing is used in design technology in the course of a lesson. Second, you should help teachers of other subjects to effectively promote numeracy within their subjects: you might for example tell the design technology teacher what approach the maths department takes to scale drawing and what difficulties are experienced by students.

PRACTICAL TASK PRACTICAL TASK **PRACTICAL TASK** PRACTICAL TASK **PRACTICAL TASK**

Working with a group of other trainees, which includes a mathematics trainee if possible, plan a cross-curricular day to focus on the theme of enhancing numeracy across the curriculum. Plan a lesson for your subject in detail, paying attention to the requirements given above. If possible, teach and evaluate your lesson.

A SUMMARY OF **KEY POINTS**

> **Numeracy is about using maths effectively outside the maths classroom and is an important skill for all students.**

> > To incorporate numeracy in your teaching, you need to identify the mathematics involved in your subject, ensure that you have confidence in your knowledge of this maths and plan to build on students' prior knowledge and understanding of mathematics.
> > Key teaching strategies are the use of discussion and questioning, in which students are encouraged to explain their methods and reasoning.
> > A supportive classroom atmosphere, in which students are not afraid to make mistakes, is important.

MOVING *ON* > > > > > > MOVING *ON* > > > > > > MOVING *ON*

Find out about the academic literature on situated cognition and mathematics. A useful paper is:

Boaler, J. (2000) Mathematics from another world: Traditional communities and the alienation of learners. *Journal of Mathematical Behavior*, (sic) 19 (4): 1–19.

This paper contains an introduction to situated cognition in mathematics and connects this perspective to students' experiences in learning mathematics in six English schools. It will enable non-specialists to see some of the issues in traditional mathematics teaching, which can lead to insights about how to more effectively incorporate numeracy in their own subjects. It also contains an extensive bibliography for further reading.

FURTHER READING FURTHER READING FURTHER READING FURTHER READING

Ledwick, M. (2001) *Numeracy Across the Curriculum in Secondary Schools*. Leicester. Mathematical Association. A resource to assist in the planning and implementation of this initiative.

Perks, P. and Prestage, S. (2001) *Teaching the National Numeracy Strategy at Key Stage 3*. London. David Fulton. A very useful discussion of the ways in which the KS3 numeracy strategy may be implemented.

10
Teaching ICT across the curriculum
Cathy Wickens with Alaster Douglas

Teachers' Standards

A teacher must

3. Demonstrate good subject and curriculum knowledge

- have a secure knowledge of the relevant subject(s) and curriculum areas, foster and maintain pupils' interest in the subject, and address misunderstandings
- demonstrate a critical understanding of developments in the subject and curriculum areas, and promote the value of scholarship
- demonstrate an understanding of and take responsibility for promoting high standards of literacy, articulacy and the correct use of standard English, whatever the teacher's specialist subject

4. Plan and teach well structured lessons

- impart knowledge and develop understanding through effective use of lesson time
- promote a love of learning and children's intellectual curiosity
- reflect systematically on the effectiveness of lessons and approaches to teaching
- contribute to the design and provision of an engaging curriculum within the relevant subject area(s).

Part 2 of the Teachers' Standards relating to professional and personal conduct will be used to assess cases of serious misconduct, regardless of the sector in which the teacher works.

Introduction

In a new century where information and communication technology (ICT) capability is prized as never before, we are duty-bound to design a curriculum for all students which will allow them to be educationally 'street-wise' with today's technology. This chapter seeks to demonstrate that the use of ICT in teaching and learning can help students learn more effectively and enjoyably with the same avid concentration and commitment that they have for computer games.

In September 2000, the new orders for the National Curriculum stated that all students in England were to be given opportunities to apply and develop their ICT capability through the use of ICT tools to support their learning in all subjects (with the exception of physical education at Key Stages 1 and 2). It is not the intention of this chapter for the reader to feel constrained by the statutory orders of the National Curriculum or the criteria for initial teacher education. Rather that through classroom examples and results from research it will demonstrate how the use of ICT can enhance and enrich the learning experience across the curriculum and form the basis for lifelong learning. Practical tasks and ideas for the use of ICT in school will enable those embarking on the teaching profession to demonstrate a developing pedagogy of ICT.

Claims

There are many claims for what ICT can do in support of teaching and learning. For example ICT can help:

- motivate learners and raise levels of attainment;
- reduce the teacher's workload;
- link school, home and the rest of the world.

Some of the key research

The research has a shorter history than other subject areas but there is growing evidence to confirm that there is a correlation between good resources, good teaching and student attainment. *Ways Forward With ICT* (Moseley *et al*. 1999), although a primary-focused report, has some very important conclusions demonstrating that ICT contributes to teaching and learning where:

- clear subject-focused objectives had been identified;
- the teacher could use the ICT to deliver those objectives;
- the teacher ensured that students had ICT skills that were sufficient to enable them to achieve the subject-specific objectives;
- students were given sufficient access to ICT to achieve learning objectives.

The findings from the ImpaCT2 report (Becta 2002), which evaluated the impact of the ICT in Schools Programme and the *Secondary School of the Future* report (Becta 2001), the purpose of which was to analyse the relationship between ICT and secondary school standards, certainly support these claims. The first three bullet points above are concerned with teaching at its best; when not meeting these standards the report shows that teachers underestimate the capability of students although the students are generally enthusiastic about using computers and they perceive using ICT as useful. Seymour Papert's book *Mindstorms* (1980) gives an account of his vision of how computers might be used in education using the Logo language as an example. His work supports that of the Swiss psychologist Jean Piaget, who spent decades studying and documenting the learning processes of young children. Piaget believed that students excel by actively building and constructing for themselves the specific knowledge they need, rather than having a teacher dictate numerous facts. Therefore I would suggest that ICT lessons which are largely skills-based are unlikely to meet the subject specific learning objectives.

Visit **www.futurelab.org.uk/research/lit_reviews.htm** for further reading.

First steps

Knowing where to start developing your own ICT capability depends very much on your own situation but personal access to modern ICT is crucial. Explore the facilities in your own institution.

As a simple baseline you should ask yourself if you can:

- word-process;
- use a spreadsheet for simple calculations and graphing;
- use a database;

- communicate effectively using ICT;
- use the internet.

The following site is a useful starting point for your own professional development.

- **www.netskills.ac.uk/onlinecourses/tonic** is an online tutorial for use of the internet.

When is it appropriate to use ICT?

A word of warning. One of the biggest mistakes made using ICT is when its use does not support the learning, the presumption being that just because the students are using ICT its use is appropriate. It is also easy to fall into the trap of using ICT as, for example, a reward for good behaviour, *I'll let you go onto the internet if you finish your work*, or awarding higher attainment for work that has been produced using ICT when the content is weak.

IN THE CLASSROOM

A student was asked to word-process a handwritten essay so that the teacher could use it for display.

Comment – A word-processor should have been used to allow for amending and refining during the drafting stage, and additional features such as thesaurus and spell checker would have made the use of ICT an integral part of the learning.

A group of Year 10 business studies students were researching on the internet for their coursework and were given a worksheet to write their results on.

Comment – The students should have been copying and pasting information as they found it into a word-processing package so that they could use it using ICT in subsequent activities, thus learning to share, exchange and present information in a variety of contexts. An extension to the learning could have been a discussion on the implications of copying information from web-based sources and plagiarism.

It should also be noted here that all use of the internet should be carefully monitored and pupils made aware of online safety. See **www.safekids.com** for easy-to-understand rules for pupils and **www.kidsmart.org.uk/** for guidance and resources.

From Figure 10.1 it can be seen that at the planning stage the learning objectives need to be addressed in the activities, so that they can then be demonstrated in the learning outcomes.

Building on the ICT strand of the National Strategy, in 2004 ICT Across the Curriculum (ICTAC) was launched as a major initiative with support materials for all subjects. The focus was on developing ICT capability, described as:

> the technical and cognitive proficiency to access, use, develop, create and communicate information appropriately, using ICT tools. Learners demonstrate this capability by applying technology purposefully to solve problems, analyse and exchange information, develop ideas, create models and control devices. They are discriminating in their use of information and ICT tools, and systematic in reviewing and evaluating the contribution that ICT can make to their work as it progresses.

(DfES 2004, p. 7)

Figure 10.1. The planning process for an ICT activity

The support packs demonstrated that teachers were not expected to teach ICT as a subject; rather they were to support the strands of the ICT National Curriculum programmes of study, as appropriate for their subject.

If we look at the distinctive features of ICT we can then begin to unpack the contribution that information technology can offer within the learning environment.

The four main features are:

- provisionality;
- speed and automatic functions;
- capacity and range;
- interactivity.

Provisionality

Work can be revised easily with ICT. For students working to extend their literacy skills or prepare a presentation this is an important feature. Word-processors can be 'thought processors' allowing ideas to be revised without the chore of a total rewrite. A number of applications can take the tedium out of traditional methods of working and open up opportunities for higher-order thinking skills and interpretation. Art and music software, for example, encourages experimentation without the fear of losing what has already been created.

IN THE CLASSROOM

A Year 8 history class was set the challenge of producing a newspaper front page with the start of World War One as its lead story. Initial research was done using a variety of sources (not all IT-based) and a class discussion was held in order for them to highlight the main issues. They worked in groups of about four students with each child initially as a journalist word-processing their own article and then taking on different roles such as editor. They were encouraged to use features such as double line spacing, thesaurus and spell checker for drafting, and writing frames were used to structure their arguments. The completed articles were imported into a desktop publishing package where images, graphics, etc. were added with audience in mind.

www.homepages.warwick.ac.uk/staff/D.J.Wray/Ideas/frames.html

PRACTICAL TASK PRACTICAL TASK PRACTICAL TASK PRACTICAL TASK PRACTICAL TASK

Find an article or section of text that you want to use with your students. Consider how the use of formatting could make the text accessible for all students.

For example:

- change the font to one such as **Comic Sans** – you will notice in the example that the 'α' is cursive (how students write it) and for many it is easier to read than usual print;
- altering font colour and size;
- use 'find and replace' for words which some may find difficult to understand;
- embolden key words.

NB If the original text is in a book, try using a scanner which can read text and import this into a word-processing package. If it is web based, use copy and paste.

Speed and automatic functions

Collecting large amounts of data and processing it rapidly are tasks that computers are very good at. The graph-plotting capability of spreadsheets allows students to examine quickly a number of ways of displaying data, allowing them to look for patterns without having to re-plot the data manually. Graphics and computer-aided design (CAD) packages engage students with design concepts. Their ideas can be developed quickly, modelling solutions and producing sophisticated outcomes. Data logging, for example using electronic sensors, allows for higher order thinking skills as students can progress into analysis of the data rather than being involved in the tedium of collecting it. Automatic control systems can be created from a range of electronic sensors and output devices such as motors, lights and loudspeakers. As with data logging this gives immediate feedback as changes can be observed as they happen. Sense and control functions often feature strongly in design and technology, and music, but I would like to contest the notion of one area of ICT 'belonging' to a particular subject. For example, a short input on how information is processed at a supermarket checkout with credit cards and 'reward cards' as the focus would work very well in a citizenship curriculum, which is not usually associated with control technology. Students could discuss and reflect critically on the economic, legal and ethical issues associated with personal data being used to monitor shopping habits. (For further information on formatting text for accessibility see Chapter 13.)

PRACTICAL TASK PRACTICAL TASK **PRACTICAL TASK** PRACTICAL TASK **PRACTICAL TASK**

Set up a spreadsheet for one or more of the classes that you teach to monitor their performance. Input test results, levels and any other data you have on the students. Use the functionality of the program to perform tasks such as exam percentages, searching for students at a particular level using graphing to compare data to predict results. Most secondary schools in England use a database called SIMS (School Information Management System); ask the SIMS manager if you can access historical data such as end of key stage results and cognitive ability testing for your students.

IN THE CLASSROOM

A physical education department used fitness data (bleep tests) on their students to allow them to monitor their own progress over a key stage. Students entered the data into a database and analysed their own results using increasingly complex queries. Identities were kept anonymous on the charts for the whole year group. Students began to take an increased interest in their own performance as they could watch it improve over time.

Modelling (answering the question 'what if?') is a difficult concept for students, especially as the examples used are often too difficult for the students to engage with. Making the example tangible (as in the next story) allows the students to visualise the possibilities and discuss the issues (for example, why people would want a low-fat sandwich). Use of an interactive whiteboard for whole-class or small group teaching can similarly engage students with the learning. Allowing students to physically touch the board, and encouraging them to hypothesise and evaluate as changes happen, concurs with the constructivist model of teaching. See **www.mirandanet.ac.uk/pubs/smartboard.htm** Visit the National Whiteboard Network for online guidance at **www.nwnet.org.uk/pages/software_guid ance/interactive_ whiteboards.html**

IN THE CLASSROOM

A Year 8 design and technology project used a failing sandwich company as a focus for a range of problem-solving tasks. The students were faced with the scenario of a sandwich company whose best-selling line – cheese sandwiches – were not selling as they should. This was a substantial project, part of which entailed looking at how food products are researched and developed. They weighed the ingredients for their sandwich using accurate electronic scales and then modelled the nutritional analysis of their 'new' sandwich looking at the marketing possibilities (e.g. low fat) and implications for cost of production and the final label. The worksheet in Figure 10.2 supported the latter part of the activity.

Modelling the nutritional analysis of your sandwich

	Cheddar Cheese	White Bread	Butter	
Weight in grams	24.5	55	10	
Protein per 100g	26	7.8	0.5	Amounts per
Carbohydrate per 100g	0	50	0	100g found in
Kcal per 100g	400	230	750	food tables
Fat per 100g	34	1.7	82	
Protein per weight used	6.37	4.29	0.05	Formulae used
Carbohydrate per weight used	0	27.5	0	to calculate amounts
Kcal per weight used	98	126.5	75	
Fat per weight used	8.33	0.935	8.2	

NUTRITIONAL ANALYSIS OF THE SANDWICH		
PROTEIN	10.71	Sum function used
CARBOHYDRATE	27.5	
KCAL	299.5	
FAT	17.465	

Now you are ready to **model** - the example above has been modelled to produce an 'under 300 kcal' sandwich for someone on a calorie-controlled diet. You could try a different one e.g. reduced fat.

Extension - now that you have learned the skill of modelling on a spreadsheet to find the nutritional analysis, see if you can use the same method and sheet to work out the cost of production for your sandwich using the prices below.

Cheese - £5.26 per 1 kg   Butter - £0.57 per 250g   Bread - £0.25 per 250g

Can you suggest a retail price?

There are additional costs (labour, buildings, transport etc.) - £0.25 per sandwich that you must consider. What will your profit be?

All of you will manage to complete the first spreadsheet with formulae and **most** of you will be able to model e.g. an under 300 kcal and a reduced fat sandwich. **Some** of you will have successfully completed the extension task.

Figure 10.2. Worksheet for nutritional analysis of sandwich

Capacity and range

This feature is concerned with the diversity of ways in which information can be presented, the ability to communicate with people all over the world and the immediacy and availability of information which is up to date, sometimes to the minute, and can bring life to research into current issues better than traditional research methods.

IN THE CLASSROOM

A teacher of a Year 9 MFL class found a class of similar age students in France for her students to correspond with using e-mail. The project began very well with the students writing half of their message in the target language and half in their own language. The theme of the first few letters tended to be all about themselves, but subsequent correspondence became difficult for both classes as they were struggling with vocabulary. The teachers realised that they had to work to common themes so that the students' correspondence was an extension activity of the learning taking place in the classroom. Other subject areas became interested to such an extent that it became a cross-curricular project with a focus on festivals and a celebration of cultural diversity. They looked at festivals that were common (such as Christmas and Easter) and those that were unique (for example, Guy Fawkes and the French Pepper Festival).

Three more schools joined the project from Portugal, Germany and Slovakia. The types of activity that have subsequently taken place include:

- recording songs in music;
- shared assembly on Europe Day – 9 May;
- exchanging recipes for use in food technology;
- videos of events;
- digital images of art work;
- a display created in each school, a 'Point Europe', regularly updated with information from all the partners.

Look at **www.epals.com/** to find partners for your students.

The feature of capacity and range can work against a teacher if the lesson isn't well planned. Students can lose valuable time, for example, by scrolling through a clip art gallery rather than doing a focused search or surfing for information from the internet in an understandable format. One of the features of Microsoft Word is that when the 'enter' key is pressed at the end of a web address it becomes a live link (it changes to blue, is underlined and when the cursor points at it there is the familiar 'pointing hand' denoting a link). Therefore interactive worksheets can be easily produced which students can use 'live' to links which have already been checked for suitability. This is not to say that students should never be offered the opportunity to do a 'free search'. The use of 'key words' and Boolean logic to refine a search on a CD-ROM or in a search engine is an important concept for students to engage with and is relevant to all subject areas. However, we would never offer students the entire works of *Encyclopaedia Britannica* or a vast library to search for information without some guidance and it is the same when using computer-based research.

Interactivity

The interactive way in which information can be processed and presented enables teacher and students to explore prepared or constructed models and simulations. They can search for and compare information from other sources, presenting it in a variety of different ways, using a range of technologies, thus making it accessible for different audiences. Interactivity actually encompasses many of the other features of ICT, pushing the boundaries of what is possible with the use of technology. The audience and the author are almost indistinguishable as the roles become blurred. Examples can be found particularly in multimedia work and web authoring. The integration of text, graphics, sound, video and hyperlinks allows for the reader to take 'excursions' into the narrative, exploring, researching, exchanging information and learning as they do so.

Visit Hackney's Highwire City Learning Centre at **www.highwire.org.uk**

IN THE CLASSROOM

A group of Year 7 students and staff went away for an enrichment week of cross-curricular activities. Each day the students took digital photographs of their experiences and in the evening they word-processed a diary of events. The images and text were then placed on the school website, not only as a record to refer to later but also for family and friends to see what they were up to. The site allowed interaction with those at home by sending messages, which were checked and then read to the whole group in the evenings.

Kettlethorpe High School, Wakefield: **www.kettworks.com/**

REFLECTIVE TASK
REFLECTIVE TASK

REFLECTIVE TASK

Building on the vision of our changing schools, as outlined in *Transforming the Way We Learn* (DfES 2002), and growth in internet access from home, school, public libraries and community centres, many activities can now be continued or developed outside normal school hours. In addition, an increasing number of schools have developed their own virtual learning environment such as **http://moodle.org/** to use e-learning, to extend discussions, exchange ideas, enhance group work, post support material, use blogs, create wikis and allow students to submit work. Explore the Moodle site for examples of what others in the profession are doing and consider the implications for your own practice.

The contribution ICT can make to SEN students and inclusion

Various references have already been made to how ICT can be used to support SEN students but as this is such a huge topic it cannot be dealt with adequately in this chapter. There is no doubt, however, of the contribution that ICT can make to inclusion. Portable writing aids, communication aids and devices, portable computers, screen magnification software, and appropriate keyboard alternatives can help to support inclusive practice. (For further information on supporting SEN students, see Chapter 13.)

www.potentialplusuk.org – a national charity supporting gifted children.

www.nasen.org.uk/ – the National Association for Special Educational Needs.

Access

Sufficient access to appropriate and up-to-date ICT for any student is of course an issue for all students. The *ImpaCT2* report (Becta 2002) reassuringly confirms that connectivity is reaching government targets, with all secondary schools having internet access. However, it also demonstrates a strong relationship between access to the internet at home and socio-economic status, with those advantaged students spending four times longer using ICT at home compared with at school. An ICT activity doesn't mean that all of the students need to be sitting in a computer suite interacting with a monitor; in fact this is often a sign of poor practice if this is all that occurs. However, it does mean that all of the students need to have sufficient time to achieve the learning objectives and this does entail careful planning, keeping abreast of new technologies and not being afraid to have a number of activities happening in the classroom at one time. Remember that e-learning can include the use of mobile technologies such as phones, PDAs and MP3 players. You could stimulate active use of them, such as encouraging pupils to download the BBC Breakfast TV daily video podcast (**www.bbc.co.uk/programmes/6006v5tb**).

Assessment

The curriculum model of ICT in schools can vary from ICT being taught as a discrete subject to being totally subject-integrated. Whatever your model there will be a member of staff who has responsibility for the co-ordination of ICT within the curriculum as well as assessment. However, teachers are often asked to assess students' work for both their own subject area and for ICT. The National Curriculum in Action website at **www.ncaction.org.uk/subjects/**

ict/index.htm uses students' work and case study material to show what the National Curriculum in ICT looks like in practice. The examples given show:

- the standard of students' work at different ages and key stages;
- how the programmes of study translate into real activities.

PRACTICAL TASK   PRACTICAL TASK   PRACTICAL TASK   PRACTICAL TASK   PRACTICAL TASK

Using students' work from an ICT activity that you have planned, assess the work for your own subject area, then look at the work again for its use of ICT. Select what you would consider to be high, middle and low achieving pieces of work and discuss these with the ICT co-ordinator in your school. How did the levels of attainment compare with the levels in your own subject area?

Were there any other issues that the discussion raised such as suitability of the task, gender bias and access to technology?

ICT for professional purposes

You will notice that a large number of the websites suggested in this chapter include discussion forums for teachers to exchange and share ideas with other professionals. Join one of these forums, read what your new colleagues are doing and be adventurous in your own teaching. Listen to your students: what are they doing with new technologies? Remember that ICT isn't just about working with computers.

A SUMMARY OF **KEY POINTS**

> **There is no substitute for good teaching. It is crucial that you always question whether the planned activity supports the learning objectives for the lesson.**

> **Never underestimate the ICT capability of students.**

> **Plan lessons to maximise the use of ICT so that time is not wasted, for example with trouble-shooting equipment, unnecessary searching for sites or formatting without a purpose.**

> **Develop strategies for linking home, school and the outside world.**

> **Do not be complacent about your own capability; take advantage of any training that is offered and keep abreast of new technologies.**

MOVING *ON* > > > > > > MOVING *ON* > > > > > > MOVING *ON*

The ever-changing world of ICT inevitably means that keeping abreast of current changes is a constant challenge. However confident you are with your use of ICT to support teaching and learning, you may like to take one subject-specific innovation and investigate its impact, for example on creativity or gender basis.

FURTHER READING FURTHER READING **FURTHER READING** FURTHER READING

www.tes.co.uk A monthly insert in the *Times Educational Supplement* called 'Online' contains useful classroom ideas, book reviews and ICT news.

Chapter glossary

Boolean logic The internet is a vast computer database and its contents must be searched according to the rules of computer database-searching. Much database-searching is based on the principles of Boolean logic. When using internet search engines (the most common method of searching), the user is often unaware that this is happening but can be disappointed with the search results. Constructing a logical search using 'or, and, not' (or +, −, = signs) with the search words can refine the search and make the 'hits' much more successful. Visit the following two sites for further information: **www.education-world.com/a_tech/tech001.htm** and **http://computer.howstuffworks.com/boolean.htm**

Capability ICT capability is characterised by an ability to use IT tools and information sources effectively to investigate and research, develop ideas, communicate, analyse and evaluate. It is not concerned with the acquisition of skills but the teaching of these skills may form part of the learning process towards capability. See also Allen *et al*. (2000, p. 2).

ICT IT is to ICT as literacy is to books, journals or screen displays. The focus of IT is on students' capability with ICT. For this reason IT is the title used for the National Curriculum subject qualifications.

Key skills The six key skill areas which are embedded in the structure of the National Curriculum – communication, application of number, information technology, working with others, improving own learning and performance, and problem-solving.

Logo A programming language plus a philosophy of education developed in the 1960s by Seymour Papert. It was designed as a tool for learning and its features – modularity, extensibility, interactivity, and flexibility – follow from this goal.

11
The 14–19 curriculum: aims and values
Richard Pring

The developing 14–19 phase

There is some arbitrariness in any division of education and training into separate phases, not least that of 14–19. But such a phase is now assumed in government policy both in England and in Wales. Indeed, developments post-14 would seem to justify this. It is the end of Key Stage 3. Young people start preparing for their GCSE examinations. Choices are made about subjects. Those choices determine what subsequent courses and employment they might follow. Certain National Curriculum subjects can be discontinued – modern languages and the humanities. Career guidance commences. Work experience becomes a requirement. And for those who are deemed to need a more practical and vocationally oriented learning experience, opportunities are now available for 14- to 16-year-olds to take part of their studies in colleges of further education.

Furthermore, although school is compulsory only to the age of 16, a large majority remain in some form of education and training beyond that. And it was government policy that all young people should remain in education or training until 18 or 19, and that 50 per cent should continue into higher education.

Therefore, there are major developments which are having a profound effect upon the educational and training arrangements for all 14- to 19-year-olds. These include:

- development of specialised diplomas, with a vocational orientation, which, from 2008 onwards, could be taken instead of more traditional 'academic' subjects;
- compulsory work experience for all 14- to 16-year-olds;
- opportunity for young people on more practical courses to undertake part of their studies in colleges of further education where there are the facilities and expertise;
- 'entitlement' of all young people to pursue the full range of 'academic' and 'vocational' subjects;
- corollary 'entitlement' to discontinue what were compulsory subjects in order to pursue what they are entitled to;
- establishment of local arrangements between schools, colleges and private training providers to ensure that this entitlement is available.

These developments are quite revolutionary and in many respects are being challenged by the coalition government. They would undermine the autonomy of schools as they enter into partnership with other providers of education and training. They put demands upon the careers advice and the counselling which all young people need in order to make appropriate choices. They require teaching expertise and skills which are not generally available within the profession. They require, especially with the new diplomas, major staff development. They necessitate a different 'framework of qualifications', as new courses are developed, new modes of assessment created and new progression routes into further education, training and employment established.

In anticipation of these developments, a working group under the chairmanship of Michael Tomlinson produced a Report in 2004, *14–19 Curriculum and Qualifications Reform*, which tried to produce a unified system of qualifications. This, to the almost universal dismay of teachers, universities and employers, was not accepted by the government. Instead, the government proposed what in effect is a divided system post-14, namely, the traditional 'academic' route for some and a more practical, 'vocational' route for others through specialised diplomas. Although the word 'vocational' is used less and less in official documents about the diplomas, each of the 15 new diplomas will have a vocational orientation. The first five were ready in 2008; the others came on line in 2009 and 2010.

Educational aims

The 2005 DfES White Paper *14–19 Education and Skills* briefly set out educational aims in terms of helping all young people to realise their potential, part of which will be to give greater 'stretch' to the more able (stretching is emphasised over 60 times in the White Paper). That, and an enormous number of other government papers, also emphasise the need to make young people more employable both for their personal sakes and for the sake of society. Such an aim is, of course, crucially important, but employability must be tempered by broader humanistic considerations. And talk of realising potential is unhelpful – there is as much potential for bad as there is for good. Indeed, despite the radical changes envisaged for education and training, little attention has been given to the aims of education and the values which should shape that system.

However, to educate is to teach and nurture those qualities and understandings which are judged to enrich life and to foster a distinctively human form of life. For example, the government, in setting the standards and content of a National Curriculum, in determining which subjects are compulsory, in requiring certain forms of assessment, in prioritising certain modes of learning, in requiring work experience, is implicitly shaping what is judged to be an educated person. Economic usefulness is one aspect of that human flourishing, but only one, and its value has to be seen within a broader moral context.

Therefore, the Nuffield Review (a three-year, independent review of 14–19 education and training in England and Wales) started with the question:

What counts as an educated 19-year-old in this day and age?

REFLECTIVE TASK

Consider this question yourselves. How would you characterise an educated 19-year-old today? What are the contemporary demands placed upon young people by society (including employment and higher education)?

In defining an 'educated 19-year-old', what educational values should prevail? 'Intellectual excellence' (traditionally excluding the majority of young people, but remaining a yardstick against which a majority is still assessed as ill-educated)? Practical usefulness (emphasising capability and economic usefulness, but relegating in status the intellectual virtues and aesthetic qualities once cherished)? Character formation (possibly embracing new definitions of citizenship)?

Those who doubt the significance of these questions might be referred to the diminishing importance of the humanities and the arts in the idea of a general education post-14, not only in the newly developed diplomas, as learning is increasingly geared to economic usefulness ('realising our potential' through the acquisition of the skills needed for a highly competitive economy). The arts and the humanities fit uncomfortably in the division of courses into academic and vocational. On the other hand, practical learning no longer plays a significant part in the prevailing idea of general education, as standards are increasingly defined in terms of written accounts even when those standards concern practical activities. Under the cover of a 'new language', education and training are being redefined. Different aims and values are being promoted. A different conception of human flourishing is presupposed. The essentially moral language of education (concerned with human fulfilment and personal development) has been trumped by other forms of discourse derived from other areas of public life. That language is increasingly one of curriculum delivery rather than of teaching, of inputs related to outputs rather than of the struggle to understand, of efficiency gains rather than of changing pedagogy to meet more challenging teaching tasks, of audits rather than of professional judgement, of performance indicators rather than of the standards internal to the activity, of economic relevance rather than of human fulfilment, of clients and customers rather than of apprentices to a form of life and a way of thinking.

It is difficult to deliberate about the aims of 14–19 education when the very language of morality has been subverted by the language of business management. In resolving this set of difficulties, one needs to address two major considerations.

The first lies in some view of what it means to be fully or distinctively human. Bruner (1966), in his pioneering social studies course, *Man: a Course of Study,* identified three questions which should shape the curriculum, namely, 'What is it that makes us human?', 'How did we become so?', and 'How can we become more so?' Education would seem to be about the development – whether through character formation, practical capability or increased understanding – of those qualities which make us distinctively human.

The second major consideration lies in the social context in which we nurture the growing humanity of young people. To flourish requires living within a particular community and making a contribution to it. Hence, the qualities, knowledge and skills need to be relevant to living within and contributing to that community – the capacity to appreciate the problems which beset it, the skills which enable one to prosper within it, the knowledge which empowers one to challenge those in authority, the moral qualities which help develop a fairer and more inclusive society.

Twenty-first century curriculum

The Nuffield Review (2004), having raised these concerns, issued a four-page document which suggests what should constitute a *21st-century curriculum*, embodying the learning achievements which might arise from the distinctively human qualities of all young people irrespective of their different talents, abilities and backgrounds. These might be summarised as follows.

1. The pursuit of excellence

Excellence refers to the attainment of standards. Those standards are defined in relation to the purpose of the activity – which could be in intellectual pursuits, art, sports, project management, making artefacts, etc. There is a need to include a wider range of standards by which young people might get a sense of achievement and be seen to excel.

2. Knowledge and understanding

Education is associated with the initiation into those forms of knowledge or understanding through which we make sense of the physical, social and moral worlds we inhabit – and which are systematically introduced through various subjects. Such initiation can be at different levels.

3. Moral responsibility

All young people have the potential to be responsible about how they conduct their lives, form relationships, decide upon future employment, treat the environment, etc. Such responsibility operates within a context of virtues which need to be nurtured. It is important, therefore, to see schools and colleges as moral, not just learning, communities.

4. Practical capability

A liberal tradition of education has too often ignored the world of practice – the world of industry, of commerce, of earning a living, of practical usefulness. There has been a disdain for the practical intelligence – indeed, for the technological and the useful.

5. Appreciation of big issues which affect all (e.g. environmental change)

The critics of a general education based almost exclusively on subjects point to the way in which the 'big issues' get squeezed out. For example, environmental change and racism are 'big issues' which should be addressed in the education of all young people 14–19. But the 'big issues' cannot avoid ethical questions and the adoption of a moral stance.

6. Basic and wider skills

Essential to everything are 'basic skills' – competence in reading, writing, listening and communicating. Added to those must now be competence in ICT. Also there is now an acknowledgement of the 'wider key skills' concerned with interpersonal relations and the organisation of one's own life and future.

7. Ideals which inspire

To educate is to open up what is humanly possible, and thereby to inspire and to enable young people to extend themselves beyond the immediate and the mediocre. In so many ways (through literature and drama, through example and narrative) they can be exposed to ideals which they find worth pursuing, and enable them to persevere when life gets tough.

8. Economic viability

A main thrust of educational policy has been to ensure that young people acquire the qualities, skills and knowledge required to meet the needs of the country and of their own economic viability. Such development is open to all at different levels and in different modes, responsive to the changing economic face of the regions in which they live.

9. Social responsibility

The current interest in citizenship, following the Crick Report (1998), emphasises the positive part young people should play in creating and sustaining a healthy society. But that part requires active participation, meeting practical challenges and engagement with the community. Citizenship as an educational aim demands attention to the school as a community.

To summarise: reform of 14–19 needs to raise questions about the qualities, skills and knowledge which are to be nurtured, if all young people are to have a fulfilling life. That requires a curriculum and a form of life in the school or college or training provider which is wider than an initiation into the traditional subjects (although not rejecting them either) and that no longer thinks in terms of academic or vocational. Rather it would include:

- the opportunity for all young people to excel in some way;
- the knowledge and understanding essential for intelligent living, with the possibility of progressing to more specialised studies;
- moral commitment and responsibility;
- practical capability;
- appreciation of big issues which affect us all;
- basic skill;
- ideals which inspire;
- economic relevance;
- social responsibility and citizenship.

Inclusion

Fundamental to government policy (and to the principles of the twenty-first century curriculum outlined above) had been that these educational ideals should apply to all young people, irrespective of ability, social background or religion. But any policy and practice aimed at greater inclusion must recognise the social reality of classrooms and the wider society in which young people live. Broader questions about 'adolescent well-being', which impinge upon the aspirations and behaviour of young people and which cannot be ignored in any arrangement for their education and training, are currently being explored by the Nuffield Foundation. Evidence gathered by the Institute of Psychiatry (see Meltzer and Gatwood 2000) on time trends in adolescent mental health indicated that the mental health of adolescents in the UK declined over the previous 25 years. Meanwhile, a UK enquiry was launched in 2004 to investigate rising levels of self-harm among young people – further evidence that many young people are finding it increasingly difficult to cope with the demands of everyday living.

This negative aspect of the social context affects profoundly how teachers see their role and find difficulty in carrying it out. They speak continually of the rising violence and indiscipline. In 2003/4, there were 10,000 permanent exclusions from schools, and over 200,000 who had one or more fixed periods of exclusion (MacBeath 2006). A large proportion of those permanently excluded is lost from the system and has a strong likelihood of subsequent imprisonment. Of the rising prison population, 18,000 are aged 20 or below, and seven tenths of these were reconvicted. The proportion of pupils in referral units rose by 25 per cent between 2001 and 2003 (Ofsted 2004, quoted in MacBeath 2006).

Any development of the 14–19 system must take this dimension into account – in particular, the implication for the diversity of provision (including the use of voluntary bodies and the youth service), the resourcing of those with special needs, the training of and support for teachers, the more personalised organisation of learning, and the criteria of accountability. As the MacBeath Report says:

> As schools widen their intake and as teachers meet more disturbed and damaged children the need for pastoral care increases commensurately. This becomes particularly acute in disadvantaged communities where the issues are compounded by poverty, violent communities and turbulent domestic circumstances.
>
> (p. 25)

Elsewhere the Report says:

> Practitioners in particular, conceived the educational system to be too inflexible to accommodate a broad range of needs, governed by the demands of the National Curriculum, by high stakes testing, parental choice and the strictures of Ofsted. All of these constrained any radical departure from the 'official' programme of study and its preferred pedagogy, based largely on whole class instruction.
>
> (p. 12)

Across a number of indicators, young disabled people experience poorer outcomes: namely, membership of NEET (not in employment education or training); 27 per cent of the 16–19 year olds with disabilities are in NEET, compared with 9 per cent of the non-disabled (Haines 2006); 21 per cent aged 16–19 having no qualifications; and much less likely to proceed to higher education.

The idea of an educated 19-year-old, as that has been argued for, embraces those with special educational needs and those with disabilities. At the same time, those same aims need to be reconceptualised to reflect the progress and achievement of young people, who, for whatever reason, are not able to progress as far or as quickly as other young people in some aspects of their learning. Alternative approaches to learning should *embody greater opportunities for them to participate fully in society as adults*. That is, however, not always easy, for as Haines says, citing Miller *et al.* (2005):

> The standards agenda depends too much on measures of success defined by summative assessment and external verification. The effect is that there is less incentive to differentiate the curriculum and use formative assessment that can benefit young disabled people's learning.

Implications for 14–19 provision

Learning and curriculum

In the light of a defensible answer to the question 'What counts as an educated 19-year-old?', five aspects of 14–19 organisation of learning require attention.

Listening to the learner's voice

In improving learning, one needs to attend to 'the learner's voice'. Rudduck's (2005) work is concerned with the responsiveness to the student voice in the teaching itself, partly (if not mainly) because the articulation of ideas or of problems is crucial in the development of understanding. The very best work in the humanities has always understood this. Drama lessons, *par excellence*, enabled young people to articulate their feelings and understandings of human relations and predicaments. The Humanities Curriculum Project put discussion, informed and challenged by evidence, at the centre of the learning experience (Stenhouse 1975), as indeed did many projects. It is generally felt that the scope for discussion has diminished under the pressure to cover content related to the ever more detailed targets measured by tests. A lively tradition of oral work in the classroom, reflected in Chapter 10 of the Bullock Report (1975) and once an integral part of the examination of young people, is now almost forgotten.

More radical, however, is the example of the voice of the young person becoming the *curriculum* – not just an aid to the learning of someone else's curriculum. This is by no means an alien concept in youth work, where so often those who have opted out of school, or have been excluded from it, find a place where their voice is taken seriously and where a better understanding of the world in which they live is made sense of (Davies 2005).

Practical and experiential learning

The antithesis between 'academic studies' on the one hand and, on the other, practical and experiential learning (wrongly confused with 'vocational') is deeply embedded in our culture. Yet the central importance of hands-on learning and learning from experience is reflected in the *14–19 Education and Skills* White Paper. It is reflected, too, in a wide range of innovative practices, both past and present. The Technical and Vocational Education Initiative (TVEI), launched in 1983, integrated theory and practice through making and designing which transformed the experience of learning for many young people across the ability range (see Dale 1990), but it ended with the National Curriculum and with a regime of accountability which put much more focus upon writing than upon 'doing'. The more recent emphasis upon practical modes of learning is usually associated with the less able and the disengaged, which does a disservice to a way of knowing which benefits all young people.

Potential of information technology

Frequent reference is made in the evidence to the benefits (some say revolutionary benefits) of advances in information technology – the use of the internet as a source of information and the communication made possible by e-mail.

Wider key skills and qualities

ASDAN is a non-profit-making examination board, whose qualifications are recognised for funding purposes by the DfE through its agency Ofqual. Its new Certificate for Personal

Effectiveness, Level 2, is seen as equivalent to one GCSE graded A–C. It is now taken in over 100,000 centres by over 20,000 young people 14–19, and illustrates the ways in which, first, a range of key skills, seen to be essential for success in employment, in higher education and in citizenship, can be taught and assessed without distorting the skills and qualities themselves, and, second, how the system of awards can accommodate a radical and student-centred innovation (**www.asdan.org.uk**).

Subjects

The idea of a subject as a 'building block' in the curriculum is contentious. Certain core subjects are seen traditionally to be the basis of a more 'academic curriculum', whereas many, who are concerned about the 'relevance' of the curriculum and the need to engage more young people in learning, argue for a curriculum more based on practical activities or on work-related experience. But this should not be seen as an 'either/or' debate, and subjects at their best represent ways of enquiring into, and of understanding, the world which have withstood critical scrutiny and the test of time. They, therefore, provide the resources upon which teachers and learners need to draw.

However, the subjects themselves, and the selection of material within each, need to be justified in terms of how they contribute to the aim of education spelt out above – and for all young people, not just the intellectual elite. For example, the humanities (history, drama, geography, literature, etc.) do particularly address the human story – what, in the words of Bruner, makes us human, how we became so and how we might become more so. That is why they should remain central to the educational experience of all young people.

Assessment and qualifications

According to the Tomlinson Report (2004), students are overburdened. They are currently expected to sit for over 100 public exams, around 40 in the last three years. This clearly affects the nature and the quality of learning, since much of the assessment is 'high stakes' both for learners (in terms of selection for post-16 provision, choice of courses, and employment) and for providers (in terms of league table places, recruitment and funding).

There is a need to rehearse the different purposes of assessment, and in the light of those purposes, to see, first, what is necessary and, second, what assessments need to be in the public domain, thereby 'raising the stakes'. The main purposes are:

- 'assessment for learning' (see Black and Wiliam, 2005) through giving accurate feedback to the learner;
- diagnosis of learning difficulties;
- statement of national standards (which contribute to but are not the same as support for learning);
- account of a student's achievement at the end of a stage in education;
- selection of students for particular purposes (e.g. university entrance);
- accountability of the various providers and of the system as a whole.

One major difficulty in the present overburdening and highly expensive system lies in the confusion of these purposes and the use of instruments of assessment which, though appropriate for some purposes, are inappropriate for others – often with considerable financial and personal costs.

Hence, the national examinations normally taken at 16, 17 and 18 unsuccessfully try to combine the different functions of setting standards (disputed by professional and academic experts within the respective areas), giving an account of individual and institutional attainment (but thereby narrowing what is to count as personal and institutional achievement), and discriminating between students for selection purposes (in which they are deemed to have failed by universities themselves). What they in fact do are: first, set, in an increasingly detailed way, what teachers must teach irrespective of their professional judgement; second, give a 'certificate of failure' to the many young people who otherwise might continue with their formal learning. They fail to provide 'assessment for learning', to motivate the disengaged to remain in education or to give the kind of information which helps universities and employers to select.

The way forward would be, first, separating 'assessment for learning' from 'assessment for accountability'; second, relying more on moderated teacher assessment (see Mortimore 2006); third, reconsideration of the continuation of public examinations for all (GCSEs) at 16; fourth, restoring relations between external assessment and curriculum development; fifth, finding ways of differentiating the most able for purposes of selection, thereby eliminating the proliferation of expensive tests now being created by separate universities.

Teachers

The pamphlet *Curriculum for the 21st century* referred to above (Nuffield Review 2004) emphasised the need to see the teacher as a curriculum developer, not just as a curriculum deliverer. It is important to see the teacher as one who is immersed in that which he or she has to teach, for it is not just the facts or formulae which have to be 'transmitted' but a love of that which has to be learnt. And that applies as much to the practical and the vocational activities as it does to the traditional subjects.

Good history teachers have a deep grasp of the historical issues; they have learnt to think and to enquire in a distinctively historical mode; they believe in the importance of what is being taught. The learner is being introduced 'to a conversation between the generations' – to arguments and understandings, to distinctive ways of seeing the world, to a social tradition of critical enquiry which itself has a history. The teacher is trying to get the learner onto the inside of a way of thinking, indeed a form of life, to which he or she already belongs and is committed. At their best, professional associations, such as NATE (National Association for the Teaching of English) or the Geographical Association or the Historical Association help sustain this identity. The teacher is a mediator of the cultural understandings we have inherited to a new generation of learners.

This applies, too, to the teachers of so-called vocational subjects – to the teachers of joinery and construction, of hospitality and hairdressing. The learner is being introduced to an activity which has its standards of accuracy and relevance, and which the teacher believes to be important and seeks to impart through example and correction. There is a wider dimension (aesthetic and economic, moral and social) to vocational areas, with which the learner needs to be acquainted. To acquire the 'vocational skills' can be an educational experience where this more holistic dimension is conveyed.

However, the specialised diplomas raise problems about the preparation and qualifications of teachers. First, few qualified teachers in schools have the experience of the skills relevant to teaching the specific vocational content. Second, those people who do have such skills and experience (e.g. bricklayers, hairdressers, engineers) may not have the degree-level background to qualify as teachers. Third, those who teach these skills in further education (FE) are not qualified to teach 14–16 in schools – and, indeed, may not want to. There are anomalies – inevitable in a rapidly changing system of education and training. Teachers qualified to teach in schools can teach in FE with no further training – their qualification carries an implicit ability to teach 'vocationally', whereas PCET (Past Compulsory Education and Training) lecturers can teach 14–16 in the colleges, but not in schools, even though many sent to college have 'challenging behaviour'. In addition, there is a shortage of quali-fied staff even in FE in some diploma areas (e.g. a major college closed a plumbing course because of shortage of staff).

PRACTICAL TASK PRACTICAL TASK PRACTICAL TASK PRACTICAL TASK PRACTICAL TASK

In your placement school, who has responsibility (in terms of overview) for 14–19 education? Talk to the person (or people) responsible about the changes in this phase and the school's development plans. Has the school started to think differently about the purposes of education and training at Key Stage 4 and above, for example?

Provision

There are intensive debates about the aims of learning and about the best ways to improve the learning experiences of everyone. This is made possible by a range of government policies and initiatives – for example, the encouragement, and now requirement, of 14–19 Partnerships (see Arnold 2006), the quite massive Building Schools for the Future Programme, the Networked Learning Communities, the development of Centres of Vocational Excellence, and many others. At the same time there are opportunities for new curriculum developments, especially in science and mathematics, arising out of the criticisms of major reports (see Smith Report 2004).

Indeed, it is difficult to reconcile the apparent tensions between, on the one hand, the apparent managerial language of accountability and of 'public service reform principles' (which exudes from government papers with their specific targets and high-stakes testing) and, on the other hand, the increasing freedom which schools and colleges, supported by government initiatives and by examination boards, seem to have to explore imaginatively different ways of addressing the learning needs of all young people.

A SUMMARY OF **KEY POINTS**

Radical changes are affecting the 14–19 curriculum, approaches to learning, assessment, teaching and institutional provision. These changes are affected by underlying aims and values. There are differences of aim, reflecting different underlying philosophical views and values. At the same time, there is an increasing opportunity for schools, colleges and teachers to shape these changes. But that means going back constantly to the aims of education. What ought to be the 'educated product' of our educa-tional and training system?

FURTHER READING FURTHER READING **FURTHER READING** FURTHER READING

Papers about the current reforms of 14–19 education and training – and details of events and conferences – are available at: **www.nuffieldfoundation.org/14-19review**

PART 4
PROFESSIONAL KNOWLEDGE: INCLUSION

12

Pastoral care, personal, social and health education and citizenship
Trevor Mutton

Introduction

The purpose of this chapter is to provide an overview of pastoral care in schools and to deal with some specific aspects of curriculum provision closely related to this area, namely personal, social, health and economic (PSHE) education, and citizenship. Secondary schools clearly place a great deal of emphasis on the teaching of separate subjects but also have a long tradition of supporting the personal development of individual students and helping them to deal with a range of issues that students might encounter as they move through adolescence. This is not an easy time for many young people but schools see it as a key part of their responsibility not only to offer their students appropriate levels of pastoral care but also to offer curriculum opportunities aimed at preparing them for life in the world beyond school. Such an approach is not an optional extra – the 1988 Education Act (which saw the introduction of a National Curriculum for the first time) stated that the curriculum as a whole should:

> *promote the spiritual, moral, cultural, mental and physical development of pupils and of society*

and should be one that:

> *prepares pupils for the opportunities, responsibilities and experiences of adult life.*

Pastoral care had been a key feature of schools and schooling well before the introduction of the National Curriculum but the recognition within a statutory framework of the importance of this pastoral dimension affirmed its value as something which goes beyond individual subject teaching and permeates the curriculum as a whole. The close relationship between the importance of personal well-being and the curriculum continues to be emphasised in the most recent version of the National Curriculum where the curriculum aims (expressed in each subject area at both Key Stage 3 and Key Stage 4) are:

> *for all young people to become:*
> - *Successful learners who enjoy learning, make progress and achieve;*
> - *Confident individuals who are able to live safe, healthy and fulfilling lives;*
> - *Responsible citizens who make a positive contribution to society.*

(QCA 2007a)

What is meant by pastoral care?

Pastoral care is an integral part of the life of all schools and contributes to the entitlement of all pupils to a broad and balanced curriculum. While contexts may have changed significantly in recent years, the definition offered by Her Majesty's Inspectors of Schools in 1989 probably still encapsulates much of what teachers would currently recognise as being covered by the term.

> *Pastoral Care is concerned with promoting pupils' personal and social development and fostering positive attitudes: through the quality of teaching and learning; through the nature of relationships amongst pupils, teachers and adults other than teachers; through arrangements for monitoring pupils' overall progress, academic, personal and social; through specific pastoral structures which support systems; and through extra-curricular activities and the school ethos.*

(DES 1989, p. 3)

In practical terms this covers:

- the specific pastoral role that many teachers have, either as form tutors or as pastoral leaders within the school;
- the organisational structures that schools adopt in order to support the well-being of all their students;
- the delivery of specific aspects of the curriculum (and in particular the provision for personal, social, health and economic (PSHE) education;
- the way in which the five outcomes of the Every Child Matters (ECM) agenda might be supported in schools.

PRACTICAL TASK   PRACTICAL TASK   PRACTICAL TASK   PRACTICAL TASK

Think about the sort of pastoral support that was provided in the school that you went to as a pupil.

- Who were the key people who played a pastoral role in your own education?
- What was the nature of their pastoral role?

- What are all the ways in which pastoral care is exemplified in the school you are in at the moment?
- Could the different aspects of the pastoral role of teachers that you have identified be grouped together into different categories? (For example, interventions to support individuals with specific problems, preventative pastoral work, establishing a group ethos.)

While schools in the United Kingdom have a long history of offering support and guidance to their students in a number of different ways, it was Michael Marland's (1974) highly influential book entitled *Pastoral Care* that captured a new wave of interest, particularly in relation to the role of the form tutor. What followed was the development of a more structured approach to the personal development of pupils and the introduction of materials specifically designed for the teaching of what were often called 'Lifeskills' and which would later be developed into what we now know as PSHE education.

Douglas Hamblin, another key contributor to this development, took forward the idea that pastoral care should focus on the needs of the pupils in relation to their own development, anticipating the transitions which are part of secondary school life and using structured materials to prepare students for what might be the 'critical incidents' in their adolescence (Hamblin 1978). Nowadays this may seem not particularly startling or innovative but at the time it represented a significant change in the development of the curriculum and in the accompanying teaching methodology. The latter entailed students playing a much more active role in the lesson, with the focus being on learning through participation and discussion, and materials began to appear to assist teachers in delivering lessons using these approaches. Alongside this was the developing role of the teacher or tutor, with Marland's phrase *tutor ascendant* being used to describe a tutor who had a significant degree of responsibility for the well-being and development of his or her form group, who was the first point of contact for any discussion involving individual students in the group and who worked in a school where such pastoral work was recognised and affirmed.

The role of pastoral care in schools has, in the intervening years, remained a critically important one although it has been argued by some that an increasing emphasis on, among other things, regular testing, performance targets for pupils, a narrowing of the curriculum and more teacher-centred classrooms could *lead pastoral care in UK schools to be de-emphasised, marginalised, or distorted* (Watkins 2004, p. 3). It could be argued however that the implementation of the Every Child Matters agenda has required schools to focus on the well-being of pupils in new and different ways, As Fergus Crow (2008) concludes:

> The future of PSHE is inextricably bound up with the transformation of schools through ECM and through the development of well-being as a school improvement imperative. Well-being is not an alternative to standards and achievement; it is its critical partner – this shift presents us with a renewed impetus. Is this an opportunity to reclaim and refocus our attention on a broad inclusive vision for education and for learning that a culture of excessive testing has gradually eroded?
>
> (Crow 2008, p. 50)

Although Crow discusses specifically the role of PSHE education, these comments could apply equally well to pastoral care as a whole.

How is pastoral care in schools organised?

Pastoral care is usually arranged in one of two ways – horizontally or vertically. The former refers to the more common arrangement of dividing the school according to the year groups within it, and within this arrangement having form groups or tutor groups, which are usually 'mixed' (although even the notion of a 'mixed' tutor group can raise important questions as to the basis on which the initial decisions relating to the formation of the group were taken). Each form group or tutor group is usually assigned a tutor, who normally sees the group on a daily basis either for registration at the beginning of the day and/or another period of time later in the day. This tutor also has an overview of all that is happening to any individual child within the group and may (or may not) also deliver some, or all, of the PSHE education curriculum to the tutor group.

Vertical structures work in different ways and can co-exist with the year-group system described above. In the case of the latter, students are also assigned to 'houses', each of which is made up of some students from each year group.

A system known as vertical tutoring is becoming increasingly popular within which tutor groups are composed of a small number of pupils from each of the year groups within the school, about five pupils from each of Years 7–11. Advocates of such a system cite a number of advantages, including the increased opportunity for peer mentoring and for individual students to develop leadership responsibilities, the fostering of improved relationships across the school as a whole, the facilitation of a whole-school approach, fewer issues related to bullying, etc. Advocates of vertical tutoring believe strongly that this is not just about pastoral reorganisation, but see it as having a much wider impact on every aspect of the school.

What are the roles and responsibilities of those involved in pastoral care in schools?

Traditionally there have been two key roles involved in pastoral care in the majority of schools: the form tutor and the head of year, the former having responsibility for a specific form group and the latter having responsibility for the year group as a whole. In recent years the role of the form tutor has changed in many schools from one that included predominantly administrative and pastoral responsibilities. Administrative tasks might include things such as formal registration of the class; monitoring attendance and following up cases of unexplained or regular absence; the distribution of messages and other information related to school life as a whole; checking homework diaries/student planners, etc. General pastoral responsibilities might involve providing support and guidance for individual students as required; following up issues raised by colleagues with regard to individual students, including dealing with behavioural issues; monitoring students who may have been identified in any way as vulnerable or a cause for concern; consulting parents as appropriate; providing support appropriate to a specific stage in the student's school life (such as the transition to secondary school, guidance on subject choices for GCSE, guidance on opportunities for further work and study beyond the age of 16; etc.).

Heads of year carried out similar responsibilities but would also follow up specific issues in consultation with the form tutor, as well as co-ordinating the work of the tutor team as a whole.

A change of emphasis within schools in recent years, combined with changes to the school workforce, has seen the nature of these pastoral roles develop and, in addition to the responsibilities described above, many tutors now take an increased level of responsibility for the academic monitoring of the students within their form group. This places an increased focus on each student in the form group as a learner and may include the monitoring of progress against predetermined targets, attainment across a range of subjects and discerning where there may be any anomalies, intervention to support individual students who may be experiencing particular difficulties at any given time and the co-ordination of provision for some students who may have specific barriers to learning. Likewise some schools now have learning managers (or a similar title) rather than heads of year, and again their role has a clear focus on learning, progress and attainment. Margaret Roberts has summarised this role as including:

- to lead the year team in systems and activities designed to ensure that students achieve their potential by promoting high-quality teaching and learning;
- to ensure that the appropriate pastoral systems and personnel effectively contribute to the educational progress of the year group;
- to maintain an ethos of high achievement;
- to offer support to the development of individual students;
- to co-ordinate monitoring and mentoring arrangements across the year group;
- to promote the highest standards of achievement and positive behaviour within the year group; and
- to be responsible for the guidance, welfare and achievement of the year group.

(Roberts 2006, p. 63)

It is also the case that whereas in the past most pastoral roles were carried out by qualified teachers, it is not unusual now to find colleagues who do not have a teaching background taking responsibility for some of the activities traditionally associated either with the role of the form tutor, or with the role of the head of year.

PRACTICAL TASK PRACTICAL TASK PRACTICAL TASK PRACTICAL TASK PRACTICAL TASK

In what way is pastoral care in your school organised?

- What are the key roles?
- What responsibilities do these roles carry with them?
- What is the specific contribution made to pastoral care by both teachers and non-teaching colleagues within the school?

What are the key processes involved in pastoral care in schools?

It is, however, important to acknowledge that definitions of what constitutes pastoral care in schools need to go beyond the describing of organisational systems. The 2005 Ofsted report into the teaching of PSHE in secondary schools asserted that:

> *Schools play a significant role in the personal and social development of their pupils by ensuring that they prepare them for the opportunities, responsibilities and experiences of later life. In most cases, this is achieved through the ethos of the school, planned curriculum outcomes including the school's personal, social and health education (PSHE) programme, and its provision for the spiritual, moral, social and cultural development of its pupils.*
>
> (Ofsted 2005, p. 2)

Ron Best, who has written extensively on issues related to pastoral care over a number of years, has produced a model (Best 1999, 2007) that highlights five key pastoral tasks, which he has subsequently summarised as follows:

Reactive pastoral casework *undertaken on a one-to-one basis in response to the needs of children with problems of a social, emotional, physical, behavioural, moral or spiritual nature;*

Proactive, preventative pastoral care, *often in the form of presentations or activities undertaken in tutor or form periods and assemblies, which anticipate 'critical incidents' in children's lives (Hamblin, 1978) and are aimed at pre-empting the need for reactive casework;*

Developmental pastoral curricula, *aimed at promoting the personal, social, moral, spiritual and cultural development and well-being of children through distinctive programmes of PSE, tutorial work and cross curricular activities;*

The promotion and maintenance of an orderly and supportive environment *by building a community within the school, through extra-curricular activities, the 'hidden curriculum' of supportive systems and positive relations between all members, and the promotion of a pervasive ethos of mutual care and concern;*

The management and administration of pastoral care *in the form of planning, motivating, resourcing, monitoring, supporting, evaluating, encouraging and otherwise facilitating all of the above.*

(Best 2007, pp. 250–251)

PRACTICAL TASK PRACTICAL TASK **PRACTICAL TASK** PRACTICAL TASK **PRACTICAL TASK**

Try to find out ways in which the various aspects of Best's model are exemplified in your current school. Try to complete the following grid with as many examples as possible. In order to obtain the necessary information you will probably need to talk to form tutors, one or more heads of year (or the equivalent), and one or more teachers who have responsibility for the organisation and/or delivery of the school's pastoral programme.

Process	Specific examples of practice
Reactive pastoral casework	
Proactive, preventative pastoral care	
Developmental pastoral curricula	
The promotion and maintenance of an orderly and supportive environment	
The management and administration of pastoral care	

How has the taught pastoral curriculum developed in recent years?

For a number of years most schools used the term 'personal and social education' (PSE) to refer to that part of the pastoral programme which was taught directly in classrooms and which focused on the development of appropriate knowledge, concepts skills and attitudes. In recent years the term PSHE has been more common (referring to personal, social and health education) but, following the review of the secondary curriculum, the term personal, social, health and economic education (shortened to PSHE education) is now the designated title for this curriculum subject. Details of what is included within each of these areas are given below.

What is the current status of PSHE education within the National Curriculum?

In spite of the expectation that PSHE education would become a statutory part of the National Curriculum following the recommendations of the Macdonald Review (2009), it nevertheless remains a non-statutory subject. Most schools, however, teach it in some form or another to the majority of students because of the importance attached to it. There are two interrelated non-statutory programmes of study for PSHE education at Key Stages 3 and 4. These are:

1. PSHE: Personal well-being (QCA 2007b, d);
2. PSHE: Economic well-being and financial capability (QCA 2007c, e).

Explanatory notes, within the appropriate National Curriculum documents, describe how the non-statutory programme of study for personal wellbeing:

> *is intended to support schools in developing coherent whole-school approaches to personal, social, health and economic well-being (PSHE). It provides a context for schools to fulfil their legal responsibilities to promote the well-being of pupils and provide sex and relationships and drugs education. It also provides schools with an opportunity to focus on delivery of the skills identified in the framework for Social and Emotional Aspects of Learning (SEAL). The presentation and headings of this programme of study are the same as the programmes of study for other subjects to support cross-curricular planning...The content is based on the Every Child Matters outcomes and on the government's guidance on sex and relationships education.*
>
> (QCA 2007b, p. 4)

The notes also explain how the non-statutory programme of study for economic well-being and financial capability:

> *brings together careers education, work-related learning, enterprise and financial capability. It supports the fifth outcome of Every Child Matters and also contributes to the other outcomes, particularly 'enjoy and achieve' and 'make a positive contribution'.*
>
> (QCA 2007c, p. 4)

Each of the above programmes of study is structured in a similar way to those for other subjects within the National Curriculum in that there is a statement of curriculum aims, a summary of the importance of the subject and the contribution that it makes, a description of key concepts, a description of the key processes involved, a section describing the range and content of the programme of study and finally a section that outlines the curriculum opportunities that the subject affords.

The key concepts and key processes from the two programmes of study specific to PSHE education are summarised in the following table.

	Key concepts	Key processes
PSHE: Personal well-being	• Personal identities • Healthy lifestyles • Risk • Relationships • Diversity	• Critical reflection • Decision-making and managing risk • Developing relationships and working with others
PSHE: Economic well-being and financial capability	• Career • Capability • Risk • Economic understanding	• Self-development • Exploration • Enterprise • Financial capability

(Adapted from QCA 2007b, d)

The 'Range and content' sections for Key Stage 3 and Key Stage 4 respectively clearly differ since each reflects development in the issues covered as students grow older. Compare for example the following extracts from the Key Stage 3 and Key Stage 4 documents for PSHE: Well-being (QCA, 2007b, d) in relation to tackling issues of diversity:

At Key Stage 3 the study of personal well-being should include:

> ...the similarities, differences and diversity among people of different race, culture, ability, disability, gender, age and sexual orientation and the impact of prejudice, bullying, discrimination and racism on individuals and communities.
>
> (QCA 2007b, p. 249)

At Key Stage 4 it should include:

> ...the diversity of ethnic and cultural groups, the power of prejudice, bullying, discrimination and racism, and the need to take the initiative in challenging this and other offensive behaviours and in giving support to victims of abuse.
>
> (QCA 2007d, p. 259)

Finally, the list of curriculum opportunities within the programmes of study differs slightly between each of the programmes and each of the key stages, but essentially provides a breakdown of the learning opportunities that students should experience through their PSHE education study. These include opportunities for them to take part in group discussion, to use case study materials and simulations, to use role-play and drama, to carry out their own research, to meet visitors who may contribute to the programme in different ways, etc.

PRACTICAL TASK ~~PRACTICAL TASK~~ PRACTICAL TASK ~~PRACTICAL TASK~~ PRACTICAL TASK

Look in detail at the two programmes of study for the National Curriculum for PSHE education.

- What are the key aspects of progression in the programmes of study from Key Stage 3 to Key Stage 4?
- Are there some aspects of the curriculum that might be more difficult to tackle than others?
- Try to find out how your current school goes about tackling these issues.

What is the relationship between pastoral care and social and emotional aspects of learning (SEAL)?

In the explanatory notes that accompany the preliminary statements in each of the programmes of study (see above), reference is made to social and emotional aspects of learning (SEAL), which can be seen to be closely related to the school's overall pastoral programme. Many schools have adopted SEAL approaches and more detailed guidance can be found in the appropriate Secondary National Strategy documentation (for example, DfES 2007) but the following extract summarises the claims for its importance made by those promoting the initiative and touches on its relationship with the wider pastoral curriculum.

> *Social and emotional aspects of learning are the underpinning qualities and skills that help us to manage life and learning effectively. They underlie almost every aspect of our lives and enable us to get on with other people and be responsible citizens. SEAL can help schools to create a safe and emotionally healthy school environment where pupils can learn effectively. The SEAL resources focus upon five social and emotional aspects of learning: self-awareness, managing feelings, motivation, empathy and social skills. They build upon effective work already in place in schools where systematic attention is paid to the social and emotional aspects of learning through whole-school ethos, initiatives such as circle time or buddying schemes and through the taught PSHE education and Citizenship curriculum. SEAL also contributes to the achievement of Healthy School status. SEAL does not, however, cover the whole of PSHE education.*
>
> (PSHE Association 2010, p. 46)

What arrangements are made within schools to deliver the PSHE education curriculum?

Most schools have a designated pastoral curriculum, often planned as a 'spiral' model where themes are dealt with in the earlier years and then revisited later on in subsequent years. For example, issues of health might, in Year 7, deal with personal hygiene but by Year 11 be dealing with matters related to sexual health. However, there seems to be an increasing trend for PSHE education to be taught as a discrete subject only within Key Stage 3, and maybe even then not throughout the first three years in the secondary school; this provision is then often replaced by a more 'flexible' approach at Key Stage 4, where timetable demands are often more difficult to reconcile. Clearly a school is responsible for the way in which it promotes the personal, social, moral and cultural development of pupils, as it is required to do under the National Curriculum, although this does not necessarily have to be through a taught PSHE education programme (since PSHE education is not a statutory subject) and may be covered through individual subject areas. The following are some of the models of delivery that might be found in schools.

- Dedicated time on a weekly or fortnightly basis assigned to PSHE education and taught by the form tutor.
- Dedicated PSHE education lessons, taught by 'specialists'.
- PSHE education delivered across the wider curriculum through subject areas.
- Individual 'enrichment' days, where students are taken off timetable for a day or a half day of intensive PSHE education work.
- Learning opportunities available through participation in the wider school community.
- A combination of the above.

Ofsted has a clear view on the question as to whether PSHE education should be delivered by form tutors or specialist teachers. The 2005 report, entitled *Personal, social and health education in secondary schools*, stated that:

> In those schools where the course is taught by tutors, the work of the tutor is not sufficiently separated from the PSHE curriculum.
>
> (Ofsted 2005, p. 14, para. 44)

and again:

> Often PSHE programmes emphasise knowledge and understanding at the expense of other objectives. Teachers with weaker subject knowledge tend to fall back on the more tangible aspects of programmes and conventional teaching methods. As a consequence, for example, four out of ten lessons taught by form tutors, as against one in ten lessons taught by teachers with specialist knowledge, fail to explore what pupils think or to challenge existing attitudes.
>
> (Ofsted 2005, p. 5, para. 2)

These findings were also evident in the subsequent report entitled *Time for change? Personal, social and health education* (Ofsted 2007). This is not to say, however, that form tutors are not able to deliver the sort of well-planned, interactive, dynamic and challenging lessons that effective PSHE education requires. Many will take this responsibility seriously and in doing so might:

- develop a greater understanding of the relevant subject matter in relation to the topic in question;
- explore a range of different teaching strategies that enable issues to be explored in a collaborative and supportive way;
- elicit effectively the views of students through carefully constructed activities within the classroom;
- develop an atmosphere of mutual trust and respect, capitalising on the effective relationships already established with the students in the form group;
- value the process of learning as well as the actual learning outcomes;
- review regularly what has been learnt and how this learning can be taken forward.

It has to be acknowledged, however, that not all teachers see the delivery of PSHE education as an integral part of their work, whether it be teaching it to individual form groups or integrating aspects of it through their subject teaching. Their arguments might come from, among other things, a personal view that PSHE education should only have a low status within the curriculum as a whole; an unwillingness to explore unfamiliar teaching strategies or a lack of sympathy with these approaches; insecurity in relation to the subject knowledge required; a perception that it is intrusive in that it explores more deeply what students think and believe; or a concern that the teaching of sensitive and controversial issues is too challenging.

While some arguments about the nature and value of PSHE education need to be addressed at a more philosophical level, many of the concerns expressed above can be addressed through effective continuing professional development and by taking a proactive approach to this. It is important for those who may not be that confident initially to take the opportunity to observe teachers who are recognised as being good PSHE education teachers and to see what teaching strategies they employ, how they engage the learners in the subject matter and establish the sort of classroom atmosphere required, how they go about teaching more controversial issues, etc. A lot can be learned from discussion with these teachers in relation to the overall strategies that they use, the decisions they have taken when planning specific PSHE education lessons, their reflections on lessons that have been observed, etc.

In relation to another model of delivery the 2005 Ofsted report also comments on the potential value of whole-school 'focus days' and concludes that:

> At their best they are well planned, pupils are well prepared for the day, external inputs are well coordinated and the school effectively follows up and evaluates the event.
>
> (2005, pp. 15–16, para. 46)

But it also states:

> Often, however, the success of these days is limited because they do not connect with pupils' prior experiences or meet their needs and there is no effective follow-up. They have the potential to enrich programmes, but not to replace them.
>
> (2005, p. 16, para. 47)

Here the argument seems to be that while 'focus days' (or 'enrichment days' as they are called in some schools) may be a way of covering various aspects of the PSHE education curriculum efficiently, there is no guarantee that this approach alone will enable the curriculum to be delivered effectively.

Finally, the materials and resources used in the classroom are clearly going to be very important. The chances are that the school will have a good supply of teaching resources but in some cases teachers may need to find their own. While PSHE education course books are available and contain many useful resources, these may not always be totally appropriate because generic materials may not always match the needs of the students at any particular stage in their adolescence, or within any particular context. Furthermore, any factual information needs to be reliable and up to date. The internet obviously represents a ready source of information, both to inform the teacher's own subject knowledge and to provide the basis for classroom materials but there has to be some caution in the initial selection of these materials in order to avoid either misrepresentation of factual information or unacknowledged bias.

How are the outcomes of PSHE education assessed?

The Macdonald Review (2009) acknowledged the importance of assessment within PSHE education and, noting *the range of innovative practice that illustrates how the essential principles of assessment can and are applied to PSHE education successfully* (para. 107) went on to state:

> *The uniqueness of the teaching and learning in PSHE education and the connection with children and young people's own personal development and well-being are factors that demand schools to be flexible, creative and innovative with assessment in order to make the process relevant and meaningful for all.*
>
> (para. 107)

The assessment of PSHE was highlighted as a concern in the recent Ofsted report (2007) which is critical of the 'misguided' idea that students enjoy PSHE education because of the *absence of any assessment framework* (para. 40). The report goes on to say that:

> *Most schools focus narrowly only on pupils' progress in developing their subject knowledge and understanding. Relatively few schools attempt to assess changes in pupils' attitudes or their developing skills. Few schools have valid data which might be used to inform planning and, where the data are available, they are not used.*
>
> (para. 41)

Some argue that PSHE education can, and should, be assessed in much the same way as all curriculum areas, with the identification of clear learning outcomes for the teaching and subsequent assessment of students to ascertain to what extent these learning objectives have been met. Guidelines have been produced (for example, QCA 2005) that advise teachers as to what should be assessed and how this can be carried out, emphasising the need for a range of different approaches and contexts for assessment (role-plays, discussions, written work, self-assessment sheets, resources produced by the students themselves, evidence from their own planning of an event, observation of group work, etc.). Such guidance also emphasises the importance of peer assessment and self-assessment as part of the overall assessment process.

What is the curriculum status of citizenship?

Citizenship is a compulsory subject of the National Curriculum at Key Stage 3 and Key Stage 4 (there are non-statutory guidelines for the subject at Key Stage 1 and Key Stage 2). The introductory statement in the citizenship programme of study outlines its importance as such:

> *Education for citizenship equips young people with the knowledge, skills and understanding to play an effective role in public life. Citizenship encourages them to take an interest in topical and controversial issues and to engage in discussion and debate. Pupils learn about their rights, responsibilities, duties and freedoms and about laws, justice and democracy. They learn to take part in decision-making and different forms of action. They play an active role in the life of their schools, neighbourhoods, communities and wider society as active and global citizens.*

Citizenship encourages respect for different national, religious and ethnic identities. It equips pupils to engage critically with and explore diverse ideas, beliefs, cultures and identities and the values we share as citizens in the UK.

Pupils begin to understand how society has changed and is changing in the UK, Europe and the wider world.

Citizenship addresses issues relating to social justice, human rights, community cohesion and global interdependence, and encourages pupils to challenge injustice, inequalities and discrimination. It helps young people to develop their critical skills, consider a wide range of political, social, ethical and moral problems, and explore opinions and ideas other than their own. They evaluate information, make informed judgements and reflect on the consequences of their actions now and in the future. They learn to argue a case on behalf of others as well as themselves and speak out on issues of concern.

Citizenship equips pupils with the knowledge and skills needed for effective and democratic participation. It helps pupils to become informed, critical, active citizens who have the confidence and conviction to work collaboratively, take action and try to make a difference in their communities and the wider world.

(QCA 2007f, pp. 27–28)

Citizenship comprises three key concepts (democracy and justice; rights and responsibilities; identities and diversity: living together in the UK). The programme of study likewise explains the scope of each of these key concepts.

- **Democracy and justice:** This focuses on the role that citizens can take within the political and justice systems in the UK. It includes: freedom as part of democracy; fairness and the rule of law as part of justice; power and authority; and accountability. Pupils should understand that accountability happens at many levels, ranging from a responsible opposition in parliament challenging, testing and scrutinising what government is doing, to citizens in local communities challenging decisions that affect them.
- **Rights and responsibilities:** There are different kinds of rights, obligations and responsibilities – political, legal, human, social, civic and moral. Pupils should explore contested areas surrounding rights and responsibilities, for example the checks and balances needed in relation to freedom of speech in the context of threats from extremism and terrorism.
- **Identities and diversity: living together in the UK:** This includes the multiple identities that may be held by groups and communities in a diverse society, and the ways in which these identities are affected by changes in society. For example, pupils could learn about: how migration has shaped communities; common or shared identity and what unifies groups and communities; and how living together in the UK has been shaped by, and continues to be shaped by, political, social, economic and cultural changes. The historical context for such changes should be considered where appropriate. (QVA 2007f, pages 28–29)

The key processes involved are:

- critical thinking and enquiry;
- advocacy and representation;
- taking informed and responsible action.

How is 'citizenship' delivered in schools?

Although citizenship is a compulsory subject of the National Curriculum at Key Stages 3 and 4 it will not always be found as a regular timetabled lesson within many schools and, like PSHE education, there are different models of delivery. These include:

- weekly or fortnightly timetabled citizenship lessons, taught by a specialist teacher;
- timetables lessons taught by 'non-specialist' teachers;
- taught within PSHE education lessons;
- delivered across the curriculum as a whole;
- delivered through enrichment days (or similar) when the normal school timetable is suspended;
- a combination of the above.

Students are also encouraged to become involved in 'active citizenship' through a response to some of the issues covered, through participation in democratic processes within the school (e.g. the school council) and through involvement in 'active citizenship' initiatives in the local community or beyond. Ofsted (2010) reported an improvement since the previous report in the overall position of citizenship education in the schools surveyed, an increase in the quality of citizenship teaching and a greater commitment on the part of schools towards its integration into the curriculum as a whole.

PRACTICAL TASK PRACTICAL TASK PRACTICAL TASK PRACTICAL TASK PRACTICAL TASK

Find out how citizenship education is delivered for each year group in your current school, both as a curriculum subject and also in the way in which it is addressed beyond the classroom within the school as a whole (e.g. assemblies, outside visitors, school council).

Year group	Curriculum method of delivery	Approaches beyond the taught curriculum
7		
8		
9		
10		
11		
12/13		

What is involved in teaching controversial issues?

One aspect that applies to both PSHE education and citizenship education is that teachers may, at times, be required to teach issues that could be categorised as 'controversial'. Oxfam (2006) draws on the QCA definition to define controversial issues as those:

> that have a political, social or personal impact and arouse feeling and/or deal with questions of value or belief.

(QCA 2001)

and then goes to offer some examples that might be encountered in the citizenship curriculum, stating that:

> (c)ontroversial issues can be local or global, such as bullying, religion, politics, personal lifestyle or values. More specific examples might include examining the effects of multinationals promoting GM crops to farmers in developing countries, or discussing whether cars should be banned from an area around the school gates. They are usually complicated with no easy answers and are issues on which people often hold strong views based on different sets of experiences, interests and values.
>
> (Oxfam 2001, p. 2)

There are a number of effective approaches that teachers can use to deal with such issues that enable different perspectives to be discussed in a balanced and dispassionate way. Useful resources to support teachers are available from a range of organisations, such as Citizenship Foundation (**www.citizenshipfoundation.org.uk**) and a search of appropriate websites will provide a number of different sources related to the teaching of controversial issues. Once again, however, care must be taken to discern any bias in the materials available.

Finally, as was the case with the teaching of PSHE education, the teaching of citizenship requires an approach that is student-centred and gives learners opportunities to explore their beliefs and attitudes through discussion, group work, role play, opportunities to meet and learn from visitors from outside the school and other activities which have been carefully planned to develop their knowledge, skills and understanding.

A SUMMARY OF **KEY POINTS**

> Pastoral care is a broad term that covers not only the organisational systems that operate in schools but also the specific pastoral role that many teachers have, the delivery of certain aspects of the curriculum (PSHE education and citizenship) and the way in which the five outcomes of the Every Child Matters (ECM) agenda might be supported in schools.

> There is not one standard model for the organisation and delivery of pastoral care in schools, and the role of those with any sort of pastoral responsibility may differ from school to school.

> PSHE education is a non-statutory subject at Key Stages 3 and 4, whereas citizenship is a statutory subject of the National Curriculum at Key Stages 3 and 4.

> Both PSHE education and citizenship are delivered in schools in a number of different ways (perhaps even integrated in some schools) and may be taught by either specialist or non-specialist teachers.

> Recent inspection evidence suggests that the quality of both PSHE education and citizenship teaching is improving, but is nevertheless still variable, and that the key issues focus on the model of delivery and the assessment of student learning outcomes.

> Teaching PSHE education and citizenship often require different teaching approaches and classroom strategies, particularly when eliciting student views and attitudes or when dealing with controversial issues, but there is lots of support available both within schools and from other sources.

FURTHER READING FURTHER READING FURTHER READING FURTHER READING

Best, R. (2007) The whole child matters: the challenge of Every Child Matters for pastoral care. *Education 3–13*, 35 (3), 249–259.

Best, R., Lang, P., Lodge, C. and Watkins, C. (eds) (1995) *Pastoral Care and Personal-Social Education – Entitlement and Provision*. London. Cassell.

Crow, F. (2008) Learning for well-being; personal, social and health education and a changing curriculum. *Pastoral Care in Education*, 26 (1), 43–51.

Watkins, C. (2004) Reclaiming pastoral care. *Pastoral Care in Education*, 22 (3), 3–6.

13
Special Educational Needs
Geraldine A. Price with Alaster Douglas

What is inclusion?

The Green Paper (DfEE 1997) entitled *Excellence for All Children: Meeting Special Educational Needs,* and the DfEE document *Meeting Special Educational Needs: A Programme of Action* (1998) embraced the principle of inclusion and set out in the educational arena the government's aim of social inclusion. The concept of inclusion is more than another word for integration. It embodies Human Rights and Equal Opportunities. Its general principles encompass the following.

- *Valuing diversity:* all students should be valued. This extends beyond a simplistic view of Special Educational Needs (SEN) and disability. It extends beyond the notion of geographical integration, which is concerned with where students with SEN are placed.
- *Entitlement:* all students are entitled to receive, with a suitable peer group, a broad, balanced and relevant curriculum.
- *Dignity:* all students, and their parents, are entitled to be treated with respect and have their views taken into account.
- *Individual needs:* inclusive practice should not create situations within which individual needs are left unmet.

An historical overview

Research, policy and practice in the education of students with SEN have moved through three broad stages since the turn of the twentieth century. These are:

- segregation;
- integration;
- inclusion.

In a sense these stages embody philosophical, sociological and political thinking over the years. It is important, therefore, to understand what has gone before in order to grasp the principles of inclusive learning environments and to be sensitive to the underlying issues that inclusion embraces. A closer examination of how the terminology in this field has evolved demonstrates changes in attitude towards those with SEN.

Terms such as handicap, impairment and disability need clarification if we are to understand the evolution of special education.

- *Handicap* is defined by the Oxford English Dictionary as 'any encumbrance or disability that weighs upon effort and makes success more difficult'.
- *Impairment* is a characteristic, feature or attribute within the individual that is long-term and may be the result of disease, injury or congenital conditions.
- *Disability* is the loss or limitation of the ability to take part in normal life on an equal level with others. This disability may be 'a physical or mental impairment which has a substantial and long-term adverse effect on his ability to carry out day-to-day activities' (Disability Discrimination Act 1995).

At the heart of these definitions is the inability of the individual who is regarded as presenting problems for society.

Segregation

At the turn of the twentieth century, emphasis was placed upon a student's handicap to determine appropriate schooling. The education of students with handicaps was in the hands of the medical profession to a large extent. Categories of handicap and the educational placement of individuals relied upon the medical model of diagnosis and treatment. In the early twentieth century, educational placement was resolved by segregation, according to the individual's handicap. Early special schools were established for those with sensory handicaps, such as deafness and blindness.

The system of categorisation relied heavily upon the concept of defect.

> ...*segregated classes and schools that were to be the repositories for all the varied kinds of students that could not fit into the regular class without creating problems for the system...*

> (Sarason and Doris 1979)

Some of the labels used at that time may appear bewildering and offensive today. Terms such 'deaf and dumb', 'deaf mute' and 'cripple' reflected prevailing attitudes to disability and impairment.

The debate still rages about the efficacy of special schooling. The predominantly medical model used for the segregation of students was placed under the spotlight. The educational value of special schooling came under fire. Major changes in the curriculum of mainstream schools have occurred, and the introduction of a National Curriculum, with its highly prescribed content, in a sense mitigated against the continuation of special schools. It was suggested that the curriculum in most ESN (educationally sub-normal) special schools was a watered-down version of that provided in mainstream schools. Those who defended the special school system would point to the adaptation of the curriculum to meet the particular needs of the students. There is no doubt that the dedicated staff in these schools possessed specialist qualifications and were often the expert practitioners. However, special education went through a period of turmoil with a groundswell of feeling that segregation of students needed to be scrutinised in terms of its educational value. New concepts of handicap were emerging which placed less emphasis upon the *individual* defect. More focus was given to the educational environment. This paved the way for integration.

Integration

The 1981 Education Act was a landmark in special education and the embodiment of new, radical thinking. The concept of integration was embraced. It was concerned with making mainstream schools 'special' and transposing the special education ethos into the mainstream setting. In retrospect, it was essentially about bringing SEN children into the mainstream setting and making physical adaptations to the buildings where necessary; differentiating the mainstream curriculum – to account for a continuum of needs (Warnock Report 1981). Integration, therefore, was embodied in the notion of *bringing them [the students] into their premises but on the schools' terms* (Gross 2002, p. 234).

The drive also came from a desire to ensure that all students, regardless of their SEN, should have the opportunity to participate in the wider context that the mainstream school provided and to be 'included' with their peers. Such moves towards integration spawned their own mechanisms for funding, which remain to some extent today.

Integration is regarded as a 'within-child' model. This implies that the difficulties lie within the student. This model aimed to ensure that students were able to fit into the educational system.

Inclusion

Inclusion embraces aspects of integration but goes beyond this. Inclusive learning and teaching environments will demonstrate flexibility and differentiated learning in order to respond to individual needs. In line with the principles set out in the SEN and Disability Act (SENDA) (DfES 2001d, chapter 10), as a teacher, you will be expected to provide suitable learning challenges for *all* students, by planning effectively to overcome potential barriers to learning and by responding to diverse learning needs.

The term 'inclusion' takes the notion of integration one stage further, and is more to do with changing the educational system to suit the needs of students, rather than making sure that students can fit into the system.

> *Inclusion implies a radical reform of the school in terms of curriculum, assessment, pedagogy and grouping of pupils. It is based on a value system that welcomes and celebrates diversity arising from gender, nationality, race, language or origin, social background, level of educational achievement or disability.*

(Mittler 2000, p. 10)

Every Child Matters

Every Child Matters (2003) set out the government's vision for procedures and frameworks for future provision of SEN children and students. Its intention was to bring together multi-disciplinary services and to reform children's services at local, regional and national levels. The government's Green Paper entitled *Removing Barriers to Achievement* (2004) built upon the 1997 Green Paper *Excellence for All Children*, and the resulting Programme of Action which followed in 1998. This set out the framework for procedures and was followed by SENDA (2001) and the SEN Code of Practice.

Children's trusts

These trusts provide integrated services whereby education, health and voluntary services work in multidisciplinary teams. The aim is to bring about early intervention and to embed inclusive practices in every school.

Removing Barriers to Achievement

> All children have the right to a good education and the opportunity to fulfil their potential. All teachers should expect to teach children with special educational needs (SEN), and all schools should play their part in educating children from their local community.
>
> (DfES 2004b, p. 5)

Removing Barriers to Achievement was published in 2004 in response to concerns that many SEN students had to wait too long before their needs were met. There were growing concerns within the teaching profession that classroom teachers were ill-equipped to meet the needs of the range of SEN in schools and the potential influx of students with complex difficulties in mainstream schools. Thus, one of the main aims of *Removing Barriers to Achievement* was to demonstrate how the barriers could be broken down by personalised learning for all students.

Personalised learning

> We need to provide a personalised education that brings out the best in every child, that builds on their strengths, enables them to develop a love of learning, and helps them to grow into confident and independent citizens.
>
> (DfES 2004, p. 16)

Personalised learning is not new. It is an approach to SEN which has been at the heart of teaching and learning for the last 50 years. It means that teachers devise a curriculum and lessons in such a way that the needs of each student are met. Teachers are required to have high expectations for all their students and provide opportunities for learning by utilising a wide repertoire of teaching approaches. Equally, students are expected to take a more active role in their learning and be part of the planning and evaluation of their progress and performance.

Brain matters: neuroscience and education

How the brain works has always been of interest to the general public, as witnessed by the popularity of programmes on television which inform the viewers of fascinating facts about how the brain works. Over the past five years, there has been increasing interest in bringing together the two disciplines of neuroscience and education which have hitherto had little dialogue. What do they have to offer each other? Will brain research, which is conducted in experimental, controlled conditions, be able to inform the naturalistic setting of the class-room?

Neuroscience is the study of the inner workings of the brain and draws upon aspects of physiology, biology and chemistry. The quest to unravel the structure of the brain, its work-ings and its organisation has been a driving force in research in neuroscience. Much has been found out about brain functioning but much is still to be explored. How the brain is wired up and how it fires up has become a fascinating topic.

However, unrealistic claims were made initially about the impact of neuroscience research upon education. The inevitable backlash has suggested that 'neuro-myths' (Bruer 1997) have emerged. The oversimplification of the research findings has led to psycho-babble discus-sions about the way in which this knowledge can be used by educationalists.

Brain-based education

It has been suggested that classroom practices, curricula and pedagogy should change in response to the unfolding knowledge of how the brain works. An example of this is the learning style movement in schools, whereby students are taught according to their indivi-dual learning style preference. This has gained ground, and the impact of VAK (visual, auditory and kinaesthetic) systems has been due in part to a growth industry of training educationalists to change the teaching and learning environment to respond to the way in which the brain takes in information. However, there is little research evidence to support the effectiveness of this in terms of increased performance.

Two findings from neuroscience research may have implications for education.

- The plasticity of the brain.
  - This refers to the brain's ability to rejuvenate and reform during a lifetime. It suggests that the brain can be retrained. For example, Guinevere Eden conducted a study with adult dyslexic people who had experienced difficulties with reading. She carried out a controlled experiment to find out if the reading pathways in the brain could be retrained using a specific reading intervention programme. She demonstrated that the blood-flow channels in the brain were changed, and the participants increased their reading skills. This has importance for those in the field of SEN. It becomes imperative to choose the most effective intervention programme, linked to scientific evidence of brain changes. However, research into this is in its early stages.
- Critical periods for learning.
  - Early research by neuroscientists has demonstrated that the brain has sensitive periods of development and that it is crucial, therefore, to use this knowledge to maximise when students are taught different skills in school.

Brain myths

It is apparent that what neuroscience has to offer education may bring about changes but research is still in its early stages and there is insufficient evidence at the moment to make radical changes to the curriculum and the teaching and learning environment. Oversimplification of what is complex and technical research in the sphere has led to many brain myths. One such example is the 'gendered brain' (Goswami 2004). The populist notion has emerged that there are two kinds of brain and that male and female brains work differently. If this is true, it could have implications for the way in which schools are organised. It would certainly fuel the debate for single-sex classroom environments which would more effectively differentiate learning to suit a specific brain type.

Nevertheless, a more cautious optimism may be the way forward. Two high-profile research studies have had an impact upon classroom practices. Madeleine Portwood's trials in Durham schools have demonstrated that performance and behaviour can be improved by giving students omega 3, a type of fish oil.

Insights into how the brain deals with number knowledge are of interest to mathematics teachers. However, it is the research conducted by Brian Butterworth and his team into possible deficits in certain areas of the brain which could help a better understanding of dyscalculia. This research could, in the long term, help teachers develop more effective and incisive identification and assessment tools. Early identification will then lead to early intervention, which is one of the main aims of Every Child Matters.

What are special educational needs?

'Special educational needs' is a catch-all term. It is used frequently in schools and often, depending upon who is using the term, it has different significance. However, you must be aware that it is a term that is embedded in current educational thinking and is defined in statutory legislation.

> A *child has* special educational needs *if they have a learning difficulty which calls for* special educational provision *to be made for them.*
>
> (Education Act 1996, Section 312)

The Education Act gives a clear definition of what can be considered a learning difficulty and what is meant by special provision. This provides us with shared working definitions to ensure that students can be identified and that there is a uniformity of provision nationally for the different categories of needs. The Act makes reference to 'significantly greater difficulty in learning' and the impact of disability on learning. Educational provision for SEN students is regarded as the provision which is additional to (or different from) that which is offered generally to all students.

All newly qualified teachers should read the Code of Practice (DfES 2001e) which is available in all schools. This is a guidance document that will inform your practice on issues such as:

- the formal assessment procedure leading to a Statement of SEN;
- characteristics of different categories of SEN;
- meeting the needs of different categories of SEN;
- monitoring students' progress;
- additional resources needed in mainstream schools.

What are the SEN categories?

The term 'special educational needs' (SEN) has undergone many facelifts over the years. It may even be feeling somewhat schizophrenic because of the many name changes it has had over the last 30 years. Nevertheless, the reason why it is constantly under scrutiny is because of its importance in the educational arena. Coping with the range of SEN may seem daunting to a trainee or a newly qualified teacher, and grappling with new terminology

– emotional and behavioural difficulties (EBD), ADHD, dyspraxia, Asperger's syndrome, to name but a few – may be overwhelming.

Nevertheless, it is important to recognise the various categories of SEN so that you can plan your lessons to ensure that you:

- set suitable challenges for all students;
- respond to 'diverse needs';
- provide access to the National Curriculum.

The Code of Practice exemplifies the following broad categories:.

- Cognition and Learning Difficulties:
  1. General Learning Difficulties
  2. Specific Learning Difficulties, e.g. Dyslexia, Dyspraxia;
- Emotional, Behavioural and Social Difficulties (EBD);
- Communication and Interaction Difficulties:
  1. Speech and Language Difficulties
  2. Autistic Spectrum Disorders, e.g. ADD/ADHD/Asperger's syndrome;
- Sensory and Physical Difficulties:
  1. Hearing Impairment
  2. Visual Impairment
  3. Physical and Medical Difficulties.

What is 'graduated response' to SEN?

'Graduated response' is a phrase that is used in the Code of Practice and signifies a staged response to the needs of students with SEN. This approach encapsulates the concept of a continuum of needs and is a method of optimising resources available within the classroom and the school to meet differential needs. It is also a way of ensuring that the individual is at the heart of the process. The procedure has been divided into two main parts: School Action and School Action Plus.

School Action

This is the initial stage of support for students. Schools are required to examine their resources to meet the individual needs of a student. Thus, classroom resources are a key feature in the support. Intervention at this level is a question of how the school and its human resources can provide an environment that enables the student to move towards independent learning. Collaboration between subject teachers and the SEN department is conducted to devise the most appropriate, differentiated environment for the student's SEN from within subject and school resources. An Individual Education Plan (IEP) is initiated so that long-term and short-term targets can be monitored carefully to measure progress.

School Action Plus

If a student is making little progress, despite school intervention, and is performing 'substantially below National Curriculum levels expected for students of a similar age' (DfEE 1999), schools may need to consider seeking advice from outside agencies, such as support services provided by the LA and other agencies. For example, a school may consult the psychological services to conduct a detailed, specialist assessment of the student's needs to inform further planning and to consider a range of different teaching approaches.

The subject teacher's role

As part of your professional duties you will be monitoring the progress of students in your care. As the person at the coalface, so to speak, you will have opportunities to observe how students learn and to monitor and record their level of achievement in your classroom. You are, therefore, in an ideal position to identify individual strengths and weaknesses. It is your responsibility to initiate the School Action stage of identification of needs. Your concerns about a student who does not appear to be achieving as you would expect will be discussed with your head of department or the school's SENCO (SEN Co-ordinator). At this stage, it is important to record and to gather evidence of the student's progress.

Gathering evidence

This will be done as part of your normal duties and will consist of some, if not most, of the following.

- Observation of the student's response to interactive oral work.
- Class/group files for comparative purposes.
- Mark book records.
- National Curriculum levels.
- Samples of the student's work output.

You may also want to look at school records for standardised assessment in reading, spelling and non-verbal reasoning. (For further information on assessment see Chapter 6.)

If you are concerned that a student's behaviour is a barrier to learning, it is important to keep records of the following.

- The type of behaviour which is cause for concern, for example, anti-social behaviour directed at peers in the form of defiling others' work; or verbally abusive responses to peers and/or the teacher.
- The frequency of the behaviour.
- When the behaviour occurs – to examine patterns of behaviour and triggers. For example, a student may demonstrate disruptive behaviour when working in groups. The behaviour may occur on specific days in which case it may be necessary to look at his/her timetable to find out if there is any significance to the occurrence.
- The degree of severity – this can be subjective but will always be made in the context of the school's rules concerning acceptable behaviour.

What is an IEP?

An Individual Education Plan (IEP) is a working document which is shared by the teacher, the student and the parent. It sets outs to record the provision 'which is additional to, and different from, the differentiated curriculum' for all children in the school (DfEE 1999).

A good IEP should adhere to the following guidelines.

- Clearly written with measurable targets wherever possible.
- Three or four focused, short-term targets.

- Appropriate teaching strategies.
- Additional provision, e.g. the use of a laptop in specified lessons; or the additional support of an LSA (learning support assistant) in specified lessons.
- Criteria for success so that the student, the parent and teacher can measure when a target has been achieved.
- Review procedures clearly stated.

What is a Statement of Special Educational Needs?

You will come across 'statemented' students in your class. This means that these students have a Statement of their Special Educational Needs. A Statement is given to students with severe and complex difficulties that cannot be met within the school's resources. This Statement is a legally binding document issued by the LA after a consultative process with the school, parents and outside agencies. The Statement specifies the student's SEN and sets out the type of provision needed to meet the individual's needs. This Statement must be reviewed annually.

As a newly qualified teacher you will be given guidance from the special needs department on the best ways to meet the student's needs in your classroom.

Inclusive teaching and learning environments

Creating an inclusive learning environment in your classroom will ensure that all students, regardless of their SEN, can make the most of their potential and can experience success in their learning. Inclusive environments will ensure that the barriers to learning are minimised.

Pupils with SEN should have the same opportunities as others to progress and demonstrate achievement.

(DfEE 1997, 1:24)

This means that you will be expected to differentiate your teaching. Differentiation is about ensuring that the way you teach and what you teach matches the individual student's needs. How you teach will take account of differentiated learning.

If a child cannot learn the way you teach, you must teach the way s/he learns.

(Chasty 1990, p. 269, cited in Pumfrey and Elliott 1990)

Considering the variety of SEN categories, mentioned previously in this chapter, which you could encounter in your classroom, planning differentiated work and providing differentiated delivery may appear to be daunting, if not overwhelming, for the NQT. It is vital, therefore, that some general principles are adhered to so that you can develop good practice which can then be modified to meet the more complex needs of some students.

General teaching strategies for SEN

Responding to students' diverse needs and overcoming potential barriers to learning will help to ensure that you provide equality of opportunity for learning. You should bear in mind the following when planning your lessons for students with SEN.

- *A multisensory environment*: this means that you need to give careful consideration to the fact that students learn in different ways. Some are visual learners, some auditory learners and some learn by doing (kinaesthetic learners). Thus, the way in which you present information to your students and the way you expect them to interact with the information and knowledge should tap into as many of these senses as possible.
- *Staged support*: in planning your lessons you must work out different levels of knowledge and understanding for a topic. You must consider what a student should know, and what a student must know within curriculum topics. In other words you will be differentiating basic knowledge from more in-depth knowledge. By asking yourself these fundamental questions you will be able to work out how you can develop competence and skills to match the student's SEN.
- *Provide structure*: this means that you will devise tasks for classroom activities and for assessment purposes whereby you have broken down the process of learning to provide practical, step-by-step procedures while the student is gaining confidence and skills.
- *Provide success*: this may seem obvious and a goal to which all teachers aspire. You must remember that success is very individual but essential for building up self-confidence as a learner. This is especially the case with secondary school students with SEN who may have experienced failure in the past and as a result have become de-motivated or anxious about new learning situations. If you examine what the student can do, you can use her/his knowledge and skill as a springboard so that s/he feels secure in the initial stages of learning a new concept and then gradually moves to new challenges. Providing success is more than the metaphorical pat on the back. Secondary school students with SEN are sensitive to praise and can often see through the empty 'well done' phrase dished out too often. If praise is to be effective and credible, you must let the students know what they have done that is successful. Thus, **targeted** praise is essential. For example, 'good work' is vague and does not let the student know what s/he has done which was good. You must target a skill which the student has used so that s/he learns to use skills and knowledge effectively. In this way you will help students to become aware of their own learning (metacognition), and you will help them to generalise skills to new learning situations. Targeted praise would then become: 'This lab report is well presented in a scientific way.' Thus, you have spelled out for the student that the way s/he has written is appropriate for the type of task.
- *Model the skills*: if you expect your students to be able to take and make notes by the end of Stage 4, demonstrate a variety of ways of presenting information as you are introducing new concepts and information. However, if this is to be effective it is vital that you make your modelling explicit and point out to the students that you have demonstrated the different ways of writing down information. In this way you can model how to use flow charts, bullet points, etc.
- *Effective management of TAs*: remember that TAs should be used to help develop a student's independence, not to create a dependency culture. Ask yourself the question: what do I want these students to do as a result of this lesson/series of lessons (learning outcomes)? A long-term target for a student may be that you want him/her to be able to read your worksheets in class. In the short-term, getting a TA to read for the student may seem the best solution. This may well get over the decoding difficulties which the student is experiencing. You might consider using the TA's time more creatively by getting him/her to record frequently used worksheets on audio tape so that the student can be more independent and still has access to your texts while developing decoding skills. This is a scaffolded approach to teaching and learning. Directing TA time to the re-presentation of frequently used texts (see guidelines in the next section) may provide differentiated worksheets which are more accessible for students with SEN.

Manageable solutions

What do students find difficult to cope with in lessons?

You can greatly improve the quality of the learning experience in your classroom and ensure that you consider student diversity by examining the main components of lessons with which SEN students in general have difficulty.

Potential sticking points in lessons for SEN students

- Verbal instructions.
- Written instructions.
- Reading.
- Writing.

Verbal instructions

- Think about when you are going to give the instructions. SEN students often tire easily in lessons – students are often at their most receptive at the beginning of your lesson. Do not leave giving out vital homework instructions to the end of the lesson as the bell is sounding. This will distract those with ADD/ADHD, for example, and they will not even 'hear' your vital instructions.
- Try to stagger the amount of information you give – setting up the lesson with all the instructions at once is placing extra pressure upon those with specific short-term memory difficulties, for example.
- Provide alternative formats – some students do not take in information if it is only given verbally and may need the back-up of a flow chart of simple instructions. (This is multisensory and differentiated learning.)
- Allow some students to tape-record verbal instructions which they can play back when memory goes into overload and so that you help them with language processing. This will enable them to hear the instructions again and again without constantly asking you to repeat – less frustrating for them, for you and for the rest of the group.

Written instructions

- Beware of just one channel of taking in information, for example the auditory channel is one way of taking in information by listening. If all-important instructions are only given in written form this makes it more difficult for the auditory learner. It will also create difficulties for those whose reading skills are hesitant or weak.
- Provide alternative formats – some students do not take in information if it is only given in written format and may need the back-up of a flow chart of simple instructions. (This is multisensory and differentiated learning.)
- Do not put vital instructions only on the board. Often SEN students are not quick enough to take down these instructions and miss out what you want them to do. Provide some typed instruction cards to distribute among groups. In this way you will not single out SEN students who may be sensitive to having 'different' work from their peers.
- Keep the instructions clear and simple. Often NQTs try to give too many instructions and make the instructions unnecessarily complicated, thinking they are helping SEN students by expanding upon the information. Clear, boxed information with practical sub-headings will direct the student and help those with language processing difficulties to make sense of written instructions.

Example

> **What you have to do**
> Write THREE note points about...

> **How to make a start**
> Use your classroom handouts to highlight relevant information.
> Use the textbook to find out more information.
> List all your information.
> Decide upon the best order to present your notes.

REFLECTIVE TASK

Choose one of your teaching groups, preferably one with some students with SEN. Examine a week's lesson notes and reflect upon how you gave instructions to the group by filling in the following table.

Describe instruction	What worked	How I would change this in the future
Verbal instructions Timing Amount of information given Use of alternative back-up instructions Use of teaching assistant		
Written instructions Timing Amount of information given Use of alternative back-up instructions Use of teaching assistant		

Worksheet production

Secondary school students have grown up in a world of computer graphics and sophisticated animation. Often teachers try to emulate these features and try to produce entertaining worksheets. This may be admirable but, if such worksheets are simply provided for visual impact, they may sadly miss the target for SEN students who experience difficulties and worries about accessing texts and worksheets. Worksheets which are too fussy and contain too many graphics and unrelated pictures are confusing for a student who is trying to make sense of the written word. These students will use pictures and graphics to help them to unravel the text so you must ensure that anything you use is complementary and is an alternative, visual method of presenting the written text or prose, not something which you have zapped in from a clipart program because it brightens up the worksheet.

Guidelines for writing worksheets
- Use of Comic Sans font is easier on the eye for those with reading difficulties.
- Key vocabulary in **bold** text.

- Use of colour – key words, for example, could always be in red. This ensures that these words stand out and those with hesitant reading skills can be taught to skim more effectively.
- Layout of written text – uncluttered information is easier to access for those with literacy difficulties. If you put boxes around information you will help the students to 'see' that certain information is linked and goes together.
- Visual representations in tandem with prose.
- Talking worksheets – these are ways of providing a multisensory environment. Your worksheets can be accessed by the 'read back' facilities of a number of computer programs.

PRACTICAL TASK PRACTICAL TASK **PRACTICAL TASK** PRACTICAL TASK **PRACTICAL TASK**

Design a worksheet for use with a class that contains students with reading difficulties. Incorporate at least three of the above features. Trial this with your class and find out which features of your design provided the best help.

Writing

Modelling how to go about the writing process for your subject is important for SEN students. You will provide them with glimpses of 'how the expert goes about the task', and will ensure that you are tapping into different learning styles. Showing students examples of the finished product, e.g. a lab report, may help students to 'see' the way the written work is presented but does not help students to understand the process involved in writing for different subject purposes.

Guided practice is essential for all students but the way in which you manage this for SEN students is critical. You must embody the principles of inclusive learning environments. Thus, you must ensure that you provide structured practice to meet the individual's needs and his/her stage of learning. It is important to provide opportunities which start at the point of need and extend the student's learning.

Writing frames are an excellent example of this. You can provide as much or as little as is needed to get the student started with writing. Key words, phrases or starting sentences are graduated ways of developing writing. Report writing for scientific purposes, giving an account of a field trip in geography etc. all lend themselves to writing frames. (For further information on writing frames see Chapter 8.)

A word of warning is needed, however. Remember that writing frames are a means to an end and should not be regarded as the pinnacle of achievement for those who are experiencing writing difficulties. Rather they should be considered as a stepping stone – or scaffold – to success. Eventually, the frame should be withdrawn so that the student can work independently.

Managing students with emotional and behavioural difficulties (EBD)

Students who find it difficult to concentrate for periods of time, who cannot seem to sit still in the classroom, who are verbally or physically abusive to their peers and/or their teachers or whose behaviour is considered anti-social, soak up a considerable amount of a teacher's time and energy. It is vital that instructions, both verbal and written, and tasks are carefully planned and designed so that learning is in small steps. Ensure that academic tasks are broken down so that attention span is constantly stimulated. (For further information see Chapter 7 Managing behaviour for learning.)

Managing the working environment for these students is essential so that opportunities for poor and unacceptable behaviour are minimised. By adopting the solutions in the previous section, you will begin to provide a more secure learning environment for EBD students.

In addition to these generic solutions, consideration should be given to the following.

- *Make explicit your classroom ground rules.* You must demonstrate some flexibility in what you expect these students to achieve while not compromising your authority with the class as a whole. One of the most effective ways of doing this is to draw up a learning and behaviour contract with the student and discuss this with him/her. This individual approach will give you a chance to show the student that you are prepared to be firm but fair in dealing with his/her particular situation but that there are lines which you will expect the student not to cross. However, remember that teenagers will not necessarily show any appreciation for your considerations.
- *Be consistent.* You must always deal with disruptive behaviour consistently. This provides the EBD student with a sense of security and reinforces the rules for classroom behaviour. It strengthens your discipline by demonstrating fairness – an attribute highly regarded by all children.
- *Keep calm and try to avoid losing your temper.* This seems such an obvious statement but one which has to be worked on when dealing with difficult classroom behaviour. Some students seem to take pleasure from trying to get their teachers angry. Remember they are past masters at argument, shouting out and causing disruption. Counter this behaviour with even, quiet speech and measured actions. Try not to retaliate when these students shout abusively but rather mentally count to ten and go over to their working area so that you minimise the upheaval. This type of restraint which is non-invasive can be most effective not only with the specific student but also your standing with the class in general.
- *Give consideration to the specific praise and rewards for individual students.* These will be effective if the EBD student really perceives the rewards as something which is valued in the culture. What you might regard as a reward may be of no value to the teenager. Discussing rewards with the individual can ensure greater success.

A SUMMARY OF **KEY POINTS**

> Read the Code of Practice for SEN to familiarise yourself with the different categories of learning needs and some general guidance for teaching.

> Examine your lesson planning to incorporate both a variety of modes of delivery of information and a range of activities to meet differing learning styles and abilities.

> Ensure that you weave in the principles of good practice to provide a differentiated curriculum that enables students to participate in the academic tasks you set, mindful of realistic targets for individual students.

> Inclusive learning environments will be multisensory, provide structure and, where necessary, give opportunities for 'small step' learning (staged support).

> Make opportunities for modelling and guiding the learning process.

MOVING *ON* > > > > > > MOVING *ON* > > > > > > MOVING *ON*

If you wish to deepen your understanding and knowledge of any category of SEN, it is worth visiting specialised websites such as the British Dyslexia Association site, **www.bdadyslexia.org.uk**, or the Dyslexia Action site **www.dyslexiaaction.org.uk**. Explore the notion of scaffolded learning to provide classroom support for all learners. Look out for Master's level training courses. There are many modular courses in the generalised category of inclusion and some for professionals who wish to specialise in a specific category, for example, specific learning difficulties (SpLD). Local universities are a rich source of information.

FURTHER READING FURTHER READING **FURTHER READING** FURTHER READING

Ainscow, M. (2003) Using teacher development to foster inclusive classroom practices. In T. Booth, K. Nes and M. Stomstad (eds) *Developing Inclusive Teacher Education*. London. RoutledgeFalmer.

Cheminais, R. (2000) *Special Educational Needs for Newly Qualified and Student Teachers.* London. David Fulton. This is a practical, easy-to-read guide for newly qualified teachers. It provides brief descriptions of the various categories of Special Educational Needs and there is a section on planning for progression.

Mittler, P. (2000) *Working Towards Inclusive Education: Social Contexts*. London. David Fulton.

Qualifications and Curriculum Authority (1998) *Supporting and Target Setting Process: Guidance for Effective Target Setting for Pupils with Special Educational Needs.* London. DfEE/QCA. This document is also practical and gives a wealth of information about how to tackle the teaching of those with different Special Educational Needs.

Stakes, R. and Hornby, G. (2000) (2nd edn) *Meeting Special Needs in Mainstream Schools: A Practical Guide for Teachers.* London. David Fulton. This is an accessible guide for busy, newly qualified teachers. It provides information to help you develop strategies for classroom management.

Wearmouth, J. (2000) *Special Educational Provision: Meeting the Challenges in Schools*. London. Open University Press.

www.bdadyslexia.org.uk British Dyslexia Association website.

www.dyslexiaaction.org.uk Dyslexia Action.

Chapter glossary

Attention deficit disorder (ADD) or attention deficit hyperactivity disorder (ADHD). Students who have been diagnosed with these disorders are recognisable in class because they can only concentrate for very short periods and often fidget and move around the class. They are often distracted by 'working' noise in the classroom and may behave inappropriately.

Asperger's syndrome is a form of autism. Many students who are identified are at the higher academic level of the autistic spectrum. They are often characterised by their difficult or unusual behaviour and their lack of social skills may cause problems in the classroom.

Auditory learners Some students may identify themselves as 'auditory learners'. These are students who believe they remember information more effectively if they listen to the teacher or work in groups where they can listen to verbal accounts.

Autistic spectrum disorders There are many disorders which are associated with autism. The degree of severity is the way in which many are distinguished. ADD, ADHD and Asperger's syndrome all form part of this continuum. Other associated disorders are speech, language and non-verbal communication disorders. Students who fall within this continuum have varying degrees of difficulty in social interaction.

Dyslexia/specific learning difficulties Dyslexia is best described as a combination of abilities and difficulties which affect the capacity to process symbolic information in either alphabetic, numeric or musical notation. Acquisition of literacy and basic numeracy is also affected. Most dyslexic students have weaknesses with working memory, sequencing and organisation. Some may be creative and demonstrate a discrepancy between oral and written performance in class.

Dyspraxia Dyspraxic students often appear clumsy and have difficulty in planning and carrying out complex movements. This sometimes affects their handwriting and motor control. They often take much longer than their peers to produce written work in class. Some dyspraxic students have difficulties co-ordinating the muscles needed for speech production.

EBD Emotional and behavioural difficulties.

Kinaesthetic learners Some students may identify themselves as 'kinaesthetic learners'. These students believe they like to learn 'by doing'. They learn best by experiential learning.

General learning difficulties Students with general learning difficulties will experience all-round difficulties in conceptualising and have been labelled as having 'moderate or mild learning difficulties' or being 'slow learners'.

Hearing impairment Students with a hearing impairment may experience some degree of hearing loss. Some students may have a severity of loss and require extra resources to access the curriculum. In severe cases the teacher will be expected to wear a radio microphone to enable the student to access verbal information.

Meares-Irlen/scotopic sensitivity syndrome This is a perceptual problem caused by light sensitivity. Students identified with this difficulty will have experienced difficulties with reading. Problems appear to be worse with black print on a white background. This has implications for the use of black markers on white boards. Often the mild difficulties can be remedied by the use of an appropriate coloured overlay on text and photocopied handouts on coloured paper to suit individual needs. Some students may have tinted/coloured lenses with spectacles. The colours of the spectacles' lenses and the overlays are not usually the same. Spectacles are useful for reading from a white board or overhead projector transparency.

Visual impairment Students with a visual impairment may experience some degree of sight loss. Some students may have a severity of loss and require extra resources to access the curriculum, such as brailled text or special software for computers to enable the student to use a word processor.

14
English as an additional language
Sue Walters

Introduction

Many of the students that you will teach will be learners who bring with them into the classroom rich experiences in and knowledge of languages and dialects other than English. Many of these students will be learning English at the same time as they are learning your subjects through English. These students are generally referred to as students with English as an additional language (EAL), bilingual students or English language learners.

In England, in 2010, provisional statistics show that 11.6 per cent of students in English secondary schools and 16 per cent in primary schools were recorded as students with EAL (DCSF, 2010). As the figures in Table 14.1 illustrate, some areas of the country have a much higher proportion of EAL students than others. However, most schools will have some EAL students at some time and many more will have students who use and speak other languages and literacies outside the classroom. The number of EAL learners continues to increase and all teachers are now very likely to teach EAL learners at some time.

Table 14.1: Percentage of students whose first language is known or believed to be other than English (DCSF, 2010)

	In maintained secondary schools	In maintained primary schools
England	11.6	16
North East	3.5	5.4
Yorkshire and the Humber	9.2	14.3
West Midlands	13.3	18.3
Inner London	48.1	54.8
South West	3.3	4.6

One of your roles as a teacher, as set out in the Standards, is to make effective provision for this group of students so that they have access to the curriculum and are able to achieve in your classroom alongside their monolingual peers. This may appear to be a daunting responsibility, one that you do not have the expertise for, especially in those cases when you need to plan for and support the learning of a student who has arrived in your classroom with very little English, or none at all, and who you need to include and teach at the same time as your other students. However, as this chapter demonstrates, by working with some clear principles in mind and utilising strategies that you are already familiar with in your teaching with monolingual learners, you will be able to support EAL learners and provide the necessary teaching and learning opportunities for them to develop their language(s) and achieve in your classroom.

While there is only space to indicate some of the key principles and strategies that can be used to support EAL students here, there are many excellent 'how to' resources available as well as more information about the principles of good practice. Details of these are given at the end of this chapter.

Why EAL and not ESL?

In schools and in policy documents you will come across the term 'English as an additional language' (EAL) used to describe learners who need support with their English in order to access the curriculum. This term is used rather than ESL (English as a second language) because the term ESL suggests that the learner already speaks one other language and is now learning their second. However, many learners, including very young children, come into our classrooms with experience and expertise in a number of languages. For example, a learner such as Afia, a seven-year-old girl born in England whose parents both come from Bangladesh, knows and uses a number of languages and literacies in her everyday life. See Table 14.2.

Table 14.2: Afia's experience and expertise in a number of languages and literacies

Afia at seven years old. She speaks:
- Sylheti at home with her mother;
- Sylheti and English with her father;
- English with her older brother;
- English at school.

She is learning to read:
- Arabic in her mosque school;
- (and write) Bengali at home, taught by her mother;
- (and write) English in her English primary school.

She watches and understands:
- TV soaps in English;
- 'Bollywood' movies in Hindi (and can sing many of the most popular songs);
- Bengali TV programmes via satellite television.

Learners like Afia bring to our classrooms a rich experience and knowledge of languages and the term EAL does not do justice to the range of languages and experiences that such learners bring with them.

It is worth noting here that Afia's languages and literacies, as do those of many of the EAL students in our classrooms, frequently remain invisible and not known about. You may have noticed that in Table 14.1 the wording was 'Percentage of students whose first language is known or believed to be other than English'. It is sadly the case that some schools fail to find out accurate information about their students' other languages and literacies or to build on or support these rich and important linguistic resources and skills. This situation flies in the face of research that consistently demonstrates that bilingual and multilingual students achieve more highly in school when they continue to use and develop both or all of their languages (Cummins 2000). As a teacher it is worth spending some time considering the ways in which you can use and build on your EAL students' expertise in other languages and literacies and how you may be able to provide ways of developing these languages alongside English.

Why are beginners in my classroom and not in a special EAL class?

EAL students, even when they are beginning to learn English, are usually educated alongside their peers in mainstream schools. Learning alongside their fully fluent peers in the class-room is the best place for EAL learners to learn. In this way EAL learners will hear and see good models of English being used and will have access to the very aspects of English language that they will need in order to learn and take part in the activities of their class-rooms and to be an achieving learner in these contexts. If you have EAL learners in your classroom then planning to support their language development is a central part of your planning for learning in the classroom. This may sound very daunting but many of the things that you plan for and do in your classroom for your EAL learners will benefit all the learners and many of these strategies are ones you may already be aware of.

EAL students and who they are

EAL students are learning both the language English in our classrooms and the content of the curriculum through English.

EAL learners do not form a homogenous group of students. Table 14.3 indicates how they may differ.

EAL students bring a wide range of life and language experiences to our classrooms. Each student will have a unique profile. To be able to provide for such students we need to find out as much as we can about their learning, their languages, the literacies they are familiar with and so on, and we need to have a clear idea of what they can already do and what kind of support we need to provide for them.

Table 14.3: Ways in which EAL students may differ

Where they were born and where they have lived	In the UK or overseas. May have moved a lot between or within countries or may have always lived in the same place. May have parents from more than one country who speak different languages. May have come from a country/countries experiencing war or internal conflict. May have come from a very secure and settled background and this is their first move to a new place.
Their schooling experiences and learning styles	May have attended schools in countries where the following are very different to England: • the starting age; • how classrooms are arranged; • what is expected in terms of behaviour and showing what you know and have learnt; • student–teacher relationships and where: • there are better or poorer or very different resources for learning; • schooling has been severely disrupted due to conflict, war, etc.
The languages they speak and have expertise in	There is no simple relationship between home=one language, school=another language. Many EAL students will speak one language with one parent, another language with the other, perhaps a different language with siblings, other relatives. May have a language for spiritual practices that is different to the language they use socially with relatives. May have very different levels of expertise in their different languages.
Their knowledge of spoken and written English	This will vary depending on previous educational and social experiences. Some will be able to read English quite well or fluently but not speak it and vice versa. Some will know dialect or 'pidgin' forms of English. Some will be complete beginners in English.
Their spiritual and cultural practices	EAL students will come from all faith groups. Even when they share a religion/faith there can be large differences in belief and practice. Care needs to be taken not to assume that all Christians, or all Muslims, practise their faith in the same way. Children may be involved in learning outside school in community and religious classes. These may have very different learning and teaching practices to the mainstream English classroom, while not detracting from children's learning in their English school.
Their socio-economic status	Some learners (and/or their parents) will be from middle-class homes, the children of professionals (e.g. doctors, university lecturers, dentists), some learners will come from working-class backgrounds and/or from very rural/agriculture-based backgrounds. Learners and their families will thus have differing access to social, cultural and economic resources (like all learners in our schools).
The value placed on their mother tongue and the languages they use outside school	Some will speak languages that are highly valued in England (e.g. French, Italian, German) while others will speak languages that are undervalued (e.g. Bengali).
Their gender and ethnicity and other people's responses to these aspects of their identity	For example, assumptions and expectations exist in the UK about South-East Asian girls and boys. Assumptions are made about ethnicity and about families. In addition, many EAL learners are also minority ethnic students and experience name-calling and other forms of racism in and outside school.
The amount of time they have lived in the UK and will continue to live in the UK	Some EAL learners will have been born and lived all their lives in the UK; they will be EAL learners because they speak and use languages other than English in the home (and sometimes in the community). Some EAL learners will have just arrived in the UK and be settling into a new home and country. Some may have moved within the UK. Some EAL learners will only be living and going to school in the UK for one or two years (learners whose parents are in the UK on short-term contracts in universities, hospitals or in the private or agricultural sectors) while for others the UK is their permanent home and they will complete their schooling in the UK.
Their life experiences	Some EAL learners will have lived very secure and settled lives; others will have lived very mobile lives; others will be asylum seekers and refugees and may be living in the UK without their families. These learners may have recently experienced violence and trauma.
Their school and community setting	Some EAL learners will be attending school and living in communities where there are other people who share their languages, cultural and faith practices and ethnicity, while others will be the only or one of a few EAL students in their school. They may be the only child who speaks a particular language and may be the only member of a particular faith group. They may not live close to people who share their cultural and faith practices or ethnicity.

Assessment and EAL students – planning for learning and teaching

Finding out about experiences, practices and skills

Finding out as much as you can about the previous experiences (and continuing out-of-school language and learning experiences) of the EAL students in your class is part of your initial and ongoing assessment of these students. This information can be gathered from the students' parents, friends, siblings and from the students themselves.

Ongoing assessment

In addition to the above, you will need to keep some record of your EAL learners' language development in the classroom in order to plan and support their learning. There have been a number of well-used methods for doing this. However, in 2000 the government introduced the 'A Language in Common' framework (QCA 2000b) which offered descriptors for EAL students' levels of English development which were in line with the descriptors used for all children's language development in the National Curriculum. There is a great deal of debate about using such descriptors. This centres around whether EAL students' language development can be considered in the same way as monolingual learners' English language development or whether a more subtle and appropriate form of assessment and description should be utilised which respects the language profiles and different learning paths of multilingual or bilingual learners. The government also introduced a new way of funding the support of EAL learners in the late 1990s, called the Ethnic Minorities Achievement Grant (EMAG). EAL learners were included with minority ethnic students and the focus was placed on achievement for these learners. The funding arrangements placed an emphasis on statistical data regarding student achievement whereby schools were encouraged to track and compare the achievement of their minority ethnic and EAL students, thus preventing such students' underachievement going unremarked and unaddressed. In 2009 the QCDA decided to update 'A Language in Common' and bring it into line with 'Assessing Pupils' Progress'. In 2010 a consultation initiated by the DCSF on school funding and recent pronouncements from the new coalition government would suggest that EMAG may be replaced by a funding formula that focuses on disadvantage rather than EAL and minority ethnic achievement.

You may come across a number of different ways of assessing and recording EAL students' language development in your placements.

PRACTICAL TASK PRACTICAL TASK PRACTICAL TASK PRACTICAL TASK PRACTICAL TASK

Find out how your placement school assesses and describes EAL learners' progress and attainment in relation to the development of their English language.
How is this method of assessment and description used in planning and teaching for these students?
What are the strengths and weaknesses of the methods used?

Care should always be taken when an EAL student appears to be struggling in school to explore whether their learning needs are connected to their EAL learning needs or whether they also have some special need that requires support. Deryn Hall's *Assessing the Needs of Bilingual Students: Living in Two Languages* (2001) is a useful resource for making such an assessment.

Social fluency and academic proficiency

As we have already seen, an important aspect of providing for EAL learners is to assess their level of language expertise and development in order to be able to plan for their language development. Care needs to be taken not to base an assessment of an EAL learner's ability to use English in your classroom simply on their oral and social English. It is easy to hear an EAL learner chatting away fluently to friends and classroom adults and to assess that student as being fluent in English and not in need of EAL support, with the result that language support and planning are not provided. Any subsequent failure of the student to complete work or take part in classroom activities is seen as a lack of interest or a lack of ability, much to the detriment of many EAL learners. They are labelled as uninterested or of poor ability when all they lack is access to the language they need as a learner in order to achieve. This is why it is important for you as a teacher to plan for language development as well as teaching the content area of your subject. We will now consider this in more detail.

Inclusive practice and effective provision

A 'language conscious pedagogy'

EAL students are supported by using what Pauline Gibbons calls 'a language conscious pedagogy'. Each subject teacher is responsible for being aware of the language that is required in order to understand, to take part in classroom activities and to demonstrate understanding in their particular subject – and for planning for and providing support to EAL learners so that they can master this language.

> *Language is integral to most of what happens in the classroom, but to a competent language user its role is like that of a window, through which we look at the content. It is transparent and although we may recognise that it is there, its transparency means that it is very hard to see. Focusing on content alone makes language the invisible curriculum in the school. And for children with poor English skills, the language becomes the block to learning. To put it another way, their window is made of frosted glass.*

(Gibbons 1991, p. 12)

Maintaining this focus on language and providing for the language development of your students is key to their ability to engage with the curriculum and achieve as students. Let's consider how this can be done.

REFLECTIVE TASK

The following extract was recorded in a classroom in which the teacher was working with the class to prepare them to write a weather forecast. This extract comes from about ten minutes into the lesson. The teacher is standing in front of the class introducing the topic and the task to the students. She has written in a list down the left side of the board some of the phrases to be found in weather forecasts that the students have suggested but she does not write anything down on the board during this extract. There are no weather forecasts available in the classroom for the students to see.

Teacher: OK. Your weather forecast. The title will be weather forecast. You're going to have to write it in two bits. There will be a sub-heading for the first bit. It will be today ... and the second bit will be a title tomorrow. So be quiet please Jack. OK. I expect you to describe the weather for today. Made up.

Remember you can choose one bad day and one good day and don't forget that the weather can change during the day.

Jaz (a student): Brightening up!

Teacher: Umm. Shh. Shh. No I didn't write that did I Jaz. Brighten up ... yeah because I couldn't get it up in the space so I wrote it below Jaz. Um so you might like to say today in the morning it will be blah, blah, blah. Shh shh shh sh! And then you might like to write later on in the afternoon it will become and you will describe how it will change. OK?

1. What might some of the difficulties be for a beginner EAL student in this classroom?
2. How might they be resolved?
3. What could the teacher be doing to support an EAL learner in this introduction to writing a weather forecast?

In the extract above we may make the following observations.

- The teacher is not using any visual images to support what is being taught and what she hopes her students will be learning.
- The learner may be unfamiliar with the vocabulary, may not have much experience of reading and seeing weather forecasts (or may have experience of them in a very different cultural form) and has no opportunity here to see a weather forecast and thus what the teacher is talking about.
- None of the children is clear about whether the teacher is referring to the weather forecast that they see on the television or one they would find in a newspaper as this has not been stated at this point in the lesson.
- There is a list of phrases on the board but they are not written up in the way they would appear in a weather forecast.
- In her explanation of the writing task, it is hard for a beginner bilingual to know which of her words are:
  – the headings they are to use in their writing (and where to position the headings);
  – the phrases they can use in the body of the writing;
  – instructions about the task that they need to listen to;
  – words aimed at controlling the behaviour of other children.
- The teacher's use of 'blah, blah, blah' will be confusing unless the child is familiar with this expression and knows that it stands in for one of the phrases the teacher has previously written on the board.
- The range and flow of the language, with very little visual support, contextualisation or demonstration, is likely to mean that the EAL student (and other students in the classroom?) will struggle to follow, will feel overwhelmed by the wash of language around them and not be able to complete the task at any level, although they may have a great deal of experience of writing in their other languages and perhaps of weather forecasts.
- It may also mean that if this is the dominant mode of teaching in the classroom the student will come to disengage from learning.

What could the teacher do? Well, the teacher in this situation could do any of the following.

- Ask the children about where they see weather forecasts and what they are used for.
- Show the class a weather forecast (either one from the television or from a newspaper or from the internet) and discuss its features with the class. The EAL learner would be able to see what the teacher was talking about and may well be able to relate some of the contributions of their classmates to the text that was in front of them and to their own knowledge.
- Use pictures and other visuals to support the language/vocabulary being used.

- Spend some time looking at the particular form and features of a weather forecast and model how to write one herself with the children contributing to this process. The EAL student would have the opportunity of hearing and seeing how specific aspects of English were deployed in such a piece of writing.
- She could then write the title, the headings and the beginnings of sentences she suggests the children use on the board or on a worksheet and allow the children to practise using the language she is trying to teach them, perhaps in pairs.
- She could use a weather forecast in the student's other language(s) with the whole class to look for common features and to explore differences and allow the student to write a weather forecast in more than one language.

In addition, instead of asking the students to move straight into writing a weather report on their own, she could provide them with opportunities to practise using the language of a weather forecast in pairs and groups or as a class. The beginning bilingual in such a class could then be given a picture-matching activity in order to develop vocabulary and this could lead into an activity using simple statements to describe the weather. This can then lead to statements that describe the weather in the past, present or future, and so on.

In doing this, the teacher would be demonstrating the most important strategies that support language development.

Start with what the learners already know. Recap what you have already covered or taught or something that you did before. Refer to other contexts where this language/subject is found or has been used. Gain their interest through relating the activity to previous experiences. Help them make connections with previous learning and make it clear what is going to be learnt (and why – give a purpose). Ask them what they know about the topic from their own experience. Remember to focus on the language that is required as well as the topic. Think about how you might be able to use (and/or develop) their other languages.

Provide a rich context for what you are teaching or demonstrating. Show the objects you are talking about or use examples. Use visuals – to indicate what you are talking about, to demonstrate a process visually. Model writing and reading. Direct attention to the language that is needed in order to engage with this topic. It may include specialist vocabulary (words change their meaning between subjects, e.g. 'face' means one thing in maths and another in an English lesson), the layout/genre of writing involved, the way connectives are used, and so on. Draw the learners' attention to the relationship between form and function. Be clear when you are 'teaching' the whole class, when you are talking to a group or a specific student, when you are dealing with administration or discipline. Using a student's name or using a phrase or gesture which makes it clear when you need them to listen is good for beginners – they will struggle with listening and filtering everything said in the classroom otherwise.

After introducing and/or demonstrating/modelling a topic or learning point, **provide many opportunities for students to comfortably practise and experiment** with the language and content that you have been teaching. This will probably involve pair or group work, can include a range of games and activities and may involve providing initial support through the use of writing frames or oral prompts. Provide learners with meaningful opportunities to use the language.

Move towards independence. Through providing many opportunities to practise and develop language and content knowledge in safe groupings, through activities that encourage language use and development (and with initial support provided by whole-class teaching/modelling, prompts and writing frames), learners are supported as they move towards being able to use a particular genre of writing or language item on their own without support. This is a gradual and iterative process.

You will have noticed that what the teacher could have done and the principles outlined above reflect much that is considered to be good classroom practice to support learning. In this way the provision you make for your EAL learners is part of the provision you make for all the learners in your classroom.

In your planning, teaching and assessment you will also need to consider the following in relation to reading and writing.

Reading and writing

EAL learners share much with monolingual English speakers with regard to learning to write in English. However, they may need to learn a new script or change the direction they write in. They will almost certainly need to learn the relationship between the written symbols of the English system and the sounds the symbols represent. As a teacher you will need to be sensitive to this, allow time for such learners to orientate themselves and to learn from you about how writing is accomplished. You can provide your students with good modelling of writing. (You can also allow your students to write in their own language if they are able to do this as a way of recording information, writing up an experiment and so forth.) Most importantly EAL students, like monolingual students, will benefit from explicit instruction in the different text types and genres of English writing that they are required to engage with and use in school.

In addition, when reading, beginner EAL students may not be able to call on many of the strategies that good readers use. They may not be able to identify the key words carrying the most information in a text. They may also have insufficient cultural or language knowledge to predict where a text is going or whether they have decoded a word they have read correctly. They may also struggle with reading for meaning because they are unfamiliar with the cohesive ties that are used in English writing. For example, EAL students may not recognise the relationship between a reference word in a text and a referent and may have difficulties with substitutions and connectives in their reading and writing.

Reference words point (usually back) to something in the text (the referent):
'*Yasmin* flashed *her torch* round the room for the last time. **She** was about to switch **it** off when Yvette cried out.'
The words 'She' and 'it' here refer back to 'Yasmin' and 'the torch'.

Substitutions are when another word is used to substitute for a word already used; nouns, verbs and clauses can be substituted:
'Somebody lend me their *mobile*', shouted Max. 'I'm afraid I don't have **one**', said Billy.
'*Your behaviour is a disgrace*', muttered the woman. Chris thought that this was probably true but did not like to be told **so**.

Connectives are words and phrases that suggest addition, opposition, cause and time: 'Clean your bedroom **or else** you won't get to play on the computer. Make your bed **and** put away your clothes. **Then** tidy away all your toys. **After that**, clean up the mess you have made downstairs' [addition and time connectives].

'We really like your work; **however** we do not have a position vacant at the moment. **As a result** we are unable to offer you anything until the end of the year' [opposition and cause connectives].

By being aware of the language you are expecting your students to use and to engage with, you can plan to include these kind of textual features in your classroom teaching by drawing attention to them and modelling their use in your work with the class as well as providing opportunities for students to practise using them. When asking your class to read the following are important.

- Give the purpose of the reading before the students read.
- Activate the students' prior knowledge – find out what they already know about the topic.
- Direct them to particular features of the text: build awareness.
- Model reading (think aloud).
- Allow uninterrupted time for reading.
- Think of ways of covering what has been read so that beginner EAL students can stay part of the lesson.

Home–school relationships

You are probably already aware of the importance of home–school relationships to students' learning. The relationship between home and school is just as important, if not more so, for EAL students although establishing such a relationship may sometimes seem more difficult. To establish good home–school relationships with parents of EAL students be aware of the following issues:

- *Parents' working hours*: Some parents may work in shops, restaurants, etc., where they have to be at work when children are picked up from school or when parent–teacher meetings happen. If a parent does not appear interested in their child's schooling then find out if this is the reason why you do not see very much of them and then find a mutually convenient time to meet.
- *Language*: Some parents do not feel confident about the English they need in order to talk to the teacher or understand what the teacher is saying and teachers feel inadequate in talking to parents when they don't share the language. Wherever possible try to provide some form of interpretation or translation for important meetings and conversations. This can be provided by an official interpreter (larger cities now provide such services), another parent, another family member (including a sibling if there is no one else). Always welcome any attempt to communicate and have a go using gestures, signs and so on.
- *School letters and forms*: In an ideal world it would be possible to have all school forms and letters translated into the languages that parents read. However, where this is not a possibility you should take care when you send letters and forms home that the font/writing is clear and easy to read. If you know that some parents are not familiar with reading in English and the information is important, then making a phone call to the home to pass on that information should follow sending a letter or a form. Where parents can read a little English then highlighting the important points (and where signatures are required) with a highlighter pen is useful. If a student needs to explain the form to their parents (and translate what is required) then make sure you give the student good, clear, oral explanation of what is in the text and what is required from the parents.
- *Don't hold children responsible*: When parents do not sign forms, return payments for school photographs and so on, do not hold the student responsible. It may well be that the student has been unable to

explain to their parents what is required. If you are in a situation like this as a teacher it is your responsibility to communicate with the parents and explain what is required, not the student's.

- *Parents' expectations*: As we noted earlier, EAL students do not form a homogenous group and neither do their parents. Parents will have diverse educational experiences of their own and may have different expectations of what a good school is. They may also have little idea of what their child is doing when they are in school because the system is very different to the system they are used to. This may be another reason why parents may not appear to be supportive. It can be remedied by providing information, in a way that can be understood, about how the school operates, what you are covering in the classroom and why.
- *Use and value parents*: The parents of EAL students will have a number of multilingual and multiliterate skills and experiences. Wherever possible use these. Parents and family members are also the most important people for helping you form a clear picture of the skills and abilities (in all their languages and literacies) of your EAL students and how you can plan for and support their language development.

Welcoming new students

This has been deliberately kept until the end of the chapter. This is because most advice provided to teachers about supporting EAL students focuses on this and just on this. It is hoped that what has come before this will support you as you effectively provide for your EAL students over the course of the first few years of their schooling and not just the first few months.

A few simple but very effective strategies for welcoming new students are as follows. They are things that you would do in your role as a form teacher rather than as a subject teacher but you might want to instigate some or all of these things for your particular subject area if they are not already in place.

Find a member of the class who will be their buddy – this will be someone who will take responsibility for showing the student to their classrooms, showing them what to do when certain bells ring and so on. The buddy doesn't have to share the new student's language(s).

Provide the new student with a bilingual dictionary so that both you and they can start to look up vocabulary. You can look up an English word and point to it and the student can read the translation in their other language.

Show new students the important places in the school (toilets, canteen, hall, school office, etc.): don't just give them a plan of the school.

Give students the language they will need in the first few days. For example, 'Can I leave the room/go to the toilet?'. You will be able to get simple introductory booklets with school language, etc. from your local authority's EAL service.

A final and most important point to make about EAL students is that if they are new to the English language they may very well remain silent for quite some time (up to a term or more) after joining your class. This is perfectly normal and is referred to as 'the silent period' by people who study second-language acquisition. Although a student may be silent it does not mean that they are not learning and taking in vast amounts of knowledge about English. They are. Students should not be forced to speak; they will speak when they are ready. And when they do speak you will probably be surprised at the level and quality of their spoken English.

MOVING *ON* > > > > > > MOVING *ON* > > > > > > MOVING *ON*

Have a look at the vignettes from your subject area on the NALDIC website (see below) and consider how these could inform your planning and teaching. Also look at the publications, research and resource pages of this excellent website.

FURTHER READING FURTHER READING **FURTHER READING** FURTHER READING

Allandina, S. (1995) *Being Bilingual: A Guide for Parents, Teachers and Young People on Mother Tongue, Heritage Language and Bilingual Education.* Stoke-on-Trent. Trentham.

Cline, T. and Frederickson, N. (eds) (1996) *Curriculum Related Assessment, Cummins and Bilingual Children*. Clevedon. Multilingual Matters. Cline Cummins Assessment – pick the D. Hall chapter and any other with good ideas.

Gravelle, M. (1996) *Supporting Bilingual Learners in School*. Stoke-on-Trent. Trentham.

Gravelle, M. (ed.) (2000) *Planning for Bilingual Learners: An Inclusive Curriculum*. Stoke-on-Trent. Trentham.

Rutter, J. (1994) *Refugee Children in the Classroom.* Stoke-on-Trent. Trentham.

Smyth, G. (2003) *Helping Bilingual Learners to Access the Curriculum*. London. David Fulton.

Useful websites

www.education2.bham.ac.uk/webapps/bilingualism/search.php Great reference list of books and articles.

www.literacytrust.org.uk Look for Professional resources under 'EAL', 'Multiculturalism'.

www.naldic.org.uk National Association for Language Development in the Classroom. Lots of very useful resources and information; the first place to look.

www.nassea.org.uk Northern Assocation of Support Services for Equality and Achievement.

www.ofsted.gov.uk

www.tes.co.uk Follow Staffroom link for EMAG forum.

www.collaborativelearning.org Collaborative Learning Project website with accessible talk-for-learning activities in all subject areas.

15
Equality and diversity
John Clay and Rosalyn George

Introduction: the changing educational context

Significant changes in educational policy were introduced by New Labour in 1997. This election ushered a raft of initiatives under the heading of modernisation and the White Paper *Excellence in Schools* (DfEE, 1997) emphasised the need for education to offer *equality of opportunity and high standards for all* (p. 3). For schools this meant in practice a renewed emphasis on literacy and numeracy and the setting of ambitious targets considered essential to raise attainment. This was coupled to national testing at the ages of 7, 11 and 14 to monitor the outcomes at these three different stages of schooling and to measure progress annually. However, such an approach, which sought to recognise and privilege the view that differences in attainment alone prevent individuals and groups from participating fully in the social, political and economic spheres, was highly problematic and contentious.

The Conservative/Liberal Democrat coalition government has not done away with national testing but is giving the impression that a centralised system that attempts to tightly control what takes place in each and every classroom at the 'micro'-level is to end. Key Stage 3

SATs have been dropped and the National Strategies teams will be disbanded while all schools – but especially those that are setting up as academies – will have considerable autonomy over both curriculum and pedagogy. The Schools White Paper, *The Importance of Teaching* (DfE, 2010), calls for recognition that the quality of teaching is the most significant variable in pupil achievement and system-wide effectiveness. The focus will be not only on assuring the quality of entrants to the profession but also on the quality of training and development that is provided.

The litmus test of the efficacy and impact of the White Paper's proposals is whether they will promote the positive changes in achievement and outcomes for all young people now and in the future. The authors of this chapter are convinced that the improvement envisaged by the current government in the quality of teaching can only happen if new entrants to the profession are both conversant with the need to tackle inequality in schools and have the capacity and confidence to do so.

Issues of equality and inclusion underpin the very foundations of the kind of society that we live in. Within this broader context, it is broadly accepted that education and schooling have a pivotal role in preparing future citizens to embrace the richness and potentialities of diversity and difference. Through an examination of the three central inequalities in education, namely, gender, 'race' and social class, we will explore:

- what inclusion and equality means in schooling and education;
- the legislative framework;
- the different patterns of achievement and expectations of pupils and students from within different communities, schooling and educational systems.

Equality

In the context of education and schools, the terms 'equality', 'equal opportunity' and 'equality of opportunity' are used interchangeably as though they all mean the same. Cole makes a distinction between equality and equal opportunities when he argues that:

> equal opportunities policies, in schools and elsewhere, seek to enhance social mobility within structures which are essentially unequal. In other words they seek a meritocracy, where people rise or fall on merit, but to grossly unequal levels or strata in society – unequal in terms of income, wealth, life chances or power. In contrast, egalitarian policies, policies to promote equality seek to go further. First, egalitarians attempt to develop a systematic critique of structural inequalities, both in society at large and at the level of the individual school. Second, egalitarians are committed to a transformed economy and a more socially just society, where wealth and ownership is shared far more equitably, and where citizens (whether young citizens or teachers in schools, economic citizens in the work place or political citizens in the polity) exercise democratic controls over their lives and over the structures of the societies they are part of and to which they contribute. While equal opportunities policies in schools and elsewhere are clearly essential they need to be advocated within a framework of a longer term commitment to equality.
>
> (Cole 2006, p. 3)

Where they are not, the false assumption will be made that there is a 'level playing field', on which we all compete as equals.

Richardson and Wood (1999) argue that within the context of education:

> equal opportunities *is concerned with ensuring that all pupils and students have genuine access to the curriculum, and that none are at an unfair disadvantage, because their distinctive experiences, concerns and identities are disregarded. The wider political task is to create and enforce legislation against unfair discrimination, both direct and indirect, in all major areas of social life, particularly in employment.*

(Richardson and Wood 1999, p. 15)

Some of the ideas embedded in these statements are complex, but despite this complexity, can be translated into everyday issues and contexts that are relevant and meaningful in the development of a deeper insight into the way our society is organised, how it operates and how this in turn impacts on schools and other educational establishments.

PRACTICAL TASK PRACTICAL TASK **PRACTICAL TASK** PRACTICAL TASK **PRACTICAL TASK**

Discuss with another student teacher the following key statements, which are intended to provoke debate and discussion.

- The classroom can be seen as a microcosm of society.
- The education system and the school reflect and reproduce society's values.
- Knowledge 'selected' for use in schools represents a particular view of the society, the perceived needs of individual, and the intrinsic value and logic of the knowledge itself.
- Behaviour that leads to the discrimination of others is learned and sometimes taught by commission and omission.
- Challenging inequalities (and supporting young people to do the same) is the responsibility of the teacher through the formal, informal and hidden aspects of the school.
- All subject areas and teachers can play a part in tackling inequality and discrimination.

Inclusion

Like equality and equal opportunities the term 'inclusion' has also become a 'catch-all' phrase. The term 'social inclusion' refers to participation in society. It includes involvement in politics, the economy and mainstream cultural life. Its opposite is social exclusion; for example, the absence of black and other minority people from key areas of social, political, recreational and economic life. Education in relation to social inclusion is concerned with equipping people with knowledge and skills, and also the paper qualifications ('educational achievement'), which they need for full participation in society. The wider political task is to combat poverty, inequality, unemployment, poor housing and poor health (Richardson and Wood, 1999, p. 15). Social deprivation that arises out of poverty, inequality, unemployment, poor housing and poor health is measured crudely within the schooling system in terms of pupils' entitlement to free school meals.

What is an inclusive school?

An inclusive school is one in which the teaching and learning, achievements, attitudes and well-being of every young person matter. Effective schools are educationally inclusive schools. This shows, not only in their performance, but also in their ethos and their willingness to offer new opportunities to pupils who may have experienced previous difficulties. This does not mean treating all pupils in the same way. Rather it involves taking account of pupils' varied life experiences and needs.

In *Evaluating Educational Inclusion: Guidance for inspectors and schools* (Ofsted 2000), the most effective schools are ones that do not take educational inclusion for granted. Instead, they constantly monitor and evaluate the progress each pupil makes, identifying pupils who may be missing out, difficult to engage, or feeling some way apart from what the school seeks to provide. They take practical steps – in the classroom and beyond – to meet pupils' needs effectively and promote tolerance and understanding in a diverse society (p. 4).

During the past three to four years, the term 'inclusion' has gained sufficient currency to become a central feature of the revised National Curriculum and a focus of the Ofsted inspection framework. The National Curriculum Inclusion Statement requires schools, in planning and teaching the curriculum, to take regard of the following three essential principles.

- Setting suitable learning challenges.
- Responding to the diverse needs pupils bring to their learning.
- Overcoming potential barriers to learning and assessment for individuals and groups.

Each of these principles has been expanded and exemplified in the National Curriculum handbook with additional information on inclusion included in the subject booklets.

Making your school more inclusive

- There needs to be a strong commitment to equal opportunities and social justice underpinned by explicit support from the head teacher.
- The perspectives of both pupil and parents need to be sought.
- Clear procedures for recording and acting on racist/sexist incidents must be developed.
- An ethos that is open and vigilant, which enables pupils as young citizens to discuss issues of justice and equity and shared concerns needs to be generated and sustained.
- Communicating high expectations accompanied by a clear view that under-performance by any group is unacceptable.
- Reviewing curricular and pastoral approaches to ensure their sensitivity and appropriateness.
- Using ethnic monitoring and other forms of data collection as a routine and rigorous part of the school's/ LA's self-evaluation and management.

The legal framework

All teachers need to be aware of the legislation with regard to equal opportunities since this has a direct impact on the school's role as a provider and an employer. The legislation is fairly complex in relation to gender, 'race' and special educational needs. It is important to note that since the passing of the 1988 Education Reform Act (ERA), governing bodies have increased responsibility for all aspects of staffing, training, grievance procedures. The specific laws that have been passed in this field are:

- the Sex Discrimination Act 1975;
- the Race Relations Act 1976 (as amended by the Race Relations Amendment Act 2000);

- the Education Act 1981 – Provision for children with Special Educational Needs;
- the Disability Discrimination Acts 1995 and 2005;
- Crime and Disorder Act 1998;
- Special Educational Needs Code of Practice 2001;
- the Children Act 2004 and the guidance on Safeguarding Children in Education (DfES 2004);
- the Equality Act 2006;
- the Equality Act 2010.

The Race Relations Act 1976 (as amended by the Race Relations (Amendment) Act 2000) places a new general (statutory) duty on public authorities (including schools) to promote race equality. The general duty has three parts. These are:

- eliminating unlawful race discrimination;
- promoting equality of opportunity;
- promoting good relations between people from different racial groups.

Specific duties (also statutory) are laid down in the Act to assist schools in meeting the general duty and include:

- a proactive approach, which builds 'race' equality into the mainstream of schools and their existing mechanisms;
- a requirement for schools to prepare and maintain a written race equality policy;
- this policy must deal with 'race' equality explicitly and transparently;
- promoting race equality and tackling discrimination.

This policy must also link with other policies and their impact on staff; pupils and parents from different racial groups must be monitored and evaluated, with particular attention being paid to pupil attainment. In practice this means:

- collecting, comparing and evaluating data to measure performance and effectiveness;
- monitoring attainment and progress, exclusions, support and guidance, parental involvement, governing body membership, punishments and rewards;
- evaluating data, establishing what more should be done, revising and setting targets in strategic plans.

There are further pieces of legislation which will have an impact on the school's role as both an employer and provider of services.

The Children Act 2004 provided the legal underpinning for *Every Child Matters: Change for Children* – the programme that aimed to transform children's services. The government paper *Every Child Matters,* which was the basis for the Children Act 2004, aimed to improve opportunities and outcomes for children, young people and families. The legislation was central to the promotion of inclusion in schools under New Labour although its current status for the Conservative/Liberal Democrat coalition government is unclear at the time of writing. *Every Child Matters* had five key outcomes for children.

- Be healthy.
- Stay safe.
- Enjoy and achieve.
- Make a positive contribution.
- Achieve economic well-being.

These five outcomes formed the basis for the structures for supporting children in local authorities as well as for Ofsted inspections. The Act placed a duty on local authorities to promote co-operation and sharing of information between health and social services agencies and education, alongside partners from the private, voluntary and community sectors in order to maximise achievement of the five key outcomes. Multi-agency working was a key element of the Children Act and therefore the inclusion agenda.

The three functions of the Equality Act (2006) were as follows.

1. To create a single commission – the Commission for Equality and Human Rights (CEHR). This replaced the Equal Opportunities Commission (EOC), the Commission for Racial Equality (CRE) and the Disability Rights Commission (DRC).
2. To make unlawful (apart from certain exemptions), discrimination on the grounds of religion or belief or sexual orientation in the provision of goods, facilities and services, the management of premises, education and the exercise of public functions.
3. To create a duty on public authorities to promote equality of opportunity between men and women and to prohibit sex discrimination in the workplace.

The Equality Act 2010 provided a cross-cutting legislative framework to protect the rights of individuals and advance equality of opportunity for all; to update, simplify and strengthen the previous legislation; and to deliver a simple, modern and accessible framework of discrimination law which protects individuals from unfair treatment and promotes a fair and more equal society.

Notably, the Equality Acts 2006 and 2010 made it illegal to discriminate against individual people on the grounds of 'sexual orientation' by businesses and public services. The year 2011 has seen a successful prosecution against the owners of a guest house for turning away a gay couple. The Acts and the Employment Regulations 2003 make it illegal for employers to discriminate on the grounds of sexuality in the treatment and protection of workers in the work-place. See **www.stonewall.org.uk** for further information. Some readers may recall a law known as 'Section 28' that attempted to prohibit discussion of sexuality in schools. That law was repealed by the Labour government in 2003. David Cameron, then a relatively new MP, voted against repeal but publicly apologised for what he then called the 'offensive' Section 28 in 2009.

The provisions of the Equality Act 2010 are being brought into force at different times to allow time for the people and organisations affected by the new laws to prepare for them. Most of the provisions came into force on 1 October 2010. The government is considering how the remaining provisions will be commenced so that the Act is implemented in an effective and proportionate way.

Implications for schools

From 1 October, the Equality Act 2010 replaced all existing equality legislation such as the Race Relations Act, Disability Discrimination Act and Sex Discrimination Act. It also provided some changes that schools need to be aware of.

The new Equality Act 2010 provided a single, consolidated source of discrimination law, covering all the types of discrimination that are unlawful. It simplified the law by removing anomalies and inconsistencies that had developed over time in the existing legislation, and it extended the protection from discrimination in certain areas.

As far as schools are concerned, for the most part, the effect of the new law is the same as it has been in the past – meaning that schools cannot unlawfully discriminate against pupils because of their sex, race, disability, religion or belief and sexual orientation. Protection is now extended to pupils who are pregnant or undergoing gender reassignment. However, schools that are already complying with the law should not find major differences in what they need to do.

The exceptions to the discrimination provisions for schools that existed under previous legislation – such as the content of the curriculum, collective worship and admissions to single sex schools and those of a religious character – are all replicated in the new Act.

However, there are some changes that will have an impact on schools as follows.

- It is now unlawful to discriminate against a transsexual pupil.
- It is now unlawful to discriminate against a pupil who is pregnant or has recently had a baby.
- New Positive Action provisions will allow schools to target measures that are designed to alleviate disadvantages experienced by, or to meet the particular needs of, pupils with particular protected characteristics. Such measures will need to be a proportionate way of achieving the relevant aim – for example, providing special catch-up classes for Roma children or a project to engage specifically with alienated Asian boys.
- Extending the reasonable adjustment duty to require schools to provide auxiliary aids and services to disabled pupils. However, this duty is not due to come into effect until a later date, following consultation on implementation and approach.
- It is now unlawful for employers to ask health-related questions of applicants before job offer, unless the questions are specifically related to an intrinsic function of the work. This means that schools should no longer, as a matter of course, require job applicants to complete a generic health questionnaire as part of the application procedure. We are considering the implications of this in relation to existing guidance for schools on establishing fitness and ability to teach (as required by the Health Standards (England) Regulations 2003). In the meantime, schools are advised to review their existing practices to ensure they are complying with both the Health Standards Regulations and Section 60 of the Equality Act. Schools may decide to ask necessary health questions after job offer. In any case, they should ensure that any health-related questions are targeted, necessary and relevant to the job applied for.
- The three existing general and specific equality duties on schools (race, disability and gender) to eliminate discrimination and advance equality of opportunity have now been combined into a single, less bureaucratic and more outcome-focused duty extending to all of the protected characteristics.

Guidance on the Act and the implications for schools is available on the Department for Education website (**www.education.gov.uk**).

Assessing and monitoring the impact of policies

Questions for assessing the impact of a school's policies, including its race equality policy, could include the following.

- Does the school help all its pupils to achieve as much as they can, and get the most from what is on offer, based on their individual needs?
- Which groups of pupils are not achieving as much as they can? Why not?
- Is the school making sure that its policies, including its race equality policy, are not having an adverse impact on pupils, parents or staff from racial groups?

- How does the school explain any differences? Are the explanations justified? Can they be justified on non-racial grounds, such as English language difficulties?
- Does each relevant policy include aims to deal with differences in pupils' attainments (or possible differences) between racial groups? Do the policy's aims lead to action to deal with differences that have been identified (for example extra coaching for pupils or steps to prevent racist bullying)?
- What is the school doing to raise standards, and promote equality of opportunity for pupils who seem to be underachieving and who may need extra support?
- What is the school doing to:
  - prepare pupils for living in a multi-ethnic society?
  - promote race equality and harmony?
  - prevent or deal with racism?

Dealing with racial and sexual harassment

While harassment may be difficult to define, it encompasses unwelcome physical, verbal or non-verbal conduct, which may be degrading, abusive and/or offensive. A resolution carried by the European Commission's Council of Ministers (May 1990) suggests that the aim of employer policies should be *to create a climate at work in which men and women respect one another's human integrity*. We have to acknowledge that harassment is frequently a function of power where power is exercised indiscriminately to the detriment of human rights. Research has indicated that harassment in schools of both a sexual and racial nature or of a more general form is a common part of a pupil/student's everyday experience. Often sexual or racial harassment in schools is not regarded as a problem because there have been few complaints. The reason for this may be that recipients:

- believe no action will be taken;
- are too embarrassed to make a complaint;
- fear reprisals for making a complaint.

PRACTICAL TASK PRACTICAL TASK PRACTICAL TASK PRACTICAL TASK

Read the letter 'To whom it may concern' in Figure 15.1. What action do you think should be taken in the light of this letter, which the head teacher has just received? What should be in place to prevent a situation like this occurring?

Including everyone in educational success

Closing the gap in educational attainment between various groups in society has been widely acknowledged as a pressing concern of national and international importance. However, it needs to be acknowledged that each of the main ethnic groups now achieves higher attainments than ever before. However, since the introduction of the GCSE there has been increasing concern among politicians, policy makers, parents, etc. that has focused upon the differences in achievement between boys and girls.

Gender is but one factor that affects schooling and achievement. Other factors such as class and ethnicity are strong determinants of educational achievement and thus it is dangerous and inaccurate to imply that all boys under-perform and all girls do well. The gender gap is widest in comprehensive schools and least pronounced in independent and grammar schools.

In the Classroom

> To whom this may concern.
>
> The girls in this class have put together their feelings towards the boys also in this class. Eversince we went into this class there has been nothing but harrisment. By now we are pretty sick of it all. if nothing is done about it we shall be forced to play truant. The facts are when we are sitting in the class we are violently assaulted, if we do not agree with them they threaten us and hit us if we answer them back. Sometimes when we want to show our feelings to them, they give us agravation. There is also a problem with them calling us insulting names, such as slags, bitch tramps, smelly cows fish, Ugly Wretch, and lots of other discusting names. Followed by a punch. They don't always hit us, unless we have sweets or something that they want. We all must state that it is not all of the boys in this class but a vast magority of them. if one of the boys start then normally the rest follow. We must confess that it is also effecting our work and giving is great stress and worry. There are so many problems that we can't take any more
>
> i hope there is something you can do to help us in the future. Thankyou.

Figure 15.1. Letter from a group of girls

National government statistics and academic reports over the last decade suggest that there is an enduring pattern of low achievement by white working-class males. DCSF (2008) statistics reveal that with the exception of traveller children, white working-class boys gained only 24 per cent 5+ GCSEs compared with the national average of 57 per cent. The 2007 Joseph Rowntree Foundation report *Tackling Low Educational Achievement* (Cassen and Kingdom 2007) using different data and a different data analysis reached similar conclusions.

Strand (2006) found that all minority ethnic groups make greater progress on average than white students between the ages of 11 and 16, with much of this improvement occurring close to or in high-stakes exams at the end of compulsory schooling.

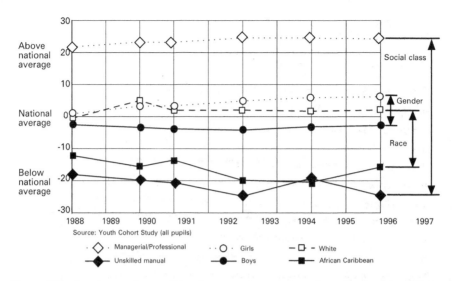

Figure 15.2. Attainment inequalities by race, class and gender – England and Wales, 1988–1997 (5 or more higher grade GCSEs relative to the national average)

Figure 15.2 illustrates how the gender gap is significantly smaller than the gap associated with class and 'race'. In relation to the national average, African Caribbean pupils and their peers from unskilled manual homes experience the greatest disadvantage. The trends highlighted by this graph concur with the research by Gillborn and Mirza (2000), that:

> *of the three best-known dimensions of inequality ('race', class and gender) the latter, gender, and in particular boys underperformance, represents the narrowest disparity. In contrast to the disproportionate media attention, {our} data shows gender to be a less problematic issue than the significant disadvantage of 'race', and the even greater inequality of class.*

(Gillborn and Mirza 2000, p. 123)

This study is still considered to be a very important piece of research because the findings reported remain pertinent today. The ethnic diversity in our schools has increased considerably over the past 20 years and classification of groups by ethnicity has changed to reflect this trend. Pupils from African backgrounds form a significant minority in many urban schools and it is acknowledged that some groups such as those of Somali background are now some of the lowest achievers in those schools. Boys achieve less than girls as it is for almost all groups but it is no coincidence that the entitlement to free schools meals (a proxy indicator for social class) is highest for pupils from Somali backgrounds.

Information from the Youth Cohort Study 1999, as cited by Gillborn and Mirza (2000), found that although African Caribbean, Pakistani and Bangladeshi boys are less likely to attain five higher-grade GCSEs than their white or Indian peers. All 'main ethnic groups' now achieve higher attainments than ever before. This study also confirmed a previous Ofsted review of research, which showed that Indian pupils as a group were the highest performing of the main South Asian categories and stated that *they are all achieving consistently in excess of their white counterparts.*

A summary of Gillborn and Mirza's research with specific reference to the three aspects of inequality, ethnicity, social class and gender, is outlined below.

- Of the three best known dimensions of inequality (race', gender and class) gender represents the smallest disparity, ethnicity next and class the greatest. This is in contrast to the amount of media attention that these dimensions receive.
- African-Caribbean, Pakistani and Bangladeshi pupils are markedly less likely to achieve five higher-grade GCSEs than their white and Indian peers nationally.
- African-Caribbean and Pakistani pupils have drawn least benefit from the rising levels of attainment.
- Since the late 1980s the attainment gap between the highest and lowest social classes has widened. The association between class and levels of attainment can be seen to operate within each of the main ethnic groups.
- Inequalities of attainment are now evident for black students regardless of their class background.
- In each of the principal ethnic groups girls are more likely to achieve five higher-grade GCSEs than boys of the same ethnic origin.
- Ethnic inequalities persist when comparing groups of pupils of the same sex but different ethnic origins.

Nevertheless, GCSE attainment has risen since the late 1980s and no group has been excluded from that improvement. Therefore, it is of paramount importance that a school's formal and informal curriculum takes into account and reflects the linguistic and cultural diversity of the intake and the community it serves. The teaching and learning in school should reflect this range of diversity.

PRACTICAL TASK PRACTICAL TASK PRACTICAL TASK PRACTICAL TASK PRACTICAL TASK

The following scenarios are based on actual events that have taken place. With one or more student teacher colleagues, discuss the issues that arise and work out your responses.
- A grandparent complained to the LA that the primary school where his granddaughter attended had used a black doll to represent the baby Jesus. He had complained directly to the head teacher the previous year and felt that his concerns had been ignored. He found it unacceptable for Jesus Christ to be portrayed as black. *I could understand it if the doll was slightly brown because we know that the Holy Land is in the Middle East and hot – so people could be a bit tanned*.
- Overheard in a staffroom – *I'm a white middle-aged and middle-class woman; what can I possibly do to help underachieving black boys? It's just so far removed from my world*.
- A parent makes a complaint that two other children are bullying his five-year-old daughter in and out of the classroom. He also reported that his daughter was having nightmares and showed extreme reluctance about going to school. He then went on to say that the daughter had recently started praying to become white.

Strategies for addressing differences in attainment

IN THE CLASSROOM

The Northwards Comprehensive school database shows that the achievement of Pakistani boys is significantly lower than the average school achievement, whereas the achievement of Pakistani girls is higher than average. The attainment gap therefore is an issue at this early stage in a pupil's secondary education. Northwards instigated an observational strategy of students in English groups in Year 7 and Year 8. The observations indicated, as would be expected, a wide range of ability, achievement and motivation within the group of Pakistani boys in these two year groups.

As a result of the observation the following actions could be initiated to possibly bring about change in outcomes for this target group.

A whole school's response may include:

- an examination of the curriculum content to reflect the interests and prior experiences of all its students;
- evaluation of its teaching and learning strategies;
- development of whole-school policies, which cover all aspects of work and behaviour.

(The school's formally taught curriculum and the informal hidden curriculum should take into account and reflect the linguistic and cultural diversity of the school and the community it serves. The teaching and learning in school should reflect this range of diversity.)

The whole-school response is aimed at creating an ethos whereby Pakistani boys can achieve without fear of ridicule. The impact of the whole school's response can then be monitored to ascertain:

- levels of attainment and progress;
- levels of engagement with school life – participation in activities both in the classroom and beyond.

A SUMMARY OF **KEY POINTS**

> The terms 'equal opportunities' and 'equality of opportunity' have to be informed by an understanding of the concept of equality.

> The concept of inclusion as used in the context of education and schooling in the present political climate refers to the role of education and its contribution to reducing disaffection and promoting participation in the political, social and economic life of wider society.

> While girls generally may be doing well in schooling up to GCSE, they fail in later life to capitalise upon this seeming success and still end up with occupying the low ranks in most areas of work, especially in the business sector.

> Since the late 1980s the attainment gap between the highest and lowest social classes has widened. The ways in which social class affects educational opportunities are multiple and complex: some factors lie outside the school, others operate through institutional processes that disadvantage particular groups of pupils.

> Social class and gender differences are closely associated with differences in attainment but neither can account for persistent underlying ethnic inequalities: comparing like with like, African-Caribbean, Pakistani and Bangladeshi pupils do not enjoy equal opportunities.

The intention of this chapter was to simplify wherever possible and make complex ideas accessible to trainee and beginner teachers unfamiliar with issues relating to equality and inclusion. It is vital that these understandings are put into practice so that they become central to your teaching and learning strategies. Promoting equality and inclusion is a cornerstone of being a member of one of the most influential professions in society.

FURTHER READING FURTHER READING **FURTHER READING** FURTHER READING

Cassen, R. and Kingdon, G. (2007) *Tackling Low Educational Achievement*. York. Joseph Rowntree Foundation.

Epstein, D., Elwood, J., Hey, V. and Maw, J. (1998) *Failing Boys? Issues in Gender and Achievement*. Buckingham. Open University Press. This is a useful and accessible text which explores the complex issues relating to masculinity, schooling and achievement.

Francis, B. and Skelton, C. (2004) *Reassessing Gender and Achievement; Questioning Contemporary Key Debates*. Abingdon. Taylor and Francis. This book draws together findings and arguments from the vast array of materials on this subject.

Gaine, C and George, R (1999) *Gender, 'Race' and Class in Schooling: A New Introduction*. London. Falmer Press. This book provides an overview of research and key problems in the field of education and the three social inequalities – gender, 'race' and class.

Lawrence, D., Richardson, B. and Ousley, H. (eds) (2006) *Tell it like it is: How our schools fail Black children*. Stoke-on-Trent. Trentham Books. This book brings the debate about 'Race' and Education firmly into the twenty-first century.

Searle, C. (2001) *An Exclusive Education: 'Race', class and exclusion in British schools*. London. Lawrence and Wishart. This text analyses the exclusionary practices of many secondary schools and puts forward policies to reverse this situation. It places educational exclusion within the wider context of social and political exclusion.

Chapter glossary

Black is sometimes used as a general term for people of African, Caribbean, South Asian and other Asian origin. Black is also one of the ethnic monitoring categories used in the census. It includes Caribbeans, Africans and others who wish to describe themselves as black.

Ethnicity and **ethnic group**. Ethnicity is an unambiguous term, which refers to culture. An ethnic group is simply a group which shares certain cultural features such as language, religion, various customs, perhaps food and clothing preferences (Gaine and George 1999).

Gender refers to those characteristics of being female or male which are socially and culturally constructed.

Gender reassignment – or, sometimes, **sex reassignment** – is usually defined as the medical and social process of a person's transition from one biological sex and the physiological features associated with that sex to the other biological sex and its features (e.g. male to female). This transition is said to accurately reflect the individual's psycho-social and cultural development. The physiological characteristics are then said to more fully represent the person's socio-cultural identity.

Institutional racism. The Stephen Lawrence Inquiry Report defines institutional racism as: *the collective failure of an organisation to provide an appropriate and professional service to people because of their colour, culture or ethnic origin. It can be seen or detected in processes, attitudes and behaviour which amount to discrimination through unwitting prejudice, ignorance, thoughtlessness and racist stereotyping which disadvantage minority ethnic people.*

'Race' is a crude and superficial classification, which began in the last century; it has no biological significance to scientists today. Perhaps a useful working definition is 'a group of people who may share some physical characteristic to which social importance is attached'. Thus, the important facet of 'race' is not the skin colour, facial features or type of hair people have but the social significance, which is placed upon these (Gaine and George 1999).

Racism. The Stephen Lawrence Inquiry Report defines racism as conduct or words which advantage or disadvantage people because of their colour, culture or ethnic origin. In its more subtle form it is as damaging as in its overt form. Using this definition, black, white or Asian people may be victims of racism. This definition of racism is consistent with the Race Relations Act. Some groups of people (for example black people, Asians, Gypsies and asylum seekers) are much more likely to suffer racism than others. Racism is sometimes used to refer to the power relationship between white people and black people. The basis for this viewpoint is that white people make most of the social, economic and political decisions and that these decisions may systematically disadvantage black people. 'Black' is used politically in this context to unite people who are not white or who are likely to be subjected to racism (for example, Jewish people).

Racist incident is any incident which is perceived to be racist by the victim, or any other person.

Sexism is discrimination against women or men on the basis of their sex.

Social inclusion refers to participation in society. It includes involvement in politics and in the economy and mainstream cultural life.

Transgender is an umbrella term that signifies individuals whose gender identity does not necessarily reflect their biological sex. Transgender does not imply any particular sexual orientation. Transgender includes individual people who were born with atypical sexual characteristics as well as people who choose to dress as the opposite sex (male/female) – cross-dressing – and people who undergo surgery to change their sexual characteristics. Transgender as a term reflects contemporary understandings of gender as a relatively mobile and contingent cultural identity in distinction to simple, biological or physiological categorisations of sex. However, transgender identities show the relationship between cultural and biological development in humans to be complex.

Appendix 1: Practising Teacher Standards (Wales)

Teachers must meet the Practising Teacher Standards (PTS) at the end of the induction period and continue to meet them throughout their teaching career.

Standards	Chapter(s)
Professional values and attributes	
1. Appreciate the diverse needs of children and young people.	**4, 12, 13, 14, 15**
2. Value fair, respectful, trusting, supportive and constructive relationships with children and young people.	**3**
3. Have high expectations of children and young people in order to improve outcomes and well-being for all learners.	**3**
4. Value the importance of building positive relationships between home and school.	**3**
5. Value the active involvement of children and young people in their progress, development and well-being.	**6**
6. Value the active involvement of parents and carers in the progress, development and well-being of children and young people.	**3**
7. Value and celebrate the contribution children and young people make within their communities.	**12**
8. Appreciate and value the contribution that support staff and other professionals make to the learning, development and well-being of children and young people.	**3**
9. Be actively involved in professional networks and learning communities which share and test beliefs and understandings with colleagues and contribute to the wider development of the school and profession.	**2**
10. Value the improvement of practice through reflection and taking responsibility for continuing professional development.	**2**
11. Have high expectations with regard to Welsh-language development in the context of the bilingual nature of Wales.	
Professional knowledge and understanding	
12. Maintain an up-to-date knowledge and understanding of the professional duties and responsibilities of teachers and the statutory framework within which they work.	**3**

13. Understand the national education policy context in Wales and the Welsh Government's national priorities for education, including an understanding of the principles of the Cwricwlwm Cymreig and how it should inform and shape their practice.	
14. Use understanding of the expectations, organizational arrangements and pedagogical approach in the key stages or phases before and/or after the ones they teach to inform their practice and planning.	
15. Understand the key factors that affect children and young people's learning and well-being.	**4, 12**
16. Maintain an up-to-date understanding of their subjects/ curriculum areas and related pedagogy in order to inform practice.	**2, 8, 9, 10, 11**
17. Understand their role in improving literacy and numeracy skills across the curriculum.	**8, 9**
18. Maintain knowledge and learning in ICT to support teaching, learning and in their wider professional role.	**10**
19. Understand and apply the SEN Code of Practice for Wales to meet the diverse needs of learners.	**13 (Note: This chapter refers to the SEN Code of Practice for England, but is worthwhile reading)**
20. Understand when appropriate and how to seek information, advice and support from internal and external sources including procedures on safeguarding.	**3**
21. Have a knowledge of a range of strategies and know how to use them to promote good behaviour and create a purposeful learning environment.	**7**
22. Understand how the United Nations Convention on the Rights of the Child and the Children and Young People's Participation Standards for Wales can be used to inform practice and improve learner outcomes.	
23. Understand the expectations in the curriculum with regard to Welsh-medium provision and/or Welsh Second Language.	
Professional skills	
Planning and target setting	
24. Set challenging teaching and learning objectives that are guided by informed expectations of individual learners based on knowledge of the expected standards of the relevant age group and the range and content of work appropriate to learners in that age group.	**5, 6**

25. Use teaching and learning objectives to plan lessons, and sequences of lessons, which clearly show how learners' knowledge, skills and understanding will be assessed.	5
26. Personalise learning in order to address individual needs including seeking the views of learners on what would help them achieve their potential.	**5, 6**
27. Identify resources to support learning that will stimulate and motivate all learners to achieve desired outcomes.	**5, 6, 8, 9, 10, 11**
28. Work effectively as a team member and collaborate with colleagues to plan work and establish targets.	**1, 3**
29. Plan for support staff to be appropriately involved in supporting learning and ensure they understand the roles they are expected to fulfil.	5
30. Plan appropriate opportunities for children and young people to learn in settings beyond the classroom.	5
31. Manage and prioritise time effectively within their wider professional role.	2
32. Instigate and maintain effective communication with children, young people, and their parents/carers.	**3, 12**
Monitoring and assessment	
33. Use a range of monitoring and assessment strategies, including both formative and summative assessment, to evaluate learners' progress towards planned learning objectives, and use this information to improve their own planning and teaching.	6
34. Meet the assessment requirements and arrangements for the subjects/curriculum areas and phases within which they teach, including those relating to public examinations and qualifications.	6
35. Use monitoring and assessment to identify and support learners including: those with additional learning needs; more able and talented learners; learners working below age-related expectations; learners failing to achieve their potential; and learners with behavioural, emotional and social difficulties.	6
36. Involve learners in target setting and in reflecting upon and evaluating their performance.	6
37. Monitor and record learners' progress and achievements to provide evidence of the range of their work, progress and attainment over time whilst taking account of the participation and views of the learner.	6
38. Provide learners with accurate and constructive feedback on their strengths, weaknesses, attainment, progress and areas for development, including action plans for improvement.	6
39. Provide colleagues, parents and carers with timely, accurate and constructive feedback on learners' attainment, progress and areas for development using supporting records and other evidence.	6

Teaching and managing learning	
40. Establish and maintain effective learning environments where all learners feel safe, secure and confident.	**7, 12, 13, 14, 15**
41. Teach the required and expected skills, knowledge and understanding relevant to the needs of the learner making appropriate use of relevant national guidance.	**8, 9, 10, 11**
42. Make effective personalised provision in their teaching including taking practical account of diversity and promoting equality and inclusion.	**12, 13, 14,1 5**
43. Challenge instances of prejudice, stereotyping, bullying and harassment, in line with school policies and procedures.	**15**
44. Teach clearly structured lessons or sequences of work so that all learners understand and meet the intended learning objectives.	**5**
45. Employ appropriate teaching strategies which develop all learners' capacity to work collaboratively and independently.	**5**
46. Build on the varying experiences, achievements and interests of learners to help them make progress.	**5**
47. Manage teaching and learning time effectively.	**5**
48. Manage the physical learning environment, equipment, materials, texts and other resources safely and effectively.	**5**
49. Employ appropriate teaching strategies to secure positive behaviour.	**7**
50. Employ appropriate teaching strategies to promote the well-being of children and young people.	**7, 12**
51. Employ appropriate teaching strategies to promote good progress and outcomes for learners over a sustained period of time.	**5**
52. Use ICT effectively in teaching and learning.	**10**
53. Encourage learners to progress independently by providing activities or other out-of-school study which consolidates and extends work carried out in school.	**4**
54. Work co-operatively and collaboratively with other teachers and colleagues, including those from external agencies, to enhance the learning and well-being of those they teach.	**3**
55. Promote learners' understanding of the bilingual nature of Wales and develop their bilingual skills as appropriate.	**14**

(Full text of Standards for Wales available at: http://wales.gov.uk/topics/educationandskills/publications/circulars/practitioners/?lang=en)

Appendix 2: The Standards for Provisional Registration GTC Scotland

Standards	Chapter(s)
1. Professional Values and Personal Commitments of all Teachers	1, 2, 3, 11, 12, 13, 14, 15
Social justice	
• Embracing the educational and social values of sustainability, equality and justice and recognising the rights and responsibilities of future as well as current generations.	
• Committing to the principles of democracy and social justice through fair, transparent, inclusive and sustainable practices in relation to:	
age, disability, gender and gender identity, race, religion and belief and sexual orientation.	
• Valuing as well as respecting, social, cultural and ecological diversity and promoting the principles and practices of local and global citizenship for all learners.	
• Demonstrating a commitment to engaging learners in real world issues to enhance learning experiences and outcomes and to encourage learning our way to a better future.	
• Respecting the rights of all learners and their entitlement to be included in their learning experiences.	
Integrity	
• Demonstrating, honesty, courage and wisdom.	
• Critically examining personal and professional attitudes and beliefs and challenging our own assumptions and professional practice.	
• Critically examining the connections between personal and professional attitudes and beliefs, values and professional practices in order to inform and shape personal and professional development effect improvement and, when appropriate, transformative change in practice.	
Trust and respect	
• Acting and behaving in ways that develop a culture of trust and respect through, for example, being trusting and respectful of others within the school community, and with all those involved in influencing the lives of learners in and beyond the school.	
• Providing and ensuring a safe and secure environment for all learners built on an ethos of care.	

• Demonstrating a commitment to motivating and inspiring learners while also acknowledging their uniqueness, individuality and specific learning needs. **Professional commitment** • Engaging with all aspects of professional practice and all members of our educational communities with enthusiasm, adaptability and constructive criticality. • Committing to lifelong enquiry, learning and professional development as a core aspect of professionalism and collaborative practice.	
2. Professional Knowledge and Understanding	
2.1 Curriculum	
2.1.1 Have a knowledge and understanding of the nature of the curriculum and its development Student teachers: • develop an understanding of the principles of curriculum design and the contexts for learning; • know about and understand the processes of change and development in the curriculum; • develop an awareness of connections with other curricular areas, stages and sectors.	4, 5, 8, 9, 10
2.1.2 Have a knowledge and understanding of the relevant area(s) of pre-school, primary or secondary school curriculum Student teachers: • acquire knowledge and understanding of theory and practical skills in curricular areas, referring to local and national guidance; • understand how to match the level of curricular areas to the needs of all learners; • understand the importance of using and designing materials for learning and teaching to stimulate, support and challenge all learners; • have an awareness of ongoing developments in curricular areas in relation to both educational and societal issues.	5, 8, 9, 10, 12, 13, 15
2.1.3 Have knowledge and understanding of planning coherent and progressive teaching programmes Student teachers: • know how to plan for effective learning in the curricular areas to be taught, or themes being studied; • know and understand how to justify what is taught within curricular areas in relation to the curriculum and the relevance to the needs of all learners; • develop an understanding of planning learning across different contexts and experiences.	5, 6

2.1.4 Have a knowledge and understanding of contexts for learning to fulfil their responsibilities in literacy, numeracy, health and wellbeing and interdisciplinary learning Student teachers: • know how to promote and support the cognitive, emotional, social and physical wellbeing of the learners in their care; and show commitment to raising these learners' expectations of themselves; • know how to apply knowledge and understanding of personal, social and health education; • have knowledge and understanding of current guidance on the use of digital technologies in schools and know how to use digital technologies to enhance learning and teaching; • demonstrate knowledge and understanding of the content of the curriculum in relation to literacy and numeracy as set out in national guidance; • demonstrate knowledge and understanding of the methods and underlying theories for effective teaching of literacy and numeracy; and select the most appropriate methods to meet all learners' needs; • know how to match the demands of work in all curricular areas with learners' skills in literacy and numeracy; • have knowledge and understanding of current educational priorities such as sustainable development education.	4, 8, 9, 12, 13, 14 15
2.1.5 Have knowledge and understanding of the principles of assessment, recording and reporting Student teachers: • know and understand that the principles of assessment, recording and reporting are integral to the process of teaching and learning; • know and understand how to use formative and summative assessment, record assessments appropriately, use assessment information to inform teaching and learning and produce clear and informed reports.	7
2.2.1 Have knowledge and understanding of the principal features of the education system, educational policy and practice Student teachers: • develop an understanding of the principal influences on Scottish education and develop awareness of international systems; • develop an understanding of current, relevant legislation and guidance surrounding education; • develop an understanding of the legal and professional aspects of a teacher's position of trust in relation to learners.	2, 3, 4, 12, 13, 14 15

2.2.2 Have knowledge and understanding of the schools and learning communities in which they teach and their own professional responsibilities within them Student teachers: • develop an understanding of the sector and schools in which they are working, including: the role of education authorities; the organisation and management of schools and resources; improvement planning; professional review and development and how these connect to teachers' professional practice; • have a working knowledge of the teacher's contractual, pastoral and legal responsibilities; • have an awareness of and respect for a school's distinctive ethos; • have an understanding of the roles and responsibilities of all staff within the school community.	1, 3, 4, 12, 15
2.3 Pedagogical Theories and Practice	
2.3.1 Have knowledge and understanding of relevant educational principles and pedagogical theories to inform professional practices Student teachers: • have knowledge and understanding of the stages of child development which they are able to use to take account of their learners' needs; • have knowledge and understanding of learning theories and the importance of these in planning, teaching and learning; • have knowledge and understanding of the ways in which natural, social, cultural, political and economic systems function and of how they are interconnected.	4, 13, 14, 15
2.3.2 Have knowledge and understanding of the importance of research and engagement in professional enquiry Student teachers: • know how to access and apply relevant findings from educational research; • know how to engage appropriately in the systematic investigation of practice.	2
3 Professional Skills and Abilities	
3.1 Teaching and Learning	
3.1.1 Plan coherent, progressive and stimulating teaching programmes which match learners' needs and abilities Student teachers: • plan appropriately for effective teaching and learning in literacy, numeracy, health and wellbeing and skills for life in order to meet the needs of all learners.	5, 13, 14, 15

3.1.2 Communicate effectively and interact productively with learners, individually and collectively Student teachers: • use communication methods, including a variety of media, to motivate and sustain the interest of all learners; • communicate appropriately with all learners, and promote competence and confidence in literacy; • demonstrate effective questioning strategies; • communicate the learning purpose and give explanations at the appropriate level(s) for all learners; • stimulate learner participation in debate and decision-making about issues which are open-ended, complex, controversial or emotional; • reflect on the impact of their personal method of communication on learners and others in the classroom.	3, 7, 11, 12, 13, 14, 15
3.1.3 Employ a range of teaching strategies and resources to meet the needs and abilities of learners Student teachers: • demonstrate that they can select creative and imaginative strategies for teaching and learning appropriate to learners as individuals, groups or classes; • demonstrate that they can select and use a wide variety of resources and teaching approaches, including digital technologies and outdoor learning opportunities; • demonstrate the ability to justify and evaluate professional practice and take action to improve the impact on all learners.	8, 9, 10, 11, 12, 13, 14, 15
3.1.4 Have high expectations of all learners Student teachers: • develop tasks and set pace of work to meet the needs of learners, providing effective support and challenge, seeking advice appropriately; • demonstrate an awareness of barriers to learning, recognising when to seek further advice in relation to all learners' needs	1, 3, 5, 13, 14
3.1.5 Work effectively in partnership in order to promote learning Student teachers: • demonstrate an ability to work co-operatively in the classroom and the wider school community with staff, parents and partner agencies to promote learning; • ensure learners contribute to planning and enhancement of their own learning programmes.	3

3.2 Classroom Organisation and Management	
3.2.1 Create a safe, caring and purposeful learning environment Student teachers: • plan and provide a safe, well organised learning environment, including effective use of display; • make appropriate use of available space to accommodate whole class lessons, group and individual work and promote independent learning; • use outdoor learning opportunities, including direct experiences of nature and other learning within and beyond the school boundary where possible; • organise and manage classroom resources and digital technologies to support teaching and learning; • know about and be able to apply health and safety regulations as appropriate to their role.	5, 7
3.2.2 Develop positive relationships and positive behaviour strategies Student teachers: • show awareness of educational research and local and national advice and demonstrate the ability to use a variety of strategies to build relationships with learners, promote positive behaviour and celebrate success; • apply a school's positive behaviour policy, including strategies for understanding and preventing bullying; • know how and when to seek the advice of colleagues in managing behaviour; • demonstrate the ability to justify the approach taken in managing behaviour.	7
3.3 Pupil Assessment	
3.3.1 Use assessment, recording and reporting as an integral part of the teaching process to support and enhance learning Student teachers: • use a range of formative and summative assessment approaches appropriate to the needs of all learners and the requirements of the curriculum and awarding and accrediting bodies; • enable learners to engage in self-evaluation and peer assessment to benefit learning; • record assessment information to enhance teaching and learning; • use the results of assessment to identify strengths and development needs which lead to further learning opportunities.	6

3.4 Professional Reflection and Communication	
3.4.1 Read and critically engage with professional literature, educational research and policy Student teachers: • read, analyse a range of appropriate educational and research literature; • use what they have learned from reading and research to challenge and inform practice to broaden understanding and improve practice.	2
3.4.2 Engage in reflective practice continually to develop and advance career-long professional learning and expertise Student teachers: • reflect and engage in self evaluation using the Professional Standards; • know how to adopt an enquiring approach to their professional practice and engage in professional enquiry and professional dialogue; • evaluate their classroom practice (taking account of feedback from others) in order to enhance teaching and learning; • model appropriate levels of literacy and numeracy in their own professional practice; • understand the processes of curriculum development, school improvement planning and professional review and development; • share their professional learning and development with colleagues; • maintain a record of their own professional development, culminating in an initial professional development action plan.	1, 2, 3

(Full text of Standards for Scotland available at: http://www.gtcs.org.uk/standards/standards.aspx)

Appendix 3: Professional Competences for Teachers (Northern Ireland)

Professional competence statements	Chapter(s)
1. Teachers should demonstrate that they understand and uphold the core values and commitments enshrined in the Council's Code of Values and Professional Practice.	
2. Teachers will have developed a knowledge and understanding of contemporary debates about the nature and purposes of education and the social and policy contexts in which the aims of education are defined and implemented.	1, 2, 3
3. (i) Teachers will have developed a knowledge and understanding of the learning area/subject(s) they teach, including the centrality of strategies and initiatives to improve literacy, numeracy and thinking skills, keeping subject, curricular and pedagogical knowledge up-to-date through reflection, self-study and collaboration with colleagues. (ii) Teachers will have developed, in Irish medium and other contexts, sufficient linguistic and pedagogical knowledge to teach the curriculum.	2, 8, 9
4. Teachers will have developed a knowledge and understanding of how the learning area/subject(s) they teach contribute to the Northern Ireland Curriculum (including the Northern Ireland pre-school curricular guidance that applies in the nursery sector) and be aware of curriculum requirements in preceding and subsequent key stages.	3
5. Teachers will have developed a knowledge and understanding of curriculum development processes, including planning, implementation and evaluation.	3, 5, 11
6. Teachers will have developed a knowledge and understanding of the factors that promote and hinder effective learning, and be aware of the need to provide for the holistic development of the child.	4, 12, 13, 14, 15
7. Teachers will have developed a knowledge and understanding of a range of strategies to promote and maintain positive behaviour, including an acknowledgement of pupil voice, to establish an effective learning environment.	3, 7
8. Teachers will have developed a knowledge and understanding of the need to take account of the significant features of pupils' cultures, languages and faiths, and to address the implications for learning arising from these.	14, 15

9. Teachers will have developed a knowledge and understanding of their responsibilities under the Special Educational Needs Code of Practice and know the features of the most common special needs and appropriate strategies to address these.	13
10. Teachers will have developed a knowledge and understanding of strategies for communicating effectively with pupils, parents, colleagues and personnel from relevant child and school support agencies.	3, 12, 13, 14, 15
11. Teachers will have developed a knowledge and understanding of how to use technology effectively, both to aid pupil learning and to support their professional role, and how this competence embeds across all of the competences.	10
12. Teachers will have developed a knowledge and understanding of the interrelationship between schools and the communities they serve, and the potential for mutual development and well-being.	12
13. Teachers will have developed a knowledge and understanding of the statutory framework pertaining to education and schooling and their specific responsibilities emanating from it.	1, 3
14. Teachers will set appropriate learning objectives/outcomes/intentions, taking account of what pupils know, understand and can do, and the demands of the Northern Ireland Curriculum (including the Northern Ireland pre-school curricular guidance that applies in the nursery sector) in terms of knowledge, skills acquisition and progression.	5, 6
15. Teachers will plan and evaluate lessons that enable all pupils, including those with special educational needs, to meet the learning objectives/outcomes/intentions, showing high expectations and an awareness of potential areas of difficulty.	5, 6, 13, 14
16. Teachers will deploy, organise and guide the work of other adults to support pupils' learning, when appropriate.	3, 12, 13, 14
17. Teachers will plan for out-of-school learning, including school visits and fieldwork, where appropriate.	
18. Teachers will manage their time and workload effectively and efficiently and maintain a work/life balance.	3
19. Teachers will create and maintain a safe, interactive and challenging learning environment, with appropriate clarity of purpose for activities.	5, 7
20. Teachers will use a range of teaching strategies and resources, including E-learning where appropriate, that enable learning to take place and which maintain pace within lessons and over time.	4, 5, 6, 10
21. Teachers will employ strategies that motivate and meet the needs of all pupils, including those with special educational needs and for those not learning in their first language.	4, 5, 13, 14

22. Teachers will secure and promote a standard of behaviour that enables all pupils to learn, pre-empting and dealing with inappropriate behaviour in the context of school policies and what is known about best practice.	5, 6, 7
23. Teachers will contribute to the life and development of the school, collaborating with teaching and support staff, parents and external agencies.	3
24. Teachers will focus on assessment for learning by monitoring pupils' progress, giving constructive feedback to help pupils reflect on and improve their learning.	5, 6
25. Teachers will select from a range of assessment strategies to evaluate pupils' learning, and use this information in their planning to help make their teaching more effective.	6
26. Teachers will assess the levels of pupils' attainment against relevant benchmarking data and understand the relationship between pupil assessment and target setting.	6
27. Teachers will liaise orally and in written reports in an effective manner with parents or carers on their child's progress and achievements.	6

(Full text of Competences for Northern Ireland available at: http://www.gtcni.org.uk/index.cfm/area/information/page/profstandard)

References

Allen, J., Loveless, A., Potter, J. and Sharp, J. (2007) *Primary ICT: Knowledge, Understanding and Practice*. Exeter. Learning Matters.

Arnold, R. (2006) *Schools in Collaboration: Federations, Collegiates, and Partnerships.* EMIE at NFER Report No. 86.

Aspect (2006) *Personalised Learning: From Blueprint to Practice*. Wakefield. Aspect.

Assessment Reform Group (1999) *Assessment for Learning: Beyond the Black Box*. Cambridge. University of Cambridge School of Education.

Barbe, W. B. and Malone, M. N. (1981) What we know about modelling strategies. *Educational Leadership*, 38, 378–80.

Barratt, R. and Barratt Hacking, E. (2000) Changing my locality: conceptions of the future. *Teaching Geography*, 25(1), 17–21.

Barrs, M. (1990) *Words Not Numbers: Assessment in English*. Exeter. Short Run Press.

Basic Skills Agency (1997) *Does Numeracy Matter? Evidence from the National Child Development Study on the Impact of Poor Numerary on Adult Life*.

Bassey, M. (1989) *Teaching Practice in the Primary School*. East Grinstead. Ward Lock Educational.

Beard, R. (1993) *Teaching Literacy Balancing Perspectives*. London. Routledge.

Beard, R. (2000) *Developing Writing 3–13*. London. Hodder and Stoughton.

Bearne, E. (1999) *Use of Language Across the Secondary Curriculum*. London. Routledge.

Becta (2001) The secondary school of the future. A preliminary report to DfEE by Becta **http://dera.ioe.ac.uk/1633/1/becta_2001_secondaryfuture_analysisreport.pdf** (Accessed 31.3.11).

Becta (2002) ImpaCT2. Norwich. HMSO.

Behets, D. (1990) Concerns of pre-service physical education teachers. *Journal of Teaching in Physical Education*, 10, 66–75.

Bereiter, C. and Scardamalia, M. (1987) The psychology of written composition, in Beard, R. (1993) *Teaching Literacy Balancing Perspectives.* London. Routledge.

Best, R. (1999) The impact on pastoral care of structural, organizational and statutory changes in schooling: some empirical evidence and a discussion. *British Journal of Guidance and Counselling*, 27(1), 55–70.

Best, R. (2007) The whole child matters: the challenge of Every Child Matters for pastoral care. *Education 3-13*, 35 (3), 249–259.

Black, P. and Wiliam, D. (1998) *Inside the Black Box: Raising .Standards Through Classroom Assessment*. London. King's College.

Black, P. *et al*. (2003) *Assessment for Learning: Putting it into Practice*. Maidenhead. Open University Press.

Bleach, K. (2000) *The Newly Qualified Secondary Teacher's Handbook.* London. David Fulton.

Booth, T., Nes, K. and Stromstad, M. (2003) *Developing Inclusive Teacher Education*. NY. Routledge.

Bruer, J. T. (1997) Education and the brain: A bridge too far. *Educational Researcher*, 26 (8), 4–16.

Bruner, J. S. (1966) *The Process of Education*. New York. Vintage.

Bruner, J. S. (1966) *Toward a Theory of Instruction*. Cambridge, MA. Harvard University Press.

Bullock Report (1975) *A Language for Life*. London. DES.

Cairney, T. H. (1995) *Pathways to Literacy*. London. Cassell.

Calderhead, J. (1987) *Exploring Teachers' Thinking*. London. Cassell.

Cano-Garcia, F. and Hughes, E. H. (2000) Learning and thinking styles: an analysis of their interrelationship and influences on academic achievement. *Educational Psychology*, 20 (4), 413–430.

Carr, W. and Kemmis, S. (1986) *Becoming Critical*. London. Falmer Press.

Chasty, H. (1990) cited in P. D. Pumfrey and C. D. Elliott (eds) (1990) *Children's Difficulties in Reading,*

Spelling and Writing. London. Falmer Press.

Cheminais, R. (2000) *Special Educational Needs for Newly Qualified and Student Teachers*. London. David Fulton.

Child, D. (1986) *Psychology and the Teacher* (4th edn). London. Cassell.

Coffield, D., Mosely, D., Hall, K. and Ecclestone, E. (2004) *Should We be Using Learning Styles: What Research Has to Say on Practice.* London. Learning and Skills Research Centre.

Cohen, E. (1994) *Designing Groupwork: Strategies for the Heterogeneous Classroom*. New York. Teachers College Press.

Cole, M. (ed.) (1999) *Professional Issues for Teachers and Student Teachers*. London. David Fulton.

Cole, M. (ed.) (2006) *Education Equality and Human Rights*. London. Routledge.

Collier, V. (1987) Age and rate of acquisition of second language for academic purposes. *TESOL Quarterly*, 21, 617–641.

Cotton, J. (1995) *The Theory of Learners: An Introduction*. London. Kogan Page.

Counsell, C. (2001) Challenges facing the literacy co-ordinator. *Literacy Today*, 24.

Cowley, S. (2001) *Getting the Buggers to Behave*. London. Continuum.

Crick Report (1998) *Education for Citizenship and the Teaching of Democracy in Schools.* London. DfEE/QCA.

Crow, F. (2008) Learning for well-being; personal, social and health education and a changing curriculum. *Pastoral Care in Education*, 26 (1), 43–51.

Cullingford, C. (2006) Children's own vision of schooling. *Education 3–13,* 34 (3), 211–221.

Cummins, J. (2000) *Language, Power and Pedagogy: Bilingual Children in the Crossfire*. Clevedon. Multilingual Matters.

Dale, R. (1990) *The TVEI Story: Policy, Practice and Preparation for the Workforce*. Milton Keynes. Open University Press.

Davies, B. (2005) Youth Work: a manifesto for our times, *Youth and Society*, No. 88.

Dean, G. (2000) *Teaching Literacy in Secondary Schools*. London. David Fulton.

Demos (2005) *About Learning: Report from the Learning Working Group*. London. Demos.

Department of Children, Schools and Families (2010) State-funded Secondary Schools: Number and Percentage of pupils by first language (Table 14b) and Maintained Primary Schools: Number and Percentage of pupils by First language (Table 14a) (both provisional) **www.dcst.gov.uk/rsgateway/ DB/SFR/S000925/sFR09_20k** last accessed 13 October 2010.

DES (1978) *Special Educational Needs: Warnock Report*. London. HMSO.

DES (1981) *Education Act*. London. HMSO.

DfEE (1995) *Disability Discrimination Act*. London. HMSO.

DfEE (1996) *Education Act*. London. HMSO.

DfEE (1997) *Excellence for All Children: Meeting Special Educational Needs* (Green Paper). London. HMSO.

DfEE (1997) *Excellence in Schools*. Cm 3681. London. HMSO.

DfEE (1998) *Meeting Special Educational Needs: A Programme of Action*. London. HMSO.

DfEE (1999) *Social Inclusion: Pupil Support*. Circular 10/99. London. HMSO.

DfEE (1999) A fresh start – improving literacy and numeracy skills. *Skills and Enterprise Briefing*, Issue 5/99. London. HMSO.

DfEE (2000) Removing Barriers: Raising Achievement Levels for Minority Ethnic Pupils. Key Points for Schools. London. DfEE.

DfEE (2001a) *Framework for Teaching English: Years 7, 8 and 9*. DfEE.

DfEE (2001b) *Key Stage 3 National Strategy Framework for Teaching Mathematics: Years 7, 8 and 9.*

DfEE (2001c) *Literacy Across the Curriculum*. DfEE.

DfEE and QCA (2000) *The National Curriculum for England*. DfEE and QCA Publications.

Department for Education and Science (1989) *Report of Her Majesty's Inspectors on Pastoral Care in Secondary Schools: An Inspection of Some Aspects of Pastoral Care in 1987-8.* Stanmore. DES.

DfES (2001a) *Numeracy Across the Curriculum Notes for School-Based Training*.

DfES (2001b) *Numeracy Across the Curriculum Support Materials for School-Based Training.*

DfES (2001c) *Schools Achieving Success*. White Paper. HMSO.

DfES (2001d) *Special Educational Needs and Disability Act*. Nottingham. DfES Publications.

DfES (2001e) *Special Educational Needs: Code of Practice*. Nottingham. DfES Publications.

DfES (2002) *Qualifying to Teach*: *Professional Standards for Qualified Teacher Status and Requirements for Initial Teacher Training* (online). Available from **www.canteach.gov.uk/itt/ requirements/qualifying/standards_printable.pdf**

DfES (2002) *Transforming the Way We Learn*. Norwich. HMSO.

DfES (2003) *Every Child Matters*. London. DfES.

DfES (2004a) *Five Year Strategy for Children and Learners*. London. DfES.

DfES (2004b) *Removing Barriers to Achievement*. London. DfES.

DfES (2005) *Higher Standards: Better Schools for All*. London. DfES.

Department for Education and Skills (2007) Secondary National Strategy. Social and Emotional Aspects of Learning for Secondary Schools. Guidance Booklet. London: DfES.

DfES (2005) *14–19 Education and Skills White Paper*. London. DfES.

Dodds, P., Griffin, L. L. and Placek, J. H. (2001) A selected review of the literature on the development of learners' domain-specific knowledge. *Journal of Teaching in Physical Education*, 20 (4), 301–313.

Doyle, W. (1979) Classroom tasks and students' abilities, in P. Peterson and H. Walberg (eds) *Research on Teaching: Concepts, Findings and Implications*, 183–209. Berkeley, CA. McCutcheon.

Doyle, W. (1981) Research on classroom contexts. *Journal of Teacher Education*, 32 (6), 3–6.

Driscoll, M.P. (1994) *Psychology for Learning*. Needham Heights, MA. Allyn and Bacon.

Ellis, V. (2007) *Subject Knowledge and Teacher Education: The Development of Beginning Teachers' Thinking*. London. Continuum.

Ellis, V. with High, S. (2004) Something more to tell you: gay, lesbian or bisexual young people's experiences of schooling. *British Educational Research Journal*, 30 (2), 213–225.

Emig, J. (1977) Writing as a mode of learning. *College Composition and Communication* 28 (2), 122–128.

Epstein, D., Elwood, J., Hey, V. and Maw, J. (1998) *Failing Boys? Issues in Gender and Achievement*. Buckingham. Open University Press.

Felder, R.M. and Silverman, L.K. (1988) Learning and teaching styles in engineering education. *Engineering Education*, April, 674–680.

Fleming, N. and Baume, D. (2006) Learning styles again: VARKing up the right tree. *Educational Developments*, SEDA Ltd 7 (4), 4–7.

Franklin, S. (2006) VAKing out learning styles – why the notion of learning styles is unhelpful to teachers. *Education 3–13,* 34(1), 81–87.

Freidson, E. (2001) *Professionalism: The Third Logic*. London. Polity Press.

Fuller, F. F. (1969) Concerns of teachers: a developmental conceptualisation. *American Educational Research Journal*, 70, 263–8.

Gaine, C. and George, R. (1999) *Gender, 'Race' and Class in Schooling: A New Introduction*. London. Falmer Press.

Galili, I. and Bar, V. (1997) Children's operational knowledge about weight. *International Journal of Science Education*, 19, 317–340.

Gardner, H. (1983) *Frames of Mind: The Theory of Multiple Intelligences*. New York. Basic Books Inc.

General Medical Council Standards of Practice. Available from **www.gmc-uk.org/Good_Medical_ Practice_0510.pdf_32611016.pdf** (Accessed 31.3.11)

Gibbons, P. (1993) *Learning to Learn in a Second Language*. Portsmouth. Heinemann.

Gillborn, D. and Mirza, H. S. (2000) *Educational Inequality: Mapping Race, Class and Gender*. London. Ofsted.

Gipps, C. and McGilchrist, B. (1999) Primary school learners. In P. Mortimore (ed.) *Understanding Pedagogy and its Impact on Learning*. London. Paul Chapman.

Gipps. C. and Stobart, G. (1997) *Assessment: A Teacher's Guide to the Issues*. London. Hodder and Stoughton.

Glaser, R. (1976) Components of a psychology of instruction: toward a science of design. *Review of Educational Research* 46 (1), 1–24.

Glaser, R. (1984) Education and thinking: the role of knowledge. *American Psychologist*, 39 (2), 93–104.

Goldstein, H. (1998) Response papers on **www.ioe.ac.uk/hgoldstn/**

Goleman, D. (1996) *Emotional Intelligence*. London. Bloomsbury.

Goswami, U. (2004) Neuroscience and education. *British Journal of Educational Psychology*, 74, 1–14.

Graff, H. J. (1987) *The Labyrinths of Literacy*. London. Falmer Press.

Gredler, M.E. (2001) *Learning and Instruction: Theory into Practice* (4th edn). New York. HarperCollins.

Griffin, L. L., Dodds, P., Placek, J. H. and Tremino, F. (2001). Middle school students' conceptions of soccer: their solutions to tactical problems. *Journal of Teaching in Physical Education*, 20(4), 324–340.

Griffiths, M. (2003) *Action for Social Justice in Education: Fairly Different*. Buckingham. Open University.

Gross, J. (2002) *Special Educational Needs in the Primary School – A Practical Guide*. London. Open University Press.

GTCE Professional Code for Teachers. Available from **www.gtce.org.uk/teachers/thecode/** (Accessed 31.3.11)

Guide to the Professional Conduct of Solicitors. Available from **www.guide-on-line.lawsociety.org.uk/**

Haines, S. (2006) *14–19 Education and Training and Young Disabled People*. Nuffield Review Working Paper No. 37. **http://81.29.86.172/~nwdatk99/toolkit/docs/57-14-19_education.pdf** (Accessed 31.3.11)

Hall, D. (2001) *Assessing the Needs of Bilingual Students: Living in Two Languages*. Abingdon. David Fulton.

Hamblin, D. (1978) *The Teacher and Pastoral Care*. Oxford. Blackwell.

Hammersley, M. (1993) On the teacher as researcher. *Educational Action Research*, 1 (3).

Hargreaves, D. (1996) *Teaching as a Research Based Profession: Possibilities and Prospects*. London. Teacher Training Agency.

Hargreaves, D. (2001) The Nuttall Memorial/Carfax Lecture. BERA. 2001.

Harlen, W., Gipps, C., Broadfoot P. and Nuttall, D. (1994) Assessment and the Improvement of Education, in A. Pollard and J. Bourne, *Teaching Learning in the Primary School*. London. Routledge.

Hart, C. (1998) *Doing a Literature Review*. London. Sage.

Haydon, G. (1996) Should teachers have their own professional ethics? *Journal of Philosophy of Education*, 30 (2), 301–306.

Heffler, B. (2001) Individual learning style and the learning style inventory. *Educational Studies*, 27 (3), 307–316.

Hill, D. and Cole, M. (eds) (1999) *Promoting Equality in the Secondary School*. London. Cassell.

Hillage, J., Pearson, R., Anderson, A. and Tamkin, P. (1998) *Excellence in Research in Schools*. London. DfEE.

Hitchcock, G. and Hughes, D. (1995) *Research and the Teacher*. London. Routledge.

Honey, P. and Mumford, A. (1982) *The Manual of Learning Styles*. Maidenhead. Peter Honey.

Hopkins, D. (1993) *A Teacher's Guide to Classroom Research*. Buckingham. Open University Press.

Hoyle, E. and John, P. (1995) *Professional Knowledge and Professional Practice*. London. Cassell.

Jasmine, J. (1996) *Teaching with Multiple Intelligences*. Westminster, CA. Teacher Created Materials.

Katz, L. G. (1972) Developmental stages of preschool teachers. *Elementary School Journal*, 73 (1), 50–54.

Koehn, D. (1994) *The Ground of Professional Ethics*. London. Routledge.

Kohl, H. (1986) *On Becoming a Teacher*. London. Methuen.

Kolb, D. A. (1976) *Teaching Students Through Their Individual Learning Styles*. Reston, VA. Reston Publications.

Kolb, D. A. (1984) *Experiential Learning: Experience as a Source of Learning and Development*. Englewood Cliffs, NJ. Prentice-Hall.

Kolb, D. A. (1985) *Learning Styles Inventory and Technical Manual*. Boston, MA. McBer.

Kyriacou, C. (1997). *Effective Teaching in Schools: Theory and Practice* (2nd edn). Cheltenham. Nelson Thornes Ltd.

Kyriacou, C. (1998) *Essential Teaching Skills* (2nd edn). Cheltenham. Stanley Thornes.

Kyriacou, C. and Stephens, P. (1999) Student teacher concerns during teaching practice. *Evaluation and Research in Education*, 13 (1), 18–31.

Lave, J. (1988) *Cognition in Practice: Mind, Mathematics, and Culture in Everyday Life*. Cambridge. Cambridge University Press.

Lave, J. and Wenger, E. (1996) *Situated Learning*. Cambridge. Cambridge University Press.

Ledwick, M. (2001) *Numeracy Across the Curriculum in Secondary Schools*. Leicester. Mathematical Association.

Lewin, K. (1946) Action research and minority problems. *Journal of Social Issues*, 2, 34–6, 286, 438.

Lewis, M. and Wray, D. (2001) Implementing effective literacy strategies in the secondary school. *Educational Studies*, (27) 1.

Long, M. (2000) *The Psychology of Education*. London. Routledge.

Luke, A. (1999) Education 2010 and new times: why equity and social justice matter, but differently. Paper presented at Education Queensland conference October 1999. Available from **http://education/qld.gov.au/corporate/newbasics/docs/onlineal.doc** (Accessed 1.4.11)

Lunzer, E. and Gardner, K. (1984) *Learning from the Written Word*. Edinburgh. Oliver & Boyd.

MacBeath, J. *et al*. (2006) *The Costs of Inclusion*. A report commissioned by the National Union of Teachers concerning inclusion in schools, University of Cambridge.

Macdonald, A. (2009) *Independent Review of the proposal to make Personal, Social, Health and Economic (PSHE) education statutory*. London. DCSF.

Marland, M. (1974) *Pastoral Care*. London. Heinemann.

Marlowe, B. A. and Page, M. L. (1998) *Creating and Sustaining a Constructivist Classroom*. Thousand Oaks, CA. Sage.

May, S. (ed.) (1999) *Critical Multiculturalism: Rethinking Multicultural and Antiracist Education*. London. Falmer Press.

McIntyre, D., Pedder, D. and Rudduck, J. (2005) Student voice: comfortable and uncomfortable learnings for teachers. *Research Papers in Education,* 20 (2),149–168.

Medwell, J. *et al*. (1998) *Effective Teachers of Literacy*, in M. Lewis and D. Wray (2001) Implementing effective literacy strategies in the secondary school. *Educational Studies*, (27) 1.

Meek, M. (1991) *On Being Literate*. London. Bodley Head.

Meltzer, H., Gatwood, R., Goodwood, R. and Ford, T. (2000) *The Mental Health of Children and Adolescents in Great Britain*. London. TSO.

Miliband, D. (2004) Personalised learning: building a new relationship with schools. Speech made to the North of England Education Conference, 8 January, Belfast.

Monk, M. (2001) Learning in the classroom, in J. Dillon and M. Maguire (eds.) *Becoming a Teacher: Issues in Secondary Teaching*. Buckingham. Open University Press.

Montgomery, D. (1989) *Managing Behaviour Problems*. London. Hodder and Stoughton.

Morgan, C. and Morris, G. (1999) *Good Teaching and Learning*. Buckingham. Open University Press.

Mortimore, P. (2006) *Which Way Forward? An Education for the 21st Century*. London. NUT.

Moseley, D., Higgins, S. *et al*. (1999) *Ways forward with ICT: Effective Pedagogy Using ICT for Literacy and Numeracy in Primary Schools*. Newcastle University.

Muijs, D. and Reynolds, D. (2001) *Effective Teaching: Evidence and Practice*. London. Paul Chapman.

Myhill, D. (2000) Misconceptions and difficulties in the acquisition of metalinguistic knowledge.

Learning and Education, 14 (3), 151–163.

Myhill, D. (2001) *Better Writing*. Westley. Courseware Publications.

National Statistics (2004) *Statistics of Education: Schools in England*. London. TSO.

Nuffield Foundation (2004) *Time Trends in Adolescent Well Being*. London. Nuffield Foundation.

Nuffield Review (2004) *Curriculum for the 21st Century*. Oxford. Oxford University Press.

Office for Standards in Education (2005) *Personal, social and health education in secondary schools*. London. Ofsted.

Office for Standards in Education (2007) *Time for change? Personal, social and health education*. London. Ofsted.

Office for Standards in Education (2010) *Citizenship established? Citizenship in schools 2006/09*. London. Ofsted.

Ofsted (1995) *Physical Education and Sport in Schools: A Survey of Good Practice*. London. HMSO.

Ofsted (2000) *Evaluating Educational Inclusion: Guidance for Inspectors and Schools*. London. Ofsted.

Ofsted (2002) *Good Teaching, Effective Departments*. London. Ofsted.

Ofsted (2004) *Standards and Quality 2002/3: The Annual Report of Her Majesty's Chief Inspector of Schools*. London. Ofsted.

Palmer, D. (2001) Students' conceptions and scientifically acceptable conceptions about gravity. *International Journal of Science Education*, 23 (7), 691–706.

Papert, S. (1980) *Mindstorms: Children, Computers and Powerful Ideas*. Brighton. Harvester Press.

Pendry, A., Atha, J., Carden, S., Courtney, L., Keogh, C. and Ruston, K. (1997) Pupils' preconceptions of history. *Teaching History*, 86, 18–20.

Perks, P. and Prestage, S. (2001) *Teaching the National Numeracy Strategy at Key Stage 3*. London. David Fulton.

Phillips, D. C. and Soltis, J. (1998) *Perspectives on Learning*. New York. Columbia University.

Placek, J. H., Griffin, L. L., Dodds, P., Raymond, C., Tremino, F. and James, A. (2001) Middle school students' conceptions of fitness: A long road to a healthy lifestyle. *Journal of Teaching in Physical Education*, 20 (4), 314–323.

Pope, S. and Sharma, R. (2001) Symbol sense: teachers' and students' understanding, in *Proceedings of the British Society for Research into Learning Mathematics*, 21(3), 64–69.

Porth Junior School (2000) Porth Junior School YEAR2KMAG (online). Available from **www.geocities. comtyear2kmag/**

Pritchard, A. (2005) *Ways of Learning: Learning Theories and Learning Styles in the Classroom*. London. David Fulton.

PSHE Association (2010) *DCSF PSHE Education Guidance*. (Available at **www.pshe-association.org. uk/content.aspx?CategoryID=1053** accessed 31.3.11)

QCA (1998) *ICT Across the Curriculum. An Overview*. Norwich. HMSO.

QCA (1998) *Supporting and Target Setting Process: Guidance for Effective Target Setting for Pupils with Special Educational Needs*. London. DfEE/QCA.

QCA (1999) *Information and Communication Technology. The National Curriculum for England*. Norwich. HMSO.

QCA (2000a) *Language for Learning in Key Stage 3*. QCA.

QCA (2000b) *A Language in Common: Assessing English as an Additional Language*. London. QCA.

QCA (2001) *Language at Work in Lessons*. QCA.

QCA (2001) *Citizenship: A scheme of work for Key Stage 3 – Teacher's guide*. London. QCA.

QCA (2005) *PSHE at key stages 1–4. Guidance on assessment, recording and reporting*. London. QCA.

QCA (2007a) *The National Curriculum statutory requirements for Key Stages 3 and 4 from September 2008*. London. QCA.

QCA (2007b) *PSHE: Personal well-being. Programme of Study (non-statutory) for Key Stage 3*. London. QCA.

QCA (2007c) *PSHE: Economic well-being and financial capability. Programme of Study (non-statutory)* for Key Stage 3. London. QCA.

QCA (2007d) *PSHE: Personal well-being. Programme of Study (non-statutory) for Key Stage 4*. London. QCA.

QCA (2007e) *PSHE: Economic well-being and financial capability. Programme of Study (non-statutory) for Key Stage 4*. London. QCA.

QCA (2007f) *Programme of study for Key Stage 3 and attainment target*. London: QCA.

Richardson, R. and Wood, A. (1999) *Inclusive Society: Race and Identity on the Agenda*. Report produced for Race on the Agenda in partnership with Association of London Government and Save the Children. Stoke-on-Trent. Trentham.

Riding, R. J. and Raynor, S. G. (1998) *Cognitive Styles and Learning Strategies: Understanding Style Differences in Learning and Behaviour*. London. David Fulton.

Rink, J. E. (2001) Investigating the assumptions of pedagogy. *Journal of Teaching in Physical Education*, 20, 112–128.

Roberts, M. (2006) Whither Pastoral Care? *Pastoral Care in Education*, 24 (2), 62–64.

Robinson, R. and Wood, A. (1999) *'Race on the Agenda': Inclusive Schools, Inclusive Society*. Stoke-on-Trent. Trentham Books.

Roblyer, M. D. (1996) The constructivist/objectivist debate: implications for instructional technology research. *Learning and Leading with Technology*, 24, 12–16.

Robson, R. (1993) *Real World Research*. Oxford. Blackwell.

Roelofs, E. and Terwel, J. (1999) Constructivism and authentic pedagogy: state of the art and recent developments in the Dutch national curriculum in secondary education. *Journal of Curriculum Studies*, 31 (2), 201–227.

Rogers, B. (1997) *You Know the Fair Rule*. London. Prentice Hall.

Ruddock, J. (2001) The Quiet Revolution: Opening address for the DfES and TTA conference, using research and evidence to improve teaching and learning.

Rudduck, J. (2005) Pupil voice is here to stay. *QCA Futures: Meeting the Challenge*. London. QCA.

Runnymede Trust (2000) *The Future of Multiethnic Britain: The Parekh Report*.

Sarason, S. B. (1993) *You Are Thinking of Teaching? Opportunities, Problems, Realities*. San Francisco. Jossey-Bass.

Sarason, S. B. and Doris, D. J. (1979) *Educational Handicap, Public Policy and Social History*. London. Macmillan.

Schön, D. (1983) *The Reflective Practitioner*. London. Temple Smith.

Schunk, D. H. (1996) *Learning Theories* (2nd edn). Englewood Cliffs, NJ. Prentice Hall.

Searle, C. (2001) *An Exclusive Education: 'Race', Class and Exclusion in British Schools*. London. Lawrence and Wishart.

Secondary Heads Association (2001) *14 and Beyond: Proposals for the Development of a Coherent Post-14 Education Framework*. Secondary Heads Association.

Shain, F. (2000) *The Schooling and Identity of Asian Girls*. Stoke-on-Trent. Trentham Books.

Sheeran, Y. and Barnes, D. (1991) *School Writing*. Milton Keynes. Open University Press.

Shipman, M. (1983) *Assessment in Primary and Middle Schools*. Kent. Croom Helm.

Siedentrop, D. and Tannehill, D. (2000) (4th edn) *Developing Teaching Skills in Physical Education*. Mountain View, CA. Mayfield.

Skinner, B. F. (1968) *The Technology of Teaching*. New York. Appleton-Century Crofts.

Smith, J. (2002) *The Learning Game: A Teacher's Inspirational Story*. London. Abacus.

Smith Report (2004) *Mathematics Counts: the Report of Inquiry into Post-14 Mathematics Education*. London. HMSO.

Stakes, R. and Hornby, G. (2000) (2nd edn) *Meeting Special Needs in Mainstream Schools: A Practical Guide for Teachers*. London. David Fulton.

Stenhouse, L. (1975) *An Introduction to Curriculum Research and Development*. Oxford. Heinemann.

Sternberg, R. J. (1997) *Thinking Styles*. Cambridge. Cambridge University Press.

Stevenson, R. J. and Palmer, J. A. (1994). *Learning Principles, Processes, and Practices*. London. Cassell.

Strand, S. (2006) Disadvantage, ethnicity, gender and educational attainment: The case of White working class pupils. Paper presented at the British Educational Research Association, 2006.

Street, B.V. (1993) 'Culture is a verb: anthropological aspects of language and cultural processes', in Graddol, D., Thompson, L. and Byram, M. (eds) *Language and Culture: Papers from the Annual Meeting of the British Association of Applied Linguistics*. Stoke-on-Trent. BAAL in association with Multilingual Matters.

Taber, K. (2001) The mismatch between assumed prior knowledge and the learners' conceptions: a typology of learning impediments. *Educational Studies,* 27 (2), 159–171.

Task Group on Assessment and Testing (TGAT) (1988) *National Curriculum, Report*. London. DES.

Teacher Training Agency (2000) *Raising the Attainment of Minority Ethnic Pupils: guidance and resource materials for initial teacher trainers*. London. HMSO.

Terwel, J. (1999) Constructivism and its implications for curriculum theory and practice. *Journal of Curriculum Studies*, 31 (2), 195–199.

Thomson, P. and Gunter, H. (2006) From consulting students to students as researchers. *British Educational Research Journal,* 32 (6), 830–856.

Times Educational Supplement (2007, 5 January) Students' personal advisers, p.1.

Tirosh, D. (2000) Enhancing prospective teachers' knowledge of children's conceptions: The case of divisions of fractions. *Journal of Research in Mathematics Education*, 31 (1), 5–25.

TLRP (Teaching and Learning Research Programme) (2004) Personalised learning: A commentary by the teaching and learning research programme. ESRC.

Tomlinson Report (2004) *14–19 Curriculum and Qualifications Reform*. London. DfES.

Tooley, J. and Darby, D. (1998) *Educational Research – A Critique*. London. Ofsted.

Tuckey, C. (1992) Who is a scientist?: children's drawings reveal all. *Education, 3-13*, 20 (2), 30–32.

Tyler, R. (1949) *Basic Principles of Curriculum and Instruction*. Chicago. University of Chicago Press.

Van Zwanenberg, N., Wilkinson, L. J. and Anderson, A. (2000) Felder and Silverman's index of learning and Mumford's learning styles questionnaire: how do they compare and do they predict academic performance? *Educational Psychologist*, 20 (3), 365–380.

Verkasalo, M., Tuomivaara, P. and Lindeman, M. (1996) 15-year-old pupils' and their teachers' values, and their beliefs about the values of an ideal pupil. *Educational Psychology*, 16 (1), 35–47.

Walker, C. and Newman, I. (1995) What teachers believe. *Educational Research*, 37 (2), 191–202.

Watkins, C. (2004) Reclaiming pastoral care. *Pastoral Care in Education*, 22 (3), 3–6.

Weber, S. and Mitchell, C. (1996) Drawing ourselves into teaching: studying the images that shape and distort teacher education. *Teaching and Teacher Education*, 12 (3), 303–313.

Wetton, N. and McWhirter, J. (1988) Images and curriculum development in health education, in J. Prosser (ed.) *Image-Based Research: A Source Book for Qualitative Researchers*. Brighton: Falmer Press.

Wiliam, D., Askew, M., Rhodes, V., Brown, M. and Johnson, D. (1998) Discover, transmit or connect? Approaches to teaching numeracy in primary schools, *Equals*, Summer 1998.

Williams, R. (1958/1989) 'Culture is ordinary', *Resources of Hope*. London. Verso.

Wood, D. (1998) *How Children Think and Learn* (2nd edn). Oxford. Blackwell.

Wray, D. (1999) Teaching literacy: the foundation of good practice. *Education 3–13*, March 1999.

Wray, D. (2001) Literacy in the secondary curriculum. *Reading*, 35(1), 12–17.

Wray, D. and Lewis, M. (1997) *Extending Literacy: Children Reading and Writing Non-Fiction*. London. Routledge.

Young, M. and Lucas, N. (1999) Pedagogy in further education: new contexts, new theories and new possibilities, in P. Mortimore (ed.) *Understanding Pedagogy and its Impact on Learning*. London. Paul Chapman.

Index

Added to the page reference 'f' denotes a figure, 'g' denotes glossary and 't' denotes a table.